𝕸𝖊𝖒𝖔𝖗𝖎𝖆𝖑 𝖁𝖔𝖑𝖚𝖒𝖊.

THE

RECORD OF ANDOVER

DURING

THE REBELLION.

COMPILED BY

SAMUEL RAYMOND.

𝕬𝖓𝖉𝖔𝖛𝖊𝖗:
WARREN F. DRAPER, PRINTER,
MAIN STREET.
1875.

Prof. A. W. Smith
¢
6-5-1925

At the Annual Town Meeting in March last, it was

Voted. To print the Record of the Town of Andover during the Rebellion, which has already been prepared by Samuel Raymond, and that every voter in town have a copy of the same, if desired.

Voted. To appropriate the sum of One Thousand Dollars to carry the same into effect.

Voted. That a Committee of three be appointed by the Chair-

In accordance with this Vote, Samuel Raymond, Francis H. Johnson, and James B. Smith were appointed.

PREFACE.

A few words seem necessary regarding the origin and purpose of the manuscript volume of which this is an abridgment.

The records show that during the late Rebellion the Town made several ineffectual efforts to keep a Register of such of its citizen's as entered the military or naval service of the United States, and who made a part of the several quotas which the Town was called upon to furnish.

It was in 1870, five years after the Rebellion had been suppressed, that the people of the Town proposed to erect, by voluntary subscriptions, a Memorial Hall, in honor of its sons who had sacrificed their lives in the war. The enterprise having been successfully inaugurated, I was chosen by my associates on the Building Committee to prepare a roll of the honored dead, to be placed under the corner-stone. The time for preparation was very brief; but, with such material as was then at hand, a list of forty-six names was furnished. Subsequent investigation proved this list to be incorrect, in that it embraced the names of six men who, at the time of their decease, were serving on the quotas of other towns.

In preparing the rolls for the tablet, as I had both ample

time and leisure, it was my purpose, not only to correct the former roll, but to prepare that Register which the Town had failed to make during the progress of the Rebellion, to record all action of the Town on affairs pertaining to the war, and collect any other kindred matter, whether local or otherwise, that might be of interest or use in the future, and to present the volume when completed to the Memorial Hall.

I do not assume that this published volume is correct in every particular; but whatever errors there may be in it are chargeable to myself or the State Records, and not to the Committee on Publication. I think, however, I may, with strict regard to truth and justice, claim that both the original and this abridged copy are far more correct than the "Record of Massachusetts Volunteers" published by the State.

It is exceedingly gratifying that the manuscript volume has in all cases received the unqualified commendation of the many prominent citizens who have carefully examined its pages, and that the Town has not only granted me a very liberal gratuity, but has ordered the publication of the present volume for gratuitous distribution among its citizens.

SAMUEL RAYMOND.

ANDOVER, January, 1875.

TO THE CITIZENS OF ANDOVER.

In the making up of the present volume we have endeavored to carry out, so far as was possible without exceeding the means at our disposal, your wishes, as expressed in the foregoing Votes. On an examination of the Record in its manuscript form, it appeared that to print the whole of its contents would involve producing a volume of more than four hundred pages, and an expense considerably in excess of the appropriation. We therefore ventured to omit from the published volume such documents as could be spared without materially lessening its value as a History of Andover's share in the War of the Rebellion.

The material omitted belongs mainly to the following classes: General Orders, issued from the War Departments at Washington and Boston, calling for quotas of troops, and prescribing rules and regulations for enrolment, volunteering, organization, equipment, etc., Laws of the State on the same subjects, and also those relating to State Aid and Bounties. All of these papers can be found in the Archives of the several Departments.

We have also omitted several speeches delivered by citizens of the Town, lists of subscriptions (being imperfect)

viii   TO THE CITIZENS OF ANDOVER.

to the Committee of Twenty-five, and a very full and interesting Report of over thirty written pages, by Provost-Marshal Herrick, of this District, to the War Department at Washington, on the subjects of enrolment, drafting, substitution, recruiting, etc.

Mention is made in this volume of all the military organizations in which the Town was represented during the war; and, in connection with the names of those who served in each one, a list of its engagements and some other statistics are given. In the case of the First Mass. Heavy Artillery, — one of the companies of which was wholly composed of soldiers from this Town, and the rolls of which contain the names of more than one-third of all the soldiers furnished by the Town,—much more has been done. A full history of this Regiment, compiled from official sources, will be found in the Appendix.

SAMUEL RAYMOND,
FRANCIS H. JOHNSON,
JAMES B. SMITH,
Committee.

ANDOVER, Jan. 23, 1875.

THE

RECORD OF ANDOVER

DURING THE REBELLION.

On the 18th of April, 1861, — six days after the bombardment of Fort Sumter, and three days after the proclamation of President Lincoln calling for 75,000 Volunteers, — the active participation of Andover in the war of the Rebellion began. On that day a meeting of citizens and others was held in the Hall at Frye Village, in response to a call of only seven hours' notice.

John Dove having been chosen Chairman, Joseph W. Poor stated that the particular object for which the meeting was called, was to see what could be done toward organizing a company of some sort, for the purpose of becoming familiar with military drill.

Remarks were made by the Chairman, Messrs. John Smith, Peter Smith, Isaac M. Hardy, William Poor, and many others; after which it was decided to await the action of the meeting to be held on the next Saturday evening, at the Town Hall.

The call for this meeting was as follows:

"CITIZENS ATTEND."

"The Citizens of Andover are requested to meet at the Town Hall, on Saturday evening, April 20th, at 7 o'clock, to take into consideration the present alarming condition of our country, and to devise such measures as may be deemed proper to sustain the General Government in preserving our National Union.

"A Military Company is being formed in this town, and the meeting will have an opportunity to tender to this object such sympathy and material aid as the occasion may suggest and the times demand.

"MANY CITIZENS."

ANDOVER, April 18th, 1861.

On Saturday evening the citizens rallied in great numbers in response to the above call.

William Chickering having called the meeting to order, was chosen temporary Chairman, and George Foster, Secretary.

A Committee appointed for the purpose of nominating a list of officers for the permanent organization of the meeting, reported as follows:

For President, — Francis Cogswell.

For Vice-Presidents, — Amos Abbott, John Aiken, Marcus Morton, Jr., Samuel Merrill, Nathan W. Hazen, William Jenkins, Solomon Holt, John Dove, Oliver H. Perry, Moses Clement, Dean Holt, Nathan Frye, David Higgins.

For Secretaries, — Moses Foster, Jr., George Foster, Albert Abbott.

Committee on Resolutions, — Marcus Morton, Jr., Calvin E. Stowe, Oliver H. Perry, William G. Means, Samuel Raymond.

On taking the Chair, the President spoke as follows:

" It was the custom of our forefathers to recognize the overruling Providence of Almighty God in public as well as private affairs. In times of national prosperity they were wont in their public assemblies to return thanks for mercies received, and to implore a continuance of the blessing. In times of great national adversity it was equally common to assemble themselves together to supplicate the interposition of Heaven to stay the evil, and avert the impending ruin.

In imitation of such a praiseworthy custom, let us look to a Higher Power for counsel, direction, and assistance, in this great national emergency. Let us devoutly look to Him who can easily control the unruly wills of men, and cause all things, however unpropitious they may appear, to work together for good to us as a nation. I feel confident, therefore, that I am but carrying out the wishes of all present, whose hearts throb with anxiety for the future welfare of our country, in calling upon Professor Stowe to lead the devotions of this great assembly."

After the earnest and appropriate Prayer of Professor Stowe, Mr. Cogswell again addressed the meeting. The Committee on Resolutions then reported, through their Chairman, Judge Morton, as follows :

Resolved, That the armed hostility to the United States Government, now assumed by a portion of the Southern people, is entirely without justification in anything which the National Administration has done or proposes to do. That the claim of a right to secede at will is utterly subversive of all government, and leaves the nation a prey to anarchy, like that of the South American republics, at the close of every election. That the robbing of the nation by the Secessionists of its money, fortifications, arms, mints, ships, custom-houses, and other property, levying war against the Government by the raising of troops, and gathering munitions of every kind, firing upon the national flag, and attempting to murder the national soldiers while in the unaggressive discharge of their duties, and the crying out against *coercion* on the part of the General Government, whenever it makes the least attempt at preparation to defend itself and its property against these open, long-continued, and insolent assaults, is absurd, malignant, and mean, beyond all parallel in civilized history, and deserves the utter contempt and detestation of mankind.

Resolved, That the present position and action of the Secessionists is not in consequence of any grievance actually endured, or even anticipated, from the General Government, but the meditated result of a plan, cherished for more than thirty years past, by certain restless and ambitious men at the South, to establish a great slave empire in the fertile regions around the Gulf of Mexico. A plan with which the better part of the Southerners themselves have no sympathy. That they are kept quiet by intimidation and violence only; and that the leaders of this rebellious movement are so well aware of the fact that they dare not, and never will, submit their own action to a fair vote of the people.

Resolved, That the exigencies of the present crisis imperatively demand of all patriots and true friends of liberty and order throughout the land that, suspending for the time the discussion of minor party differences, they unite heart and soul to sustain the Government against its lawless assailants; and that the zeal and energy with which all parties among us are now actually pursuing this course gives the best evidence of the sincerity of their patriotism, and affords the most encouraging indications of the final success of their efforts, and of the perpetuity of the free institutions which have been so wisely established in this Western world, at the expense of so much labor and self-denial, so much treasure and blood.

Resolved, That, as the present violent proceedings of the Secessionists can be successfully resisted in no other way than by an overpowering military force at the disposal of the National Government, we hereby pledge ourselves to do all in our power to raise, sustain, and encourage such a force; and that, either by bearing arms ourselves, or by contributing according to our ability to support the men who do bear arms, and their families, we will take our full share in this great struggle, and fight as our fathers fought when compelled by a like necessity.

Resolved, That the young men of Andover who are about organizing themselves into a Military Company to be at the disposal of the Government, have now, and shall continue to have, our warmest sympathy and most cordial support.

These resolutions were received with great applause, and

were subsequently unanimously adopted. The President then announced that the meeting was open for the discussion of the resolutions, and introduced to the audience Professor Stowe, who was greeted with deafening applause. He was followed by John K. Tarbox, Ex-Mayor Saunders of Lawrence, Amos Abbott, J. A. Bent of Phillips Academy, Joseph W. Poor, Peter Smith, Joseph Holt, William G. Means, and others.

The gallery of the hall, reserved for ladies, was completely filled. Music was furnished by the Andover Brass Band, whose stirring airs contributed not a little to the enlivenment of the occasion.

This meeting voted, That a Committee of twenty-five be chosen, whose duty it shall be to devise and carry into effect such measures as they deem expedient for the support and defence of our National Government during the present rebellion. That this Committee shall organize itself by the choice of a President, two Vice-Presidents, a Secretary, and a Treasurer, and have power to fill vacancies. That this Committee be authorized to raise money by subscription to be expended as they shall deem proper for the assistance of Volunteers and the families of Volunteers, and to carry out the purposes for which they were chosen.

It was also voted, That the Chair appoint a Committee of five to nominate the aforesaid Committee of twenty-five, and report at the adjourned meeting. The following gentlemen were appointed, viz. Peter Smith, Abraham J. Gould, Willard Pike, Benjamin Boynton, and John E. Farnham. At a late hour the meeting adjourned to the evening of the following Monday.

April 22d (Monday). A large and spirited meeting was held in the Town Hall. The President, Mr. Cogswell, being unavoidably absent, Judge Morton, one of the Vice-Presidents, assumed the Chair, and after a short address the meeting proceeded to the transaction of the business for which it had assembled. Peter Smith, Chairman of the Committee of five chosen on Saturday evening last, reported the following names as the Committee of twenty-five :

Francis Cogswell, Peter Smith, John Dove, William Chickering, Amos Abbott, Joseph Holt, William P. Foster, Nathan Frye, Jedediah Burtt, Stephen D. Abbott, Willard Pike, Isaac O. Blunt, James Shaw, George Foster, William Jenkins, Calvin E. Stowe, Moses Foster, Jr., Benjamin F. Wardwell, John Aiken, Benjamin Boynton, William Abbott, Nathan Shattuck, John Abbott, James Bailey, and Warren F. Draper.

After the above Committee had been unanimously accepted by the meeting, speeches were made by John Aiken, O. H. Perry, Prof. Stowe, Rev. Mr. Murray, N. W. Hazen, Amos Abbott, William Poor, Jonas Holt, Warren F. Draper, and others.

Mr. Peter Smith then proposed, That for the encouragement of our young men who compose the Military Company, and that they may have some guaranty of what our citizens will do for their families after they have been called into service, a subscription paper be opened here and now ; one-half of the sums subscribed to be paid within ten days, the balance when called for.

Mr. John Smith, in a short speech, pledged the firm of Smith, Dove, and Company for three thousand dollars; others followed with liberal amounts.

The Committee of twenty-five, chosen at the above meeting, met at the Town Hall, pursuant to notice, on Thursday evening, April 25th, at seven o'clock.

The meeting was organized by the choice of the following officers:

President, — Francis Cogswell.
Vice-Presidents, — Amos Abbott, Peter Smith.
Secretary, — Moses Foster, Jr.
Treasurer, — John Dove.

Voted, That we will provide each member of the Military Company now being formed in this town with a good revolver, the same to be his private property when said Company shall be organized; also a suitable uniform, the same to be provided forthwith.

Voted, That a Committee of three be chosen to locate, by the several Highway Districts in town, the labors of the Committee in soliciting subscriptions, and report as soon as possible.

George Foster, William Chickering, and Benjamin Boynton were chosen, who subsequently made the following assignments:

District No. 1. — Moses Foster, Jr., William Chickering, Nathan Frye.
District No. 2. — John Aiken, John Abbott.
Districts No. 3 and 5. — Calvin E. Stowe, Warren F. Draper.
Districts No. 4 and 7. — Stephen D. Abbott.
Districts No. 8 and 9. — William Jenkins.
District No. 10. — B. F. Wardwell.
Districts No. 11 and 12. — John Dove.
District No. 13. — Peter Smith, Francis Cogswell.
Districts No. 14, 15, and 18. — Benjamin Boynton.
Districts No. 16 and 17. — Jedediah Burtt.
Districts No. 19 and 24. — James Bailey.
District No. 20. — Nathan Shattuck.
District No. 21. — William Abbott.
Districts No. 22 and 23. — Isaac O. Blunt.
Districts No. 6 and 25. — Joseph Holt.
District No. 26. — Willard Pike.
District No. 27. — George Foster.
District No. 28. — James Shaw.

This report was accepted.

Messrs. George Foster, William Chickering, and Benjamin Boynton were chosen an Executive Committee.

The following form of a subscription paper was adopted by vote:

"When bad men combine the good must associate."

We, the inhabitants of Andover, hereby agree to pay the sums herein set against our names to the Committee chosen April 22, 1861, to aid in the national defence, for the assistance of Volunteers from this town and their families, and to carry out the purposes for which the Committee was chosen. Twenty per cent thereof to be paid forthwith, and the balance in such installments as said Committee shall deem necessary.

Voted, That a Committee of three be chosen to act in concert with the officers of the Military Company in the purchase of uniforms and equipments. John Dove, William Chickering, and Nathan Frye were chosen.

Voted, That the Committee enter at once upon their duty of taking up subscriptions.

Voted, That the meeting be adjourned to Saturday evening next, May 4th, at seven o'clock.

The newly organized Military Company having been chartered by the Governor, elected the following officers on the afternoon of April 30th.

Captain, — Horace Holt.
First Lieutenant, — George W. W. Dove.
Second Lieutenant, — Charles H. Poor.
Third Lieutenant, — Moses W. Clement.
Fourth Lieutenant, — Orrin L. Farnham.

The Company numbered seventy-nine men, and were daily drilled by Captain Samuel C. Oliver of Salem.

May 4th. The "Committee of twenty-five" met pursuant to adjournment.

The record of the previous meeting having been read and approved, the Committee appointed to solicit subscriptions in the several Highway Districts reported the amount subscribed, as follows:

District.	Amount.	District.	Amount.
No. 1,	$ 769 00	Nos. 19 and 24,	$ 62 00
No. 2,	1000 00	No. 20,	41 00
Nos. 3 and 5,	794 00	No. 21,	35 00
Nos. 4 and 7,	271 00	Nos. 22 and 23,	162 00
Nos. 8 and 9,	280 00	Nos. 6 and 25,	154 00
No. 10,	30 25	No. 26,	1307 00
Nos. 11 and 12,	3105 00	No. 27,	263 00
No. 13,	421 00	No. 28,	135 00
Nos. 14, 15, and 18,	166 00		
Nos. 16 and 17,	149 00	Total,	$9144 25

Voted, That the officers of the Military Company be invited to be present to answer certain inquiries of the Committee. Captain Holt and Lieutenant Clement appeared in response to the invitation.

Voted, That the Executive Committee be authorized to pay fifty cents for each day's drill that each member of the Military Company has served since April 26th, and at the same rate for such further like service as may be rendered before they are called into the service of the Government.

Voted, That the Committee on the purchase of revolvers be requested to ascertain by inquiry as to the propriety of furnishing the Military Company with those weapons; and if they are considered objectionable, that they be authorized to dispose of the same for the benefit of the soldiers.

Voted, That a Committee of three be chosen to prepare votes to be submitted to the Town Meeting on Monday next. Moses Foster, Jr., John Dove, and W. F. Draper were chosen as such Committee.

Voted, To adjourn to Tuesday evening next, at half-past seven o'clock.

May 6th. At a legal meeting of the inhabitants of the Town, qualified to vote in town affairs, the following articles in the warrant were acted upon; Professor Stowe being moderator.

Article 2d. — To see if the Town will make an appropriation to defray the expense of organizing, uniforming, and equipping such Military Companies as may be raised in the town at the present time.

Article 3d. — To see if the Town will grant free use of the Town House to said Companies for such purposes as they may require.

Article 4th. — To see what other action the Town will take in reference to the exigency of the times, and what appropriations the Town will make to carry out such action.

These articles were acted upon in the following resolutions and votes.

Resolved, That the rebellion of the Southern States of the Union is, in its principles, not only subversive of the most wise and beneficent Government which our patriotic fathers labored and fought to establish and a flagrant violation of our dearest rights, but is equally at war with the most cherished principles of our civil liberties, wrought out by ages of struggle and toil, and fatal to all institutions founded on the right of a people to govern themselves by the expressed will of the majority.

Resolved, That we will respond to the call of the President of the United States for the means to suppress this rebellion, by encouraging Volunteers in this town to enlist in the service of the Government, and by providing for their comfort and the comfort of their families in their absence, and by such other means as we, as good and loyal citizens, shall have the wisdom and the ability to devise and execute, and by adopting the language of one of the resolutions passed by this town in 1787, as follows:

"*Resolved*, That the inhabitants of the town of every description, but heads of families in particular, are hereby solicited, as they would falsify the predictions, and disappoint the hopes of those who are inimical to our independence and happiness, as they would gratify the anxious wishes of our best friends, and the friends of freedom in general, as they regard the political well-being of themselves and posterity, as they hold precious the memory of the heroes and patriots and of our own kindred who have sacrificed their lives that we may enjoy the fruits of virtuous freedom, to unite in these resolutions and to exert their utmost influence in every proper way to promote the important design of them."

Voted, To furnish each person, resident of this town, who has been or shall be enrolled as a Volunteer in any Military Company duly organized [1] in the town under the authority of the State, and offering service to the same, with a uniform not exceeding in value fourteen dollars, and the sum of seventeen dollars ; and the same to any member of any future Company which shall be duly organized, when such Company shall be called into actual service.

Voted, To furnish each member of any Company from this town, when called into the service of the Government, with a rubber blanket, and such other articles as shall be deemed necessary, not exceeding together in value the sum of six dollars.

Voted, To remit the poll-tax for the current year, of every Volunteer duly enrolled in any Military Company offering service to the Government, who shall perform the regular drill of said Company.

Voted, To pay the family of each married volunteer, except the Commissioned Officers, the sum of eight dollars per month, during the continuance of such Volunteer in the service of the Government, or until otherwise ordered by the Town.

Voted, To pay to each duly enrolled Volunteer of this town, the sum of fifty cents for each day's drill, not exceeding in all sixty days.

Voted, That a Committee of National Defence, consisting of the Selectmen, Town Treasurer, and three persons to be chosen at this meeting, be appointed to examine into the claims of any persons contemplated in the foregoing votes ; and to carry into effect the several provisions thereof, and to

---

[1] The term "duly organized," in the judgment of this meeting was defined to be when a Company had received its charter, and was accepted by the State authorities.

keep a record of their doings, and report the same to the Town.

Voted, To grant the free use of the Town Hall to any Military Companies of this town for the purposes of drill and storage of equipments, under the regulations of said Committee.

Voted, That the Town appropriate a sum not exceeding eight thousand dollars for the aforesaid purposes, and that the Treasurer be authorized to hire money therefor.

Whereas, At a preliminary meeting of the citizens of this town, on the twenty-second day of April last, a Committee of twenty-five was chosen to devise measures for the defence of our National Government during the present rebellion, and said Committee have adopted certain measures and assumed certain responsibilities, it is

Voted, That these proceedings of the Town, so far as they cover the action of said Committee, shall operate to relieve said Committee from the obligations thus far assumed by them ; so that all monies raised by them shall be at their disposal, as an emergency fund, for such measures of relief as they may see fit hereafter to adopt.

To carry out the sixth vote above, the Selectmen were chosen a nominating Committee to present the names of three persons to be chosen on said Committee. They reported the names of William Chickering, Jedediah Burtt, and John B. Jenkins, who were chosen.

May 7th. The " Committee of twenty-five " met agreeably to adjournment. The Executive Committee made a verbal report, accompanied by a written statement of the payments which had been made to the members of the Military Company for drill service.

Voted, That the Executive Committee be authorized to receive from the Committee of National Defence a return of money's advanced in payment for drill service, the same to be refunded to the Treasurer of this Committee.

Voted, That the meeting be adjourned to Saturday evening, May the 18th, at seven o'clock.

May 9th. The Committee of National Defence chosen by the Town on May 6th, consisting of Asa A. Abbott, William S. Jenkins, Benjamin Boynton, Selectmen ; Edward Taylor, Town Treasurer ; William Chickering, John B. Jenkins, and Jedediah Burtt, having met at the Selectmen's room, chose William Chickering, Chairman, and William S. Jenkins Clerk.

Voted, That William Chickering and William S. Jenkins, serve as a Committee for arranging a temporary armory in the Town Hall.

Voted, That the Selectmen be a sub-committee to economize the janitor's bills for opening the Town Hall.

Voted, That Edward Taylor and William S. Jenkins take charge of the bills contracted by George W. W. Dove.

Adjourned to Tuesday evening, May 14th.

May 11th. The ladies of the town showed their patriotism by the hearty zeal with which they provided the following articles for the Military Company about to leave for the war.

One hundred and fifty-eight shirts, one hundred and fifty-eight pairs flannel drawers, one hundred and fifty-eight towels, one hundred and fifty-eight pairs stockings, one hundred and fifty-eight handkerchiefs, seventy-nine hats, bound and trimmed, seventy-nine needle-cases filled with needles, pins, thread, scissors, etc. They also prepared bandages, lint, etc., for each knapsack.

On the 4th of May the Ballard Vale Company flung to the breeze a splendid flag of ample dimensions, with a streamer seventy-five feet in length. Hundreds of people were present ; addresses were made by several gentlemen, interspersed with the singing of the " Star Spangled Banner," the " Red White and Blue," the " Flag of our Union," "America," etc. ; closing with a prayer by Rev. Henry S. Greene.

May 14th. The "Committee of National Defence" met according to adjournment; absent Messrs. Boynton and Burtt. No particular business coming up, adjourned to Friday evening, May 17th.

May 17th. The "Committee of National Defence" met according to adjournment; absent, John B. Jenkins.

Voted, The use of the uniform to the Company for attendance upon religious worship, and such parades as the Committee and Captain shall approve. The bill for drill paid by the "Committee of twenty-five," was accepted and ordered to be paid.

Voted That the Treasurer pay the Company for drill once in two weeks, the Captain and Clerk certifying the rolls.

William S. Jenkins resigned as Clerk and Edward Taylor was chosen.

Adjourned for one week.

May 18th. The "Committee of twenty-five" met pursuant to adjournment. The record of the previous meeting was read and approved.

Voted, That the Executive Committee ascertain by inquiry the number of those Volunteers who have families, together with the number and condition and statistics of those families, and report thereon at a subsequent meeting of this Committee.

Voted, That the Executive Committee be authorized in case of pressing necessity, to afford such relief as they may think proper.

Meeting dissolved.

May 19th. In accordance with a notice issued some days previous, Professor C. E. Stowe preached a sermon before the Andover Light Infantry, in the evening, from 2 Tim. ii. 3, "Endure hardship as a good soldier."

The soldiers, in uniform, occupied the centre of the house, which was crowded to its utmost capacity, many not being able to obtain admittance.

May 24th. The "Committee of National Defence" met according to adjournment.

Voted, To choose a sub-committee of two to make inquiries and procure a suitable uniform for the Military Company already formed; this Committee to confer with the Captain of the Company. Edward Taylor and William Chickering were chosen as this Committee.

Voted, That this Committee approve all bills for articles purchased for the use of the soldiers before said bills are accepted and paid by the Town.

Voted, To adjourn for one week, unless sooner called together by the sub-committee.

Adjourned.

May 31st. The "Committee of National Defence" met according to adjournment. The sub-committee made a verbal report of their doings in contracting for a uniform, at a cost of eleven dollars a suit.

Report accepted.

Voted, That the sub-committee examine the uniforms when received, and ascertain that all is correct before using them.

Voted, That, for the present, the uniforms be returned after use.

Adjourned for one week.

June 4th. At six o'clock in the evening a beautiful flag was unfolded over the Theological Seminary, in the presence of the Academic Military Companies and a large concourse of citizens.

The exercises of the occasion were opened with the singing of the "Army Hymn," written by Oliver Wendell Holmes. After an earnest and eloquent prayer by Professor Park, the presentation address was delivered by Professor Phelps; at the conclusion of which the flag was given to the breeze, and cheer after cheer went up. The singing of the "Star Spangled Banner" followed, after which Professor Stowe delivered an address. The exercises closed with the "Banner Song," written for the occasion by Mrs. Harriet Beecher Stowe.

June 5th. In the afternoon a flag was raised over the Mansion House. Mr. Bodwell, the landlord, having procured a flag, invited the several Military Companies, and citizens to assist in placing it upon its staff. A large crowd of ladies and gentlemen assembled at six o'clock to witness the display. The " Havelock Greys," composed of students in the Theological Seminary, and the " Phillips Guards," composed of students in Phillips Academy, were early on the ground ; and they were soon followed by the Andover Light Infantry, accompanied by Hobbs and Williams' Band, of Lawrence. Speeches were made by Captain Clark, of the " Havelocks," and by others. After the speaking, the Companies engaged in a drill.

June 8th. A meeting of the " Committee of twenty-five " was held pursuant to notice. The Executive Committee, through Mr. Chickering, made a statement relative to the amount of indebtedness incurred by, and on account of, the Volunteers ; showing the same to exceed the sum appropriated by the Town.

Voted, That the unpaid accounts, with the other items proposed by Captain Holt, be referred to the Executive Committee, with directions to prepare a statement thereof, and report at a future meeting of this Committee. The same Committee also made a report relative to the statistics of the families of the Volunteers.

Voted, That the Executive Committee be a Committee of conference to consult with the officers of the Military Company relative to any expenses. incurred for which said Company expects to be reimbursed by this Committee, and that the Company be requested to incur no further indebtedness without authority.

Voted, That this meeting be adjourned, to convene at the call of the Executive Committee.

June 22d. By order of the Executive Committee a meeting of the "Committee of twenty-five" was duly notified and holden. The Executive Committee, through George Foster, made a statement presenting the outstanding claims on account of the Military Company, to be acted upon separately.

The following claims were then ordered to be paid by vote:

	Amount.		Amount.
John H. Dean,	$3 93	Shreve and Brown,	$71 00
Dodge and Beard,	7 54	Shreve and Brown,	12 50
A. W. Pollard,	32 00	Shreve and Brown,	37 50
A. W. Stearns and Co.,	163 54	George W. W. Dove,	3 20
E. A. G. Roulstone,	40 00	Chandler and Co.,	9 55
John Earl, Jr.,	164 75	Bill for additional Belts,	3 75
Abbott and Holt,	94 91		
Shreve and Brown,	26 00	Total,	$673 77
John H. Dean,	3 60		

A claim for two drums was referred to the Executive Committee, to be settled at their discretion.

A claim of eleven dollars and fifty cents for the drill service of Mr. Lovejoy, a Volunteer resident of North Andover, was referred to the Executive Committee, with power. The President of the Committee was requested to address the Volunteers on the occasion of their departure to camp on Monday next.

After which the meeting dissolved.

June 24th. Andover sent out her first Company of Light Infantry to the war. They went first to Fort Warren, there to await orders. The Company had been drilled daily for two months; part of the time under Colonel Samuel C. Oliver and Captain Fellows, and the remainder of the time under Captain Holt.

They had made good progress, and compared favorably with other Companies in this vicinity.

On the morning of the 24th, they assembled at the Town House to receive the bounty voted by the Town, and to make their final preparations for departure. At half-past eleven o'clock they partook of a generous collation, which the citizens had prepared in the Town Hall; after which they were drawn into line, and were addressed by Francis Cogswell, President of the Citizens' " Committee of twenty-five."

After the address of the President, the Company was escorted to the depot by the " Ellsworth Guards " of Phillips Academy, the " Havelock Greys " of the Seminary, and a large concourse of citizens and friends who had assembled to witness their departure.

At a meeting of the citizens in April, called to give expression to their sentiments respecting the attack upon Fort Sumter, a banner was promised by the members of Phillips Academy to the Company then forming in town. In fulfilment of that promise, a beautiful banner was presented in the afternoon of June 22d, in front of the South Church. The exercises were attended by a large number of people, among whom was Ex-President Franklin Pierce. The banner was of white silk, bearing upon one side the State arms, and on the reverse a pine tree, with this inscription : " Presented to the Andover Light Infantry by the members of Phillips Academy."

The presentation address was made by J. A. Bent of the Senior Class, and was suitably replied to by Captain Holt.

July 8th. A Town Meeting was held to see what action the Town will take in relation to an Act of General Court, Chapter 222, entitled, "An Act in Aid of the Families of Volunteers, and for other purposes " (Approved May 23, 1861), and to make such regulations for carrying out the provisions of said act as the Town may judge expedient.

Voted, That all the votes passed at the Town Meeting held May 6th, 1861, be, and the same hereby are, ratified, confirmed, and re-enacted.

1861.] DURING THE REBELLION. 19

Voted, That all the acts and contracts performed and made under and by virtue of said votes, passed May 6th, 1861, by the Selectmen, Treasurer, or " Committee of National Defence " be, and the same are, hereby ratified, confirmed, and adopted.

Voted, That the " Committee of National Defence " be discharged, and that the duties of said Committee be hereafter performed by the Selectmen.

Voted, That the pay of families of Volunteers commence from the time the Company received their charter.

Voted, That the Selectmen be authorized to pay to the family of each Volunteer, in addition to the sum of eight dollars per month, appropriated by the votes above-named, such sum as in their judgment shall be necessary and proper for the comfortable maintenance of such family during the continuance of such soldier in the service of the Government, or until otherwise ordered by the Town ; and that the Selectmen be authorized to furnish such aid as they may deem necessary for each parent, brother, sister, or child, who at the time of his enlistment was dependent on such Volunteer for support.

August 7th. The Andover Light Infantry was mustered into the service of the United States July 5th, and was designated as Company H. 14th Regiment Massachusetts Volunteer Infantry. The Regiment left Boston at about ten o'clock, P. M., by the way of the Providence Railroad, for Washington, D. C.

The following is a list of the officers of the Regiment :
Colonel, — William B. Greene, of Haverhill.
Lieut.-Colonel, — Samuel C. Oliver, of Lawrence.
Major, — Levi P. Wright, of Lawrence.
Adjutant, — Charles F. Simmons, of Boston.
Quartermaster, — Andrew Washburn, of Newton.
Surgeon, — David Dana, Jr., of Lawrence.
Assistant Surgeon, — Samuel K. Towle, of Haverhill.

Sergeant-Major, — Amos Henfield, of Salem.
Quarter-Master Sergeant, — William Glass, of Boston.
Commissary-Sergeant, — Arthur Lee Drew, of Haverhill.

The following is a complete roll of the Company as it left Fort Warren.

Captain, — Horace Holt.

1st Lieut. — Charles H. Poor.
2d Lieut. — Moses W. Clement.

1st Sergt. — Samuel C. Hervey.
2d Sergt. — George T. Brown.
3d Sergt. — Orrin L. Farnham.
4th Sergt. — Newton Holt.
5th Sergt. — Frank B. Chapin.

1st Corp. — George S. Farmer.
2d Corp. — Geo. A. W. Vinal.
3d Corp. — Peter D. Smith.
4th Corp. — John Clark.
5th Corp. — Alonzo P. Berry.
6th Corp. — Horace W. Wardwell.
7th Corp. — George F. Hatch.
8th Corp. — Phineas Buckley, Jr.

Musicians, — Newton G. Frye,
George M. Smart.

PRIVATES.

Anderson, James I.
Ashworth, James,
Bailey, Thomas R.
Beale, William,
Bell, Joseph,
Berry, Daniel,
Bodwell, Willard G.
Bohonnon, Albert L.
Brown, La Roy S.
Bryant, Epaphrus K.
Burris, Stephen,
Chandler, George W.
Cheever, Benjamin,
Cocklin, John,
Costello, James,
Coulie, John D.
Craig, George,
Cummings, Charles S.
Currier, Charles,
Curtis, A. Fuller,
Cusick, John,
Cutler, Granville K.
Cutler, Abelino B.

Dane, George,
Dugan, Charles,
Edwards, Francis W.
Farmer, Edward,
Farnham, Samuel P.
Findley, James S.
Findley, John A.
Foster, T. Edwin,
Gilcreast, David D.
Gillespie, William,
Goldsmith, Albert,
Grant, Farnham P.
Gray, Jesse E.
Greene, Charles,
Greene, William H.
Hardy, Franklin,
Hardy, John,
Hatch, Andrew J.
Hatch, Enoch M.
Hatch, Lewis G.
Hart, William,
Holt, Lewis G.
Holt, Warren E.

Howarth, Oberlin B.
Hunt, Amos,
Jenkins, E. Kendall,
Jennings, William E.
Kennedy, John,
Lavalett, Phillip C.
Logue, John,
Lovejoy, Benjamin C.
Lovejoy, Henry T.
Mahoney, Michael,
McClennen, Charles W
McGurk, Bernard,
Mears, Charles,
Mears, Warren, Jr.
Melcher, Sylvester C.
Morse, William B.
Nichols, William W.
O'Hara, Edward,
Pasho, William A.

Pike, George E.
Rea, Aaron G., Jr.
Richardson, Silas, Jr.
Russell, John B. A.
Russell, Joseph, Jr.
Russell, William,
Russell, Winslow,
Sargent, John S.
Saunders, Ziba M.
Shannon, William,
Shattuck, Charles W.
Sherman, Henry T.
Smith, James,
Stevens, Benjamin F.
Townsend, Milton B.
Townsend, Warren W.
Wardwell, Alfred,
Wardwell, William H.
Wood, Elliot,

Feb. 22d, 1862. In pursuance of the recommendation of the President of the United States, the citizens assembled at the Town Hall early in the afternoon to listen to the reading of Washington's Farewell Address, and such other exercises as might be volunteered for the occasion.

The Hall was appropriately decorated with flags, drums, and various arms, the standard presented to the Andover Company by the members of Phillips Academy, and a life-sized portrait of Washington.

The meeting was called to order by Samuel Raymond, and Francis Cogswell was unanimously chosen President. Prayer having been offered by Professor Barrows of the Theological Seminary, and an appropriate song sung by the Lockhart Society, the President delivered an address. The reading of the Farewell Address by Professor Shedd followed, after which the meeting was addressed by Professor Stowe, Rev. Charles Smith, Rev. Benjamin B. Babbitt, and others. Rev. James H. Merrill made the closing prayer.

March 3d. Annual Town Meeting. The 10th Article in the Warrant reads as follows: " To see if the Town will continue aid to the families of Volunteer soldiers as provided in Massachusetts General Laws, Chapter 222."

Voted, To continue aid to the families of Volunteers the same as last year.

July 1st. The President of the United States issued an order calling for three hundred thousand Volunteers to serve three years, or until the end of the war, to form new Regiments and to fill up the ranks of those already in the service. The proportion assigned to Massachusetts was fifteen thousand men.

July 7th. The Governor of the Commonwealth issued an order, numbered twenty-six, calling for fifteen thousand Volunteers. This order was accompanied by a table showing the proportion of each city and town, which was based upon the annual returns made to the Adjutant-General's office by the assessors of the several cities and towns of men liable to do military duty. The number assigned to this town was fifty-two.

July 14th. A Citizens' meeting was held in the evening to aid enlistments in this Town.

Professor Stowe was chosen President, and Warren F. Draper, Secretary. The President offered prayer, and afterwards made an address. Rev. Dr. Cleveland of Lowell, Chaplain of the 30th Massachusetts Regiment addressed the meeting by invitation. The audience joined in singing "America," after which the special business of the meeting was taken up. The following resolution was adopted.

" That in the judgment of this meeting, it is expedient for the Town to offer a bounty of seventy-five dollars to each person who shall volunteer to fill the quota of recruits, now called for by the Government.

Mr. John Aiken addressed the meeting, pledging the above bounty to two of fifty-two recruits required.

Messrs. Peter Smith and John Dove each offered the sum of five dollars, in addition to what the Town should pay, to each recruit to the full number required from the Town.

It was also voted to request the Selectmen to open a recruiting office immediately.

Mr. Warren F. Draper pledged the expenses of the same, there being at that time no provisions therefor.

The Selectmen were requested by vote to call a Town Meeting at the earliest practicable day.

July 19th. A Citizens' Meeting was held in the evening to encourage the enlistment of recruits.

The Meeting was called to order by George Foster, and organized by the choice of the following officers.

President, — Francis Cogswell.

Vice-Presidents, — Governor Berry, of N. H. ; Rev. Dr. Kirk, of Boston, Amos Abbott, John Aiken, Nathan Frye, Capt. Sawyer, of 23d Mass. Reg., William G. Means, Edward Buck, John Dove, Peter Smith, S. C. Leonard, Samuel C. Jackson, James H. Merrill, Charles Smith, Abraham J. Gould, Benjamin Boynton, Asa A. Abbott, and William S. Jenkins.

Secretary, — Warren F. Draper.

The meeting was opened with prayer by Rev. Mr. Smith. Short addresses were made by Professor Barrows, Rev. Mr. Smith, Rev. Mr. Leonard, Edward Buck, John Dove, Peter Smith, William E. Park, Governor Berry, Rev. Dr. Kirk, Captain Sawyer, Amos Abbott, Rev. Dr. Jackson, George W. Stephens one of the recruits, and others.

The following resolutions were unanimously adopted.

Whereas, The Chief Magistrate of this Commonwealth has called upon the Towns of the State to furnish their respective quotas of recruits demanded by the exigencies of the Government, and whereas, he has urgently requested the Selectmen of the towns to use their official and personal influence to furnish their quotas,

Resolved, That this meeting heartily approve the action of the Selectmen of this town in their offer of a bounty of one hundred dollars, and in such other measures as they are taking to fill up the quota of recruits allotted to Andover under the order of the Government of the State, and that we will support these measures in the Town Meeting notified to be holden on the 28th instant.

Resolved, That the Selectmen be requested to employ suitable persons to aid in securing the quota of recruits called for from this Town.

Resolved, That is is expedient for the Town to authorize their Treasurer to borrow money to pay the foregoing bounty, and to defray the expenses incurred by the Selectmen in raising recruits.

Resolved, That a bounty of seventeen dollars be raised by private subscription, and paid to those members of the Andover Company now in service who did not receive a bounty when they were mustered into the service, that thus the Town may be relieved from the necessity of further action thereon.

July 24th. By order of the Executive Committee a meeting of the Citizens' " Committee of twenty-five " was duly notified and holden at the Town House.

The record of the previous meeting was read.

The Treasurer reported the balance of funds on hand to be three hundred and twenty-four dollars and seventy-five cents.

Voted, To authorize the Treasurer of this Committee to pay over to the Selectmen of the town a sum sufficient to pay seventeen dollars to each Volunteer belonging to Andover, now in the service, who had joined Company H. 14th Regiment, previous to July 1, 1862, and who has not received the bounty of seventeen dollars from the Town.

Voted, That the Committee appointed to solicit subscriptions be requested to deliver to the Clerk the Subscription Lists now in their hands, and that the names of the subscribers, with the amount of their subscriptions, and the sums paid thereon be recorded.

Meeting dissolved.

July 28th. At the Town Meeting held this day, the following Articles in the Warrant were acted upon.

Article 2d. — To see if the Town will pay a bounty to all persons who may enlist, and are mustered into the service, to fill Andover's quota of Volunteers now called for.

Article 3d. — To see if the Town will direct that the bounty of seventeen dollars be paid to the members of the Andover Company now in service who did not receive said bounty when they were mustered into service.

Article 4th. — If the foregoing pass in the affirmative, to see if the Town will authorize their Treasurer to hire money if necessary, and adopt such measures as may be thought necessary to carry the same into effect.

Article 5th. — To transact any other business that may come before said meeting.

Took up Article 2d, and

Voted, That a bounty of one hundred dollars be paid to each Volunteer enlisted under this call for Andover's quota.

Took up Article 3d, and the following action was taken:

Whereas, Provision has been made by a Committee of the citizens of this town, known as the "Citizens' Committee of twenty-five," for the payment of the bounty mentioned in Article 3d, thereby relieving the Town from further action relative to the same.

Voted, That the said Article be indefinitely postponed.

Took up Article 4th, and

Voted, That the Treasurer be authorized to hire a sum not exceeding fifty-three hundred dollars, under the direction of the Selectmen, to be expended in the payment of bounty as now voted, and other incidental expenses.

Under Article 5th, patriotic speeches were made by several citizens; also by Captain Sumner Carruth who was wounded in the battle before Richmond. A hearty vote of thanks was given to Captain Carruth for his heroism and bravery in the several battles in which he has been engaged, when the 5th Article was dismissed and the meeting dissolved.

Aug. 4th. President Lincoln ordered a draft for three hundred thousand militia to serve in the army of the United States for nine months; also a special draft from the militia in States whose quota of Volunteers under the last call shall not be filled by the 15th of August.

Aug. 7th. Andover's quota of fifty-two under the Presidents call of July 1st, was completed this day. Their names, age, occupation and bounties, are as follows:

Names.	Age.	Occupation.	Town Bounty.	Smith & Dove Bounty.
Abbott, Noah B.	21	Farmer.	$100 00	$10 00
Abbott, Edward P.	28	Painter,	100 00	10 00
Aiken, Samuel,	37	Stone-mason,	100 00	10 00
Allen, Fletcher T.	21	Farmer,	100 00	10 00
Bailey, Henry H.	27	Farmer,	100 00	10 00
Barnard, George N.	21	Cordwainer,	100 00	10 00
Barnard, Charles P.	21	Cordwainer,	100 00	10 00
Bell, Charles H.	30	Cordwainer,	100 00	10 00
Blunt, Samuel W.	40	Bookseller,	100 00	10 00
Burnham, Henry O.	38	Cordwainer,	100 00	10 00
Burton, Joseph,	41	Flax-dresser,	100 00	10 00
Davis, Charles H.	17	Farmer,	100 00	10 00
Dearborn, John,	19	Operative,	100 00	10 00
Eastes, James,	23	Harness-maker,	100 00	10 00
Gooch, John F.	18	Clerk,	100 00	10 00
Grant, George W.	18	Machinist,	100 00	10 00
Hall, Henry H.	21	Farmer,	100 00	10 00
Hall, William S.	24	Farmer,	100 00	10 00
Hayward, George E.	21	Farmer,	100 00	10 00
Holt, Jonathan A.	21	Farmer,	100 00	10 00
Hussey, Wyman D.	19	Miller,	100 00	10 00
Jenkins, Harrison,	21	File-cutter,	100 00	10 00
Jenkins, Omar,	21	Farmer,	100 00	10 00
Jones, Charles E.	30	Farmer,	100 00	10 00
Joyce, Redmond,	18	Operative,	100 00	10 00
Lindsey, Robert,	30	Teamster,	100 00	10 00

Names.	Age.	Occupation.	Town Bounty.	Smith & Dove Bounty.
Logue, James,	18	Operative,	$100 00	$10 00
Luscomb, Aaron E.	22	Farmer,	100 00	10 00
Maynard, Charles,	18	Farmer,	100 00	10 00
McCabe, Frank,	31	Operative,	100 00	10 00
Mears, John,	18	Operative,	100 00	10 00
Mears, William,	31	Cordwainer,	100 00	10 00
Merrill, William F.	20	Student,	100 00	10 00
Morgan, David S.	27	Medical Student,	100 00	10 00
Morton, Douglas,	28	Baker,	100 00	10 00
Murray, James R.	21	Clerk,	100 00	10 00
Nolan, Malachi,	27	Blacksmith,	100 00	10 00
O'Brien, John,	20	Farmer,	100 00	10 00
O'Conner, Patrick,	23	Operative,	100 00	10 00
Parker, John F.	18	Operative,	100 00	10 00
Ridley, Charles W.	20	Farmer,	100 00	10 00
Rothwell, James H.	21	Carpenter,	100 00	10 00
Russell, Augustine K.	42	Cordwainer,	100 00	10 00
Russell, James,	18	Farmer,	100 00	10 00
Saunders, James,	18	Operative,	100 00	10 00
Shattuck, Leonard G.	22	Farmer,	100 00	10 00
Shattuck, William C.	19	Farmer,	100 00	10 00
Smith, Thomas,	42	Cordwainer,	100 00	10 00
Stephens, George W.	18	Student,	100 00	10 00
Trull, Charles F.	20	Cordwainer,	100 00	10 00
Tuck, M. Warren,	26	Cordwainer,	100 00	10 00
Winchester, Charles H.	35	Farmer,	100 00	10 00
Total,			$5200 00	$520 00

Aug. 8th. The Governor issued the following Proclamation:

COMMONWEALTH OF MASSACHUSETTS.

EXECUTIVE DEPARTMENT,
BOSTON, August 8, 1862.

Pursuant to requirement of the President of the United States, I hereby direct that a new enrolment of militia of Massachusetts be forthwith made and returned to the Adjutant-General of the Commonwealth. This enrolment is to conform to the provisions of the recent Act of Congress (Approved July 17, 1862), entitled, "An Act to amend the Act calling forth the Militia to execute the Laws of the Union, suppress insurrections, and repel invasions," etc. All able-bodied male citizens between the ages of eighteen and forty-five will be included. No exemptions will be considered in making the enrolment. The proper exemptions will be made on proceeding to draft, if any draft shall be made. All Assessors of the cities and towns respectively, will please proceed without delay to execute this duty.

JOHN A. ANDREW,
Governor of Massachusetts.

By order, etc.
OLIVER WARNER,
Secretary of State.

Aug. 14th, A Citizens' meeting was held in the Town Hall in the evening to consider the expediency of offering a bounty for Volunteers to fill the Andover quota of nine months' men.

The meeting was organized by the choice of the following officers.

President, — Francis Cogswell.

Vice-Presidents, — T. N. Haskell, John L. Taylor, Samuel C. Jackson, Peter Smith, Edward Buck, Daniel Logue, James Howarth, George Foster, James S. Eaton, C. M. Cordley, William S. Jenkins, Amos Abbott, Stephen Tracy, William Poor, James Shaw, Henry G. Tyer, Asa A. Abbott, Benjamin Boynton, Henry A. Bodwell, J. Q. A. Edgell, Abraham J. Gould, James Byers, Willard Pike.

Secretary, — Warren F. Draper.

After the meeting had been addressed by the President, Rev. Mr. Haskell, Dr. Jackson, Rev. J. L. Taylor, Rev. Mr. Cordley, and Dr. Howarth, the following resolutions were offered by the Secretary.

Whereas, The Government of the United States by an order from the War Department dated August 4th, 1862, calls for a draft from the loyal States of the Union for three hundred thousand men, to serve nine months in the armies of the United States, and whereas in responding to this demand of the Government many towns in this State are raising their quotas by the enlistment of Volunteers with the inducement of bounties ; therefore,

Resolved, That the quota of Andover under the above specified call of the Government, as it shall be appointed by the Governor of this Commonwealth be raised by the recruitment of Volunteers ; and to the end that this plan may be successfully and speedily consummated, the citizens of this town, now assembled, respectfully request their Selectmen to offer to each Volunteer the bounty of ———— dollars, to be paid as soon as he shall be sworn into service.

Resolved, That the Selectmen are hereby requested to open a recruiting office without delay, and to adopt such other measures as they may deem expedient for securing the quota of this town.

Resolved, That we will uphold and sustain our board of Selectmen in carrying out the provision of these resolutions, and give them our support at a formal meeting of the Town, which they are requested to call at once.

Resolved, That a copy of these resolutions be placed in the hands of the Selectmen.

On a motion of John Flint the blank was filled by inserting one hundred dollars as the bounty. The resolutions were then unanimously adopted.

COMMONWEALTH OF MASSACHUSETTS.

HEADQUARTERS, BOSTON, Aug. 21, 1862.

GENERAL ORDER, No. 38.

Whereas, The provisions of the Statutes of this Commonwealth are defective for the purpose of carrying into effect the draft of militia under the Order of the President of the United States, bearing date August 4th, 1862. It is therefore, ordered,

First, That the quota of a draft of three hundred thousand militia, to be called into the service of the United States to serve for the period of nine months, unless sooner discharged, which the State of Massachusetts has been required to furnish, to wit: nineteen thousand and eighty men to be raised by a draft, which will be conducted in conformity with the regulations of the War Department of the United States contained in General Order No. 99 of said Department, bearing date August 9, 1862, a copy of which is published with, and as a part of, the present Order (marked A).

Second, It is further Ordered, That the Assessors of the several towns and cities use all possible dispatch in completing and returning the new enrolment in the manner heretofore ordered, which is in no respect modified by this Order.

Third, And that the Selectmen of the several towns, and Mayors and Aldermen of the several cities, immediately return to the office of the Adjutant-General a sworn statement of the names and number of their inhabitants who have heretofore been mustered into the service of the United States, whose stipulated term of service has not expired, with the Companies and Regiments into which they have been enlisted. This return is directed in order that the draft may be equalized as far as possible, and towns and cities which have heretofore furnished more men them their just proportion may have due allowance for the same in the draft.

Fourth, Commissioners to superintend drafting in each County will be forthwith appointed, and Surgeons to determine claims of exemption on account of disability. These officers will receive minute instructions from the Commander-in-chief as to the mode of executing their respective duties.

Fifth, Copies of the enrolment lists for each town and city will be kept in the office of the town or city clerk for inspection. The copies to be returned to the Adjutant-General will be filed with the Sheriff of the several Counties for two days previous to the commencement of drafting in any city or town.

Sixth, The Commissioners and Surgeons will themselves appoint times and places for receiving and determining claims for exemption, conformably to the regulations of the

War Deparment, and all exemptions must be then and there claimed and determined, and not afterwards ; but all exemptions known to the Commissioners to exist, will be allowed whether claimed or not.

Seventh, After all not liable to draft have been stricken from the list in any town or city by the Commissioner, he will at once report the number remaining thereon to the Adjutant-General, who will proceed to fix the exact quota of said town or city, and order the Commissioner to make a draft for the same in the manner prescribed in the regulations of the War Department.

Eighth, Rendezvous and commandants of the same will be seasonably appointed.

Ninth, The drafting will commence in accordance with the Order of the War Department, dated August 4, 1862, which is herewith published as a part of this Order (marked B).

Tenth, The instructions relating to enrolment promulgated through the State Department are herewith republished for the information of all.

Eleventh, Although every arrangement will be made as speedily as possible to execute this draft, — and the same will be promptly and rigidly carried out in any place which fails to furnish Volunteers to the number of its quota of militia, — yet the Municipal Authorities and Citizens of Massachusetts are earnestly exhorted to furnish at once the requisite number of Volunteers in order to avoid wherever possible, and if possible everywhere, any necessity for drafting.

To this end the Adjutant-General will at once publish for the information of the people an approximate estimate of the number of men due from each place, although an accurate statement cannot be made until the enrolment is completed, and the names of all not liable to draft have been stricken out.

To prevent all misunderstanding, notice is given that all Companies of Volunteer Militia which do not volunteer will be disbanded before the exemptions are arranged upon the enrolment lists; this course is rendered necessary because otherwise the members of Volunteer Companies would be exempt from draft.

The Commander-in-chief has never for a moment doubted that the patriotism of the people of Massachusetts already illustrated by so much devotedness to the cause of their country from the beginning of the present struggle, would voluntarily furnish all the support of means, and of men, which the exegencies of the service and their duty may require. Nor does he believe it now doubtful that Volunteers for the quota required will be enlisted as rapidly as the means can be accumulated for their care, equipment, and organization. But, as from the first, it has been the purpose and duty of the State Government to obey all lawful orders emanating from the President and the Department of War, so now it is the purpose of the Governor of Massachusetts faithfully to pursue the directions he may receive in this behalf. And he relies on the unshrinking courage, the loyal patriotism, and the ancient manly character of the people of Massachusetts for all the support and encouragement which may be needed in the future.

By command of His Excellency, JOHN A. ANDREW, Governor and Commander-in-Chief.

WILLIAM SCHOULER,
Adjutant-General.

Aug. 25th. A Town Meeting was held in the afternoon which was largely attended. The meeting was organized by the choice of S. C. Jackson as Moderator. The following Articles were in the Warrant calling the meeting.

Article 2d. — To see if the Town will pay a bounty of one hundred dollars to Volunteers for filling Andover's quota of nine months' men.

Article 3d. — If the second article pass in the affirmative, to see if the Town will authorize their Treasurer to hire money to pay said bounty, if necessary.

Article 4th. — To see if the Town will ratify the resolutions passed at the Citizens' meeting of August 14th, requesting the Selectmen to open a recruiting office.

Took up Article 2d, and adopted the following, proposed by Dr. Jackson.

Whereas, The State of Massachusetts has been required under an Order of the President of the United States, bearing date August 4, 1862, to furnish her quota of a draft of (300,000) three hundred thousand militia, amounting to (19,080) nineteen thousand and eighty men, to serve for nine months, unless sooner discharged, in the service of the United States, and

Whereas, The citizens of this town would cordially respond to said Order of the President by furnishing *Volunteers* rather than *conscripts* to fill up its quota of the proposed draft, and would deem it a dishonor and a stain upon their patriotism to send soldiers raised by conscription for the defence of Liberty and the Union; and,

Whereas, The said citizens desire to equalize, as far as may be, the pecuniary burdens imposed upon the people by the present war against a most wicked rebellion; therefore,

Voted, That each Volunteer to fill the quota of men to be assigned to this town under the aforesaid Order of the President for a draft of militia, shall receive from the treasury of the town the sum of one hundred dollars as a bounty, when duly accepted and sworn into the service of the United States.

Took up Article 3d, and

Voted, That the Treasurer be authorized to hire a sum not exceeding six thousand dollars, if necessary, to pay said bounty.

Took up Article 4th, and,

Voted, To ratify the doings of the Selectmen, in opening a recruiting office.

The foregoing votes having passed unanimously, and the business of the meeting being disposed of, Mr. Benjamin F. Wardwell offered the following preamble and resolution, which was adopted, with but one negative vote.

Whereas, The institution of slavery is the cause of the present insurrection, threatening the subversion not only of Democratic and Republican principles, but of the nation ; therefore,

Resolved, That the President of the United States is hereby called on to declare the abolition of slavery throughout the length and breadth of the land, without delay.

Aug. 29th. In accordance with the 3d Section of General Order No. 38, issued by order of the Governor on the 21st day of August last, the Selectmen returned the following

Roll of the Inhabitants of this Town, who have been mustered into the Service of the United States, whose stipulated term of Service had not expired.

Abbott, Edward P.	14th Regt.	Bolton, William A.	11th Regt.
Abbott, Frank,	33d Regt.	Brady, James L.	Deserted.
Abbott, George B.	33d Regt.	Brown, George T.	14th Regt.
Abbott, Moses B.	18th Regt.	Brown, Leroy S.	14th Regt.
Abbott, Noah B.	14th Regt.	Bryant, Epaphrus K.	14th Regt.
Aiken, Samuel,	14th Regt.	Buckley, Phineas, Jr.	14th Regt.
Allen, T. Fletcher,	14th Regt.	Buguay, George A.	20th Regt.
Anderson, James I.	14th Regt.	Burnham, Henry O.	14th Regt.
Armstrong, Thomas,	19th Regt.	Burris, Stephen,	14th Regt.
Ashworth, James,	14th Regt.	Burton, Joseph,	14th Regt.
Bagley, Thomas,	22d Regt.	Callahan, Charles H.	20th Regt.
Bailey, Thomas R.	14th Regt.	Campbell, Colin,	14th Regt.
Bailey, Henry H.	14th Regt.	Carlton, Oscar F.	Battery.
Bailey, George A.	26th Regt.	Carter, William S.	6th Regt.
Barker, Samuel S.	5th Regt.	Chandler, George W.	14th Regt.
Barnard, George N.	14th Regt.	Chandler, Joseph, Jr.	26th Regt.
Barnard, Charles P.	14th Regt.	Chapin, Frank B.	14th Regt.
Barrows, William E.	19th Regt.	Cheever, Benjamin,	14th Regt.
Bell, Robert,	14th Regt.	Cheever, Samuel,	14th Regt.
Bell, Charles H.	14th Regt.	Christian, William T.	23d Regt.
Berry, Alonzo P.	14th Regt.	Clark, Aaron S.	14th Regt.
Berry, Israel,	Sharp Shooters.	Clark, George B.	14th Regt.
Blunt, Samuel W.	14th Regt.	Clark, John,	14th Regt.
Bodwell, Willard G.	14th Regt.	Clement, Charles,	13th Regt.
Bohonnon, Albert L.	14th Regt.	Clement, Moses W.	14th Regt.

Cocklin, John,	14th Regt.	Green, William H.	14th Regt.
Conley, Jeremiah,	14th Regt.	Hall, Henry H.	14th Regt.
Cooper, Thomas H.	6th Regt.	Hall, William S.	14th Regt.
Costello, James,	14th Regt.	Hanson, Charles,	4th Regt.
Costello, James,	22d Regt.	Hardy, Franklin,	14th Regt.
Coulie, John D.	14th Regt.	Hardy, John,	14th Regt.
Craig, George,	14th Regt.	Hart, William,	14th Regt.
Critchett, George D.	15th Regt.	Hastie, Thomas,	14th Regt.
Cummings, Charles S.	14th Regt.	Hatch, George F.	14th Regt.
Currier, Charles,	14th Regt.	Hatch, Enoch M.	14th Regt.
Curtis, A. Fuller,	14th Regt.	Hatch, Lewis G.	14th Regt.
Cusick, John,	14th Regt.	Hatch, Andrew J.	14th Regt.
Cutler, Granville K.	14th Regt.	Hayes, John,	14th Regt.
Cutler, Abalino B.	14th Regt.	Hayes, Patrick,	22d Regt.
Dane, George,	14th Regt.	Hayward, George E.	14th Regt.
Dane, A. L.	6th Regt.	Hervey, Samuel C.	14th Regt.
Dane, Elmore,	26th Regt.	Hervey, Albert G.	1st Cavalry.
Davis, Charles H.	14th Regt.	Higgins, Archibald, Jr.	19th Regt.
Dearborn, John,	14th Regt.	Holt, Horace,	14th Regt.
Dugan, Charles,	14th Regt.	Holt, Jonathan A.	14th Regt.
Eastes, James,	14th Regt.	Holt, Lewis G.	14th Regt.
Edwards, Francis W.	14th Regt.	Holt, Newton,	14th Regt.
Farmer, Edward,	14th Regt.	Holt, Warren E.	14th Regt.
Farmer, George S.	14th Regt.	Howarth, Oberlin B.	14th Regt.
Farnham, Orrin L.	14th Regt.	Hovey, John C.	14th Regt.
Farnham, Samuel P.	14th Regt.	Hunter, William,	22d Regt.
Findley, James S.	14th Regt.	Hussey, Wyman D.	14th Regt.
Findley, John A.	14th Regt.	Jenkins, E. Kendall,	14th Regt.
Foster, Thomas E.	14th Regt.	Jenkins, Harrison,	14th Regt.
French, Henry P.	2d Regt.	Jenkins, Omar,	14th Regt.
Frorz, James A.	6th Regt.	Jennings, William E.	14th Regt.
Frye, Newton G.	14th Regt.	Johnson, John,	14th Regt.
Frye, Enoch O.	14th Regt.	Johnson, John,	22d Regt.
Gallon, James,	20th Regt.	Joice, Redmond,	14th Regt.
Gilcreast, David B.	14th Regt.	Jones, Charles E.	14th Regt.
Gillespie, William,	14th Regt.	Keating, John,	11th Regt.
Goldsmith, Albert,	14th Regt.	Kennedy, John,	14th Regt.
Goldsmith, Joseph C.	14th Regt.	Lavalette, Phillip C.	14th Regt.
Gooch, John F.	14th Regt.	Lindsey, Robert,	14th Regt.
Grant, Farnham P.	14th Regt.	Lovejoy, Benjamin C.	14th Regt.
Grant, George W.	14th Regt.	Lovejoy, William W.	2d Regt.
Grandy, Henry C.	5th Regt.	Lovejoy, Newton,	3d U S. Inf.
Gray, Jesse E.	14th Regt.	Lovejoy, George W.	1st Regt.
Gray, Nathan H.	20th Regt.	Logue, John,	14th Regt.

Logue, James,	14th Regt.	Russell, James,	14th Regt.
Luscomb, Aaron E.	14th Regt.	Russell, John B. A.	14th Regt.
Mahoney, Michael,	14th Regt.	Russell, William,	14th Regt.
Marland, William,	6th Regt.	Russell, Winslow,	14th Regt.
Mason, Josiah,	Sharp Shooters.	Sanborn, Frank,	6th Regt.
Mason, Warren,	26th Regt.	Sargent, John,	14th Regt.
Maynard, Charles,	14th Regt.	Saunders, James,	14th Regt.
McClenna, Charles W.	14th Regt.	Saunders, Thomas,	24th Regt.
McCabe, Frank,	14th Regt.	Saunders, Ziba M.	14th Regt.
McGurk, Bernard,	14th Regt.	Shannon, John,	11th Regt.
McLaughlin, John,	14th Regt.	Shannon, William,	14th Regt.
Mears, Charles,	14th Regt.	Shattuck, Leonard G.	14th Regt.
Mears, Warren, Jr.	14th Regt.	Shattuck, C. William,	35th Regt.
Mears, John,	14th Regt.	Sherman, Henry T.	14th Regt.
Mears, Daniel, Jr.	11th Regt.	Shield, Nicholas,	14th Regt.
Mears, George,	11th Regt.	Smith, James,	14th Regt.
Mears, William,	14th Regt.	Smith, James B.	33d Regt.
Melcher, Sylvester C.	14th Regt.	Smith, Peter D.	14th Regt.
Merrill, F. H.	6th Regt.	Smith, Thomas,	14th Regt.
Merrill, William F.	14th Regt.	Stephens, George W.	14th Regt.
Morgan, David S.	14th Regt.	Stevens, Benjamin F.	14th Regt.
Morton, Douglas,	14th Regt.	Stowe, Frederick W.	14th Regt.
Morse, William B.	14th Regt.	Stott, Joshua H.	1st Cavalry.
Murray, James R.	14th Regt.	Townsend, Milton B.	14th Regt.
Nickerson, Ephraim N.	26th Regt.	Townsend, Warren W.	14th Regt.
Nichols, William W.	14th Regt.	Townley, John J.	12th Regt.
Nolan, Malachi,	14th Regt.	Trulan, William,	22d Regt.
O'Brien, John,	14th Regt.	Trull, Charles F.	14th Regt.
O'Conner, Patrick,	14th Regt.	Tuck, M. Warren,	14th Regt.
O'Hara, Edward,	14th Regt.	Tulkinton, Henry,	6th Regt.
Parker, George W.	24th Regt.	Turner, John,	26th Regt.
Parker, John F.	14th Regt.	Vaux, Walter R.	20th Regt.
Pasho, William A.	14th Regt.	Wallace, Alexander,	11th Regt.
Peterson, George,	14th Regt.	Wardwell, Horace W.	14th Regt.
Pike, George E.	14th Regt.	Wardwell, William H.	14th Regt.
Poor, Charles H.	14th Regt.	Wardwell, Joseph W.	1st Cavalry.
Raymond, Jefferson N.	26th Regt.	Welch, Robert,	11th Regt.
Rea, Aaron G. Jr.	14th Regt.	Winchester, Charles H.	14th Regt.
Ridley, Charles W.	14th Regt.	Winthrop, Thomas F.	19th Regt.
Richardson, Silas, Jr.	14th Regt.	Woodlin, Elgin,	11th Regt.
Rowley, R. Augustus,	R. Rangers.	Wood, Elliot,	14th Regt.
Russell, Augustine K.	14th Regt.	Worthley, Daniel E.	16th Regt.

As the foregoing list of two hundred and twenty-two inhabitants was the starting point of all succeeding quotas, it is desirable that the facts in relation to it should be somewhat fully stated. When the President made his first call for Volunteers on the 15th day of April, 1861, it does not appear that any quotas were assigned to the several municipalities. Recruiting offices were opened at any place where it was apparent a Company could be raised. During the interval between this and the second call in July 1862, many of our citizens had left town and enlisted in other places, wherever fancy, friendship, or interest dictated ; often giving as their place of residence, on the enlistment rolls, the name of the place where they happened to enlist.

It was in the interest of this second call, the call under which the fifty-two recruits were furnished from this town, that quotas were assigned and bounties paid. The quotas were computed on the basis of the very imperfect returns made by the assessors of "men liable to do military duty"; returns which for years they had been required to make annually.

As a third call was about to be made, and these returns were imperfect, the Governor by Proclamation of August 8th, 1862, ordered a new enrolment; and on the 21st issued General Order No. 38.

It will be noticed by referring to the Order which precedes the list, that the Selectmen were required to immediately return to the Adjutant-General's office, "a sworn statement of the number and names of the inhabitants who have heretofore been mustered into the service of the United States, whose specified term of service has not expired," etc.

The list returned by the Selectmen, pursuant to this Order, was again an imperfect one. But in view of the fact that it was *the* list accepted by the State authorites, and by the Town as true, it is given in this volume without alteration.

The most material errors in it are as follows:

It claims eleven men as in the 4th, 5th, and 6th Regiments. These were all three months' Regiments which on the expiration of their term of service, nearly or quite a year previous, had been mustered out. Baker and Hanson had re-enlisted in the 1st Company of Sharp-Shooters, and Marland in the 2d Battery, and the name of Frorz is not found in either Regiment. Costello's name appears in the 14th where he belonged, and again in the 22d. Welch was not in the 11th; the Regiment to which he belonged, if any, is unknown. The name of John Johnson in the 14th, probably should have been Solon Johnson.

On the other hand the names of a large number of men, whose "specified terms of service had *not* expired," were omitted. Of these, some had died in the service, some had been discharged for disability; but by far the larger number still remained in active service. A list of these omitted names will be found on a subsequent page.

The other errors are perhaps unimportant, and consist principally in placing some twelve men, more or less, in Regiments to which they did not belong.

It was ascertained early in August that this town's quota of nine months' men would be about twenty-three, the Town authorities without awaiting the official notification of its quota, proceeded without delay to enlist that number of men, and before the publication (October 1st) of General Order No. 52, assigning to the several cities and towns their respective quotas, there had been mustered into service the following

Roll of Nine Months' Volunteers, mustered into Service in response to General Order No. 38, of August 21st, and in anticipation of General Order No. 52, of October 1st.

Name.	Regt.	Age.	Occupation.	Town Bounty.
Allen, Walter B.	44th,	31	Mason,	$100 00
Bowen, Albert L.	45th,			*
Burtt, J. Albert,	43d,	21	Farmer,	100 00
Carruth, Isaac S.	43d,	22	Farmer,	100 00
Clarke, Amasa,	44th,	18	Student,	100 00

* Paid by Frederick L. Church.

DURING THE REBELLION.

Name.	Regt.	Age.	Occupation.	Town Bounty.
Cogswell, Thomas M.	44th,	18	Student,	100 00
Fulton, Joseph W.	50th,	23	Clerk,	100 00
Harnden, George W.	50th,	23	Clerk,	100 00
Holt, Ballard, 2d,	44th,	25	Carpenter,	100 00
Holt, Samuel M.	45th,	37	Farmer,	100 00
Kimball, Henry G.	44th,	43	Shoemaker,	100 00
Lovejoy, George W.	44th,	27	Carriage Maker,	100 00
Lovejoy, Joseph T.	43d,	22	File Cutter,	100 00
Marland, Charles H.	44th,	19	Operative,	100 00
Merrill, James W.	45th,	21	Farmer,	100 00
Raymond, Edward G.	44th,	19	Clerk,	100 00
Raymond, Walter L.	44th,	16	Student,	100 00
Rogers, L. Waldo,	44th,	24	Clerk,	100 00
Tracy, William W.	45th,	18	Student,	100 00
Tyler, Herbert,	44th,	18	Clerk,	100 00
Vinal, George A. W.	6th,	28	Dentist,	100 00
Young, George W.	44th,	20	Clerk,	100 00
Young, Francis C.	44th,	18	Student,	100 00
Total Town Bounty,				$2200 00

Sept. 15th. A Town Meeting was called to act upon the following Articles, Amos Abbott being Moderator.

Article 2d. — To determine what action the Town will take in reference to extending the payment of the bounty voted at the last Town Meeting to all Volunteers who shall enlist from this town, on petition of Marcus Morton, Jr., and others.

Article 3d. — To see if the Town will authorize the Treasurer to borrow money to carry the above vote into effect.

Took up Article 2d, and

Voted, That the Selectmen be authorized to pay a bounty of one hundred dollars to all able-bodied men who shall enlist from this town for nine months or more, and be duly sworn into the service of the United States.

Took up Article 3d, and

Voted, That the Treasurer be authorized to hire money necessary to carry the above vote into effect.

Complaints having been made that cities and towns whose quotas of nine months' men were not completed were inducing inhabitants of other places, by the payment of large bounties, to enlist to their credit, and were also claiming credit for men omitted in the returns called for by General Order No. 38, the Governor issued the following Order.

COMMONWEALTH OF MASSACHUSETTS.

HEADQUARTERS, BOSTON, Oct. 1, 1862.

GENERAL ORDER NO. 52.

Ordered, That the numbers of the militia to be furnished by the several towns and cities for nine months' service, in accordance with General Order No. 51, and in answer to the call of the President of the United States, dated August 4, 1862, be those stated opposite their respective names in the third column of figures in the Schedule herewith published.

Ordered, That the Selectmen, or Mayor and Aldermen of those towns and cities which shall furnish, as a part of their proportion for such nine months' service, men who are inhabitants of other places, return to the office of the Adjutant-General on or before the eleventh day of October, instant, a sworn statement of the names of such men, with the places of their residence, and the Regiments in which they shall have enlisted, together with the written consent of the Selectmen, or Mayor and Aldermen of the town or city in which they may reside.

Ordered, That the Selectmen, or Mayor and Aldermen of towns and cities claiming credit towards their quotas of nine months' men, for men enlisted for three years and not named in the previous returns called for by General Order No. 38, return to the office of the Adjutant-General on or before the eleventh day of October, instant, a supplementary statement, under oath, of such additional names, and the Regiments into which they have enlisted.

By order of his Excellency, JOHN A. ANDREW, Governor and Commander-in-Chief.

WILLIAM SCHOULER,
ADJUTANT-GENERAL.

In the Schedule appended to this Order, the quota of
Andover is stated as 245
Three years' men in the service (as by the Selectmen's
returns), ... 222
Nine months' men now called for, ... 23

COMMONWEALTH OF MASSACHUSETTS.

HEADQUARTERS, BOSTON, Nov. 1, 1862.

GENERAL ORDER No. 56.

Whereas, Since the promulgation of General Order No. 52, fixing the numbers of the militia to be furnished by the several towns and cities for nine months' service, in answer to the call of the President of the United States, dated Aug. 4, 1862, a portion of those towns and cities have been allowed, upon their petition, setting forth equitable reasons therefor, to have the names of men stricken from their lists of enrolled militia as exempts from draft, numbering in the aggregate (4097) four thousand and ninety-seven, by which means deductions have been made from the numbers to be furnished, amounting in all to (1802) eighteen hundred and two; and

Whereas, Since the promulgation of said General Order, credits have been allowed to several towns and cities for men previously in service who had been omitted from their previous returns, amounting in all to (1952) nineteen hundred and fifty-two, and

Whereas, These two classes of allowances have diminished the number of nine months' men furnished by the Commonwealth to the extent of (3754) thirty-seven hundred and fifty-four men, and a new apportionment is thereby rendered necessary to supply the deficiency, which it is estimated will be about (2000) two thousand, after deducting the surpluses of those places which have exceeded the number required of them, and

Whereas, Several other towns and cities have represented that, from their not understanding its importance or effect, they neglected to have stricken from their rolls the names of persons entitled to be exempt from draft, thereby rendering their proportions higher than those of other places where more attention was paid to that subject, and

Whereas, Several towns and cities have represented that of the number of men whom they have in service, a large portion are aliens, and persons not liable to draft, — which fact does not appear on their sworn returns of men in service, — and that in consequence, their relative capacity has been rated higher than it would have been if the facts had appeared on their returns.

Now therefore, For the purpose of a new apportionment to supply the deficiency above-mentioned, and to render the same as just and equal as possible, it is hereby

Ordered, That the Drafting Commissioners, appointed by General Order No. 43, sit again to hear claims to exemption, in the manner directed by the instructions to the said Commissioners issued from the Executive Department of this Commonwealth under the date of September 5, 1862, and that they give notice of their hearings, revise the lists of enrolled militia, strike the names of exempts therefrom, and report to the Adjutant-General the number of names remaining on lists of each city and town in their respective counties, in the manner directed by the said instructions. And it is further

Ordered, That the Selectmen of every town, and the Mayor and Aldermen of every city who had, prior to the first day of October, 1862, returned to the Adjutant-General the names of any men enlisted in the military service of the United States who were aliens, or exempted from being drafted for any other reason not arising from their enlistment, report to the Adjutant-General the names of all such enlisted persons so exempted, and the reasons of such exemption ; and it is further

Ordered, That all reports and returns called for by this Order, be made to the Adjutant-General on or before the fifteenth day of November, instant, *and that no report or re-*

turn shall be received or considered in making up such apportionment, unless received by the Adjutant-General on or before the said fifteenth day of November, and that no revision of militia rolls, and no returns of men in service shall afterwards be allowed to vary the said apportionment. And it is further

Ordered, That each of the said Commissioners make a particular report of the cases, if any, in which they have reason to believe that certificates of physical disability have been improperly executed, in order that such cases may be investigated at Head-Quarters. Such certificates if found to be erroneous will not be conclusive.

By order of his Excellency, JOHN A. ANDREW, Governor and Commander-in-Chief.

WILLIAM SCHOULER,
ADJUTANT-GENERAL.

Nov. 22d. The Governor issued General Order No. 58, ordering a draft to be executed on the 8th of December. A Schedule attached to this Order shows that in this Town

The whole number of non-exempts by the Commissioners
returns was 537
Whole No. of non-exempts in three years' service . . 203
    Leaving liable to draft 334
Andover's whole quota as assigned by General Order
No. 58, ... 287
Whole No. of men in 3 years' service (19 being exempts), 222
    Whole No. of nine months' men required . . 65
The number that has been mustered in . . . 23
    Leaving the number to be furnished at this date, 42

Nov. 25th. A Citizens' Meeting was held in the Town Hall to take action with regard to the new demand for nine months' men. A Committee was appointed, consisting of Samuel Raymond, Jacob Chickering, Henry A. Bodwell, John Cornell, and Warren F. Draper, to act in concert with the Selectmen in effecting specified measures.

Nov. 29th. Mr. Draper, one of the Committee, and Mr. Asa A. Abbott, one of the Selectmen, subsequently waited upon the Governor, and presented the following petition.

To his Excellency John A. Andrew, Governor of the State of Massachusetts:

The Selectmen of Andover on Tuesday last, the 25th instant, called a meeting of the citizens at which they announced the fact that, by an Order (No. 58) from the State authorities, the Town was called upon to furnish more men to fill its quota for nine months' service in the United States Armies. The citizens were startled and mortified by the announcement of a deficiency of nearly double the number of the first call which they had fully filled, and with alacrity. As neither the Selectmen nor other citizens were able to explain the fact, a Committee of investigation was appointed.

In the brief time which has since elapsed, the following facts have been developed.

First, That the Selectmen acting under orders from the State authorities, have made a return of the names of two hundred and twenty-two men from this town who were in the three years' military service of the United States previous to the call for the nine months' quota.

Second, That they have returned the names of twenty-three men to fill the nine months' quota, being the whole number called for by the Order of the State under the previous apportionment.

Third, That there are not less than thirty, and we believe there are nearly forty more names on the regimental rolls at the State House belonging to Andover, several of whose families have received and are receiving State Aid through the agency of the Selectmen of Andover, but whose names have not been returned to the State authorities, a list of which names, together with the Regiments and Companies in which they serve, is hereto annexed.

Fourth, That adequate notice of the times and places for obtaining exemptions has not been given to the enrolled inhabitants of the town since the first apportionment was filled, while the impression has prevailed that the quota of the town was filled; and consequently few have known the importance, or have embraced the opportunity, of claiming exemptions.

Fifth, That during the interval between the first and second apportionment of nine months' quotas, several cities and towns of this State, particularly those which had failed promptly to fill up their quotas under the first apportionment, have employed the interval in obtaining exemptions for their citizens, in some cases paying the Surgeon's fees from the public treasury, and by other means encouraging persons to claim exemption, thereby reducing their quotas in the new apportionment, while Andover, whose quota was early filled, has not been aware of these efforts, and has not made corresponding exertions. Thus great inequality has been produced in the new apportionment, and great injustice will be done by the enforcement of a draft under it. An unequal burden will be imposed upon those towns most prompt in responding to the early calls of the Government As an illustration, we state that the enrolled militia of Andover, aside from those in service, as appears by the returns in the office of the Commissioners, number three hundred and seventy; of whom thirty-seven have been exempted or just one in ten, while the neighboring town of North Andover has two hundred and ninety-four enrolled, of whom seventy-six are exempted, more than one in four of their enrolment.

It can be shown that, had proper returns been made by those in service from Andover, and had the efforts been made to obtain exempts here that have been made in some other towns, Andover would have to-day a surplus above all demands upon her.

If it be objected that the Town of Andover in common with all the rest has had an opportunity to correct its returns, and that if its Selectmen have failed or neglected to make full returns, the responsibility rests upon the Town; it is unfortunate, but not unjust, we reply, that the Selectmen are in this matter the appointees of the State authorities, that they have not submitted their doings to the Town. No complete list of Andover soldiers, or list of men returned to the office of the State authorities has been accessible in the town ; consequently, the citizens have remained to a great extent, in ignorance of the doings of the Selectmen under the belief that the quota of the town was full. Justice seems to demand that at least credit should be given to the town for those she had sent to the war, that her citizens should not be subjected to the mortification and cruelty of an unjust draft, after so promptly answering the calls of the Government for men, in consequence of the omission or oversight of those whom the State itself appointed to conduct these matters.

We, therefore, pray your Excellency that a further opportunity be given to Andover to make additional returns of her men in service, and for further exemptions.

ASA A. ABBOTT, *one of the Selectmen.*
W. F. DRAPER, *one of the Committee.*

ANDOVER, Nov. 29, 1862.

Dec. 1st. A Town Meeting was held to act on the following Articles.

Article 2d. — To see what action the Town will take to fill up the quota of men called for from this town, for the Military Service of the United States by General Order No. 58.

Article 3d. — To act on any other business that may legally come before said meeting.

Took up Article 2d, and the following report was made.

By a recent Order (No. 58) from the State, dated Nov. 22d, the town of Andover is called upon to furnish forty-two more men to fill up the quota of nineteen thousand and eighty to be sent from this State under the last call from the Government; and in case this number of forty-two is not otherwise furnished and mustered into service before the 8th of December, instant, the deficiency will be supplied by a draft, to commence on that day, at nine o'clock. On receiving the Order the Selectmen called a meeting of the citizens last Tuesday evening. Several questions arose at that meeting which could not then be satisfactorily answered, and a Committee was chosen to make investigation.

This Committee ascertained that the names of several Andover men, who were, and are now in service, had not been returned to the State authorities, and consequently had not been credited to the Town in making out its quota called for by the Order above mentioned. Could these names now be returned they would reduce the quota accordingly. It was found that, during the interval between the first enrolment and the second closing of the returns (Nov. 15), some towns had encouraged their citizens to obtain exemptions at the expense of the town treasury, thereby greatly reducing their quota, while Andover had made no corresponding effort to exempt its citizens.

These facts were communicated to the Governor, accompanied by a petition that further opportunity might be allowed to Andover to make her returns of men in the service, and for its citizens to claim exemption. A formal answer has not been received to this petition. But the Adjutant-General and the Governor submitted a report upon another case, involving the same principles which govern our own, wherein the conclusion is reached that no relief can be granted. The Town of Andover having had equal opportunity with all others in the State, must submit to whatever inconvenience any failure on its own part may subject it. The Committee have made efforts to ascertain how many of its citizens have entered the service, who can be made available toward making up the forty-two men lacking of its quota, according to General Order No. 58. It is believed that there are such men. If these are accepted there still remain —— men to be furnished to fill the quota from this town. Whereupon, it was

Voted, That a complete list of the enrolled militia of this town be entered in a book suitable for the purpose ; in which the exempts shall be designated by drawing a red line through their names as ordered by the State in its rolls. Also, that there shall be made a complete list of men in the service, who are counted to the Town as part of its quotas ; to which shall be added from time to time, the name of every man who shall contribute any part of any quota called for from this town, together with the Regiment and Company which he joined, the date of his being mustered into service, of his discharge, death, etc., as far as can be ascertained ; and that this book shall be kept at the Town House for inspection, at suitable times, for all citizens of the town.

Voted, That a Committee acting in conjunction with the Selectmen, be chosen to prepare, and keep these lists.

Voted, That a Committee of one or more persons be chosen from each school district, to aid in obtaining these names and facts, and report the same to the recording Committee ; also to aid the Selectmen in procuring enlistments to fill the quota of the town under General Order No. 58.

Voted, That the Selectmen of the town be authorized to pay to every Volunteer, who shall be credited to the town on its quota under General Order No. 58, a bounty of one hundred dollars on being mustered into service — whether such Volunteer be a resident of this town or otherwise, — and the sum of ten dollars expenses, in case of those enlisted out of town.

Chose as Committee first named above, — Samuel Raymond, Jacob Chickering, Henry A. Bodwell, John Cornell, and Warren F. Draper.

Chose as Committee from School Districts :
South Centre, — John Cornell, George Foster.
Phillips, — Warren F. Draper, Henry A. Bodwell.
Holt, — Benjamin Jenkins.
Scotland, — Hezekiah Jones.
Ballard Vale, — John E. Farnham, Isaac O. Blunt.
Village, — David Higgins, William Frye.
Centre, West Parish, — Charles Shattuck.
North, — Nathan G. Abbott.
Abbott, — Moses B. Abbott.

Bailey, — Simeon Bardwell.
Osgood, — Henry Boynton.
The meeting then adjourned to Thursday evening, December 4th.

Dec. 4th. The Town Meeting met according to adjournment.

Voted, That the Selectmen be requested to inquire into all facts in reference to a list of names reported in service, and report at an adjournment.

Voted, To reconsider the vote of Monday last, offering a bounty of one hundred and ten dollars.

Voted, That the Selectmen be required to pay a bounty of one hundred and fifty dollars to all men required to fill the quota of this town.

Amos Abbott gave notice that he should move a reconsideration of this vote at an adjournment of this meeting.

A motion to dissolve this meeting was decided by a yea and nay vote, the check-list being used; yeas forty-three, nays sixty-four.

Adjourned to one week from this evening, at half-past seven o'clock.

Dec. 4th. The Governor issued General Order No. 60, suspending the draft for ten days in such cities and towns as adopt the suggestions therein made.

Dec. 11th. The Town Meeting was held according to adjournment.

The matter of the notice of Amos Abbott was laid on the table, to hear the Selectmen's report of their doings.

The Chairman of the Board reported that after the meeting of December 1st, and prior to the meeting of December 4th, they made an arrangement with a recruiting officer in Boston to furnish men for the three years' service, at the bounty offered by the Town; and that in compliance with said arrangement, twenty-six men had been recruited. It was hoped to get seven men allowed, which would leave but nine men wanted to fill the quota of this town.

Motion taken from the table, and

Voted, To reconsider the vote of December 4th, in offering a bounty of one hundred and fifty dollars.

Voted, That the Town will conform to General Order No. 60, in its future efforts to fill the quota of men called for by General Order No. 58, and that the Selectmen be authorized to pay each Volunteer, who shall be credited to the town on said quota, a bounty of one hundred dollars, on being mustered into service, — whether such Volunteer be a resident of this town or otherwise, — and the sum of ten dollars each for expenses, in case of those enlisted out of town.

Voted, That the District Committee chosen December 1st, be requested to report to the Selectmen once a month.

Roll of Thirty-four Recruits for Three Years' Service who were mustered on or before the 10th of December, as a part of the quota of Nine Months' Men due from this town; all were attached to the 22d Regiment of Infantry. They were enlisted at Recruiting Offices in Boston, and it does not appear that any of them ever joined the Regiment.

Name.	Age.	Where Born.	Occupation.	Town Bounty & Expenses.
Boyle, John,	23	Waterford, Ireland,	Bronzer,	$110 00
Boyd, Patrick,	22	Sligo, Ireland,	Laborer,	110 00
Boyden, James,	19	Providence, R. I.,	Painter,	110 00
Boyce, Thomas,	27	Dublin, Ireland,	Hatter,	110 00
Clarkson, John,	21	Philadelphia, Pa.,	Shoemaker,	110 00
Clark, John,	21	—— England,	Farmer,	110 00
Collins, James,	22	Wicklow, Ireland,	Brass Finisher,	110 00
Coombs, James,	23	Oswego, N. Y.,	Sailor,	110 00
Delany, Edward,	29	New York, N.Y.,	Silversmith,	110 00
Durant, George,	23	Boston, Mass.,		110 00
Flood, Thomas,	24	Limerick, Ireland,	Teamster,	110 00
Gorman, Joseph E.	22	—— England,	Clerk,	110 00
Gorman, William B.	23	Lowell, Mass.,	Farmer,	110 00
Green, Joseph,	22	Dublin, Ireland,	Sailor,	110 00
Jameson, John,	23	Marblehead, Mass.,	Shoemaker,	110 00
Johnson, James,	23	Boston, Mass.,	Carver,	110 00

1862.] DURING THE REBELLION. 51

Name.	Age.	Where Born.	Occupation.	Town Bounty & Expenses.
Lyons, John,	21	Galway, Ireland,	Laborer,	$110 00
Malone, John,	24	Liverpool, England,	Teamster,	110 00
McAndrews, John,	23	Havre de Grace, Md.,	Shoemaker,	110 00
McCarty, Charles,	21	Boston, Mass.,	Teamster,	110 00
Morrison, John,	29	Albany, N. Y.,	Wheelwright,	110 00
Morton, Charles H.	21	Oswego, N.Y.,	Shoemaker,	110 00
Murphy, William,	21	London, England,	Baker,	110 00
O'Brien, John,	21	Boston, Mass.,	Nailor,	110 00
Riley, John,	22	——— Ireland,	Plumber,	110 00
Smith, Charles,	22	Philadelphia, Pa.,	Shoemaker,	110 00
Stanton, Michael,	23	——— Ireland,	Sailor,	110 00
Sylvester, William,	27	——— England,	Clerk,	110 00
Thompson, William,	—			110 00
Turney, Peter,	21	Galway, Ireland,	Laborer,	110 00
Walsh, William,	21	Cork, Ireland,	Laborer,	110 00
Wilson, Charles,	39	Salem, Mass.,	Longshore man,	110 00
Woods, William,	20	Salem, Mass.,	Laborer,	110 00
Young, Samuel,	22	Philadelphia, Pa.,	Laborer,	110 00

Total Town Bounties, $3740 00

Dec. 17th. By General Order No. 63, the draft was postponed for twenty-one days; that is, to the 8th of January, 1863.

Roll of Recruits mustered in Service for Three Years by Amos A. Lawrence of Boston, as a part of the quota of Nine Months' Men.

			Town Bounty.	Expenses.
Lawrence, John H.,	Co. D.	2d Cavalry,	$100 00	$10 00
Green, Michael,	Co. D.	2d Cavalry,	100 00	10 00

Additional Roll of Nine Months' Men which was allowed by the State Authorities, in partial correction of the Selectmen's List, in consideration of having mustered in Thirty-six Recruits for Three Years, instead of Nine Months.

Holt, Joseph F., Co. G. 50th Reg.	Logue, James,	Co. G. 48th Reg.
Mooar, Charles J., Co. I. 44th Reg.	Hunt, William,	Co. D. 47th Reg.
Farnham, David T., Co. K. 47th Reg.	Noyes, Aaron,	Co. D. 6th Reg.

These rolls complete the Town's quota of sixty-five men, as called for by General Order No. 58.

Roll of Nine Months' Men mustered in August,	23
Roll of Three Years' Men, "Bounty Jumpers,"	34
Roll of Three Years' Men mustered by A. A. Lawrence,	2
Roll of Nine Months Men allowed as above,	6
Total number required to fill the quota,	65

March 2d, 1863. The Annual Town Meeting was held this day. The only matter to be acted upon that resulted from the war, was

Article 10th. — To see if the Town will continue aid to the families of Volunteer Soldiers, as provided in Massachusetts General Laws, Chapter 222 of 1861, and Chapter 66 of 1862.

Took up the 10th Article, and

Voted, To continue aid to the families of Volunteer Soldiers, the same as last year.

Through the exertions of Rev. James H. Merrill, and others, the following contributions have been made to procure a Meeting Tent for Company H. 1st Heavy Artillery — formerly 14th Regiment of Infantry.

South Church and congregation,	$43 00
West Church and congregation,	37 28
Theological Seminary,	12 58
Free Church and congregation,	18 10
Ballard Vale Union and congregation,	6 33
Baptist Church and congregation,	6 23
Christ Church and congregation,	5 00
Collection at the Young Men's Lecture in January,	13 00
	$141 52

Cost of Tent, as per bill of R. M. Yale and Co., of Boston,	$135 00
Adams and Company for freight,	5 00
Other expenses,	1 25
	$141 25

April 13th. A Meeting of the Citizens was held in the Town Hall in the evening for the purpose of forming a Union League. Peter Smith was chosen temporary Chairman, and John Cornell, Secretary.

The meeting was addressed by Peter Smith, Rev. Mr. Colver, Amos Abbott, George Foster, A. J. Gould, and others, when the following Resolutions and Articles were adopted unanimously.

Resolved, That in these solemn hours of peril to the Republic, which is menaced by a rebellion of unparalleled magnitude and atrocity, and by the suspicious attitude of foreign nations, it is the duty of all citizens to support cordially and unswervingly the measures adopted for the maintenance of the Government, in all its departments, by those who have been chosen to administer its offices. And whereas, there are many manifestations in several of the Northern States of a defiant and factious spirit of opposition to the Administration, and of sympathy for the cause of the Rebels, now therefore,

Resolved, That we deplore the existence of this treasonable spirit. We denounce the expression of any sympathy with the rebellion as reckless, insolent, and wanton approval of the greatest crime in history ; and holding these manifestations to be dangerous to the well-being of the Republic, and to the cause of civil liberty throughout the world, we unite in declaring that we will not give aid or support to any person, circulate or encourage the publication of any book or paper, or approve of or countenance any public appeals which are employed in defending the rebellion, or any of the steps thereto, or attacking the Administration, or any of the measures it has adopted for carrying on the war, — a war brought about solely by traitors and rebels, and which must be continued till the final suppression of the rebellion. And be it further

Resolved, That whereas it is at all times magnanimous conduct, but *now* especially the solemn duty of all patriots, to bear cheerfully the public burdens, to aid and encourage the ministers of the Government in the performance of their responsible and often painful duties, and to exhibit a spirit of liberality and fraternity toward all honest and patriotic political opponents ; now therefore, we invite all good citizens to join with us in the earnest efforts, which we pledge ourselves to make, to promote the patriotic objects set forth in these resolutions. And to that end, we constitute ourselves an Association to be called "The Andover Union League," and to be organized as follows :

Article 1st. — The Organization shall consist of a President, five Vice-presidents, Treasurer, and Secretary.

Article 2d. — It shall be the object of the Association to encourage and disseminate patriotic sentiments in our social intercourse by public addresses, and by printed publications.

Article 3d. — The conditions of membership shall be, unqualified loyalty to the Constitution of the United States, and unwavering support of the Federal Government in whatever efforts it may use for the suppression of the rebellion, and subscription to these Resolutions and Articles, with the annual payment of fifty cents towards defraying the expenses of the League.

A Committee chosen for the purpose, reported the following permanent officers.

President, — Francis Cogswell.

Vice-Presidents, — Samuel C. Jackson, William Jenkins, Willard Pike, George Foster, and Isaac Carruth.

Secretary and Treasurer, — Samuel Raymond.

A vote was passed directing the Secretary to procure the printing of the Resolutions and Articles of Association in season for the next meeting, which was to be held in the Town Hall on the next Monday evening at half-past seven o'clock.

April 29th. The Legislature passed an Act. entitled "An Act to provide for the reimbursement of Bounties paid to Volunteers, and to apportion and assess a tax therefor."

DURING THE REBELLION.

Under the provisions of this act the Town made returns of

	Bounties Paid.
Fifty-two men enlisted and mustered under the second call,	$5200 00
Twenty-two men for Nine Months' Service,	2200 00
Thirty-four " Bounty Jumpers " procured in Boston,	3740 00
Two " Bounty Jumpers " enlisted in the 2d Cavalry by A. A. L.	200 00
	$11,340 00
Deduct the excess of ($10) ten dollars each on 34 men,	340 00
Leaving the amount of the Town's claim,	$11,000 00
From which deduct amount assessed to the Town,	9469 63
Town received, as per Auditor's Report,	$1530 37

July 18th. The following named men were drafted from the enrolled militia of this Town during the week ending this day. The reasons why many of them were discharged are placed opposite their names.

Abbott, Nathan F.	Physical disability.
Abbott, Moses B.	Paid commutation.
Allen, William, Senior,	Physical disability.
Bacon, James K.	Left for parts unknown.
Bailey, John B.	Physical disability.
Bailey, J. M. (Dentist),	Physical disability.
Bailey, Charles H.	Only son of a dependent widow.
Baker, George F.	Physical disability.
Ballard, Edward,	Physical disability.
Barclay, Peter,	Physical disability.
Battles, Otis W.	Physical disability.
Berry, Milton,	Physical disability.
Berry, Alonzo P.	Physical disability.
Birnie, David,	Alien.
Bodwell, Horace,	Physical disability.
Boutwell, George,	Physical disability.
Boutwell, Edward H.	Physical disability.
Boyd, Pliny B.	Physical disability.
Boynton, F. H.	Physical disability.
Bridgeman, Isaac,	Physical disability.
Brown, Frederick,	Physical disability.
Carr, Peter,	Physical disability.
Carter, Edward,	Physical disability.
Chambers, Aaron,	Physical disability and unsuitable age.
Chickering, Milton,	Physical disability.
Chickering, George E.	Physical disability.

Clark, Charles,	Not of Andover, enrolled in Methuen.
Clark, Lewis,	Physical disability.
Cornell, John,	Physical disability.
Cummings, Amos,	Non-resident of Andover.
Drew, Charles,	Physical disability.
Eames, Samuel,	Physical disability.
Fessenden, Edward M.	Physical disability.
Foss, Samuel,	Physical disability.
Flint, John H.	Paid commutation.
Giddings, Isaac E.	Only son of a dependent widow.
Goldsmith, George,	Physical disability.
Greene, William B.	Physical disability.
Griffin, Stuart,	Physical disability.
Grover, Lyman,	Physical disability.
Hardy, George A.	Physical disability.
Higgins, Charles W.	Physical disability.
Hill, George O.	Dependent widow elects one son.
Holden, Jones,	Physical disability.
Holt, Timothy A.	Paid commutation.
Horner, John,	Physical disability.
Jones, Edwin,	Physical disability.
Macomber, Norman,	Only son of a dependent widow.
Manahan, Horace G.	Enrolled in 2d District of N. H.
Marland, John T.	Physical disability.
Marston, Leander,	Not a citizen of this District.
Mason, Edward,	Physical disability.
McCusker, James,	Physical disability.
Merrill, James G.	Physical disability.
Mellen, Reuben,	Physical disability — less than 5 feet.
Morse, Grandison,	Paid commutation.
Myrick, William C.	Unsuitableness of age.
Newman, Henry J.	Physical disability.
Newman, Samuel,	Physical disability.
Noyes, Henry A.	Physical disability.
Parker, William F.	Physical disability.
Penny, Frank D.	Left town, said to have enl. in Boston.
Poor, Joseph W.	Paid commutation.
Rea, John H.	Physical disability.
Richardson, A. Clark,	Physical disability.
Richardson, Francis,	Physical disability.
Rowe, Alphonso B.	Physical disability.
Russell, Joseph, Jr.	Physical disability.
Shattuck, George T.	Physical disability.
Stone, Henry A.	Paid commutation.

Trampleasure, Thomas E.	Physical disability.
Upton, Abiel A.	Physical disability.
Ward, James,	Held for service.
Walsh, Edward,	Physical disability.
Webster, Henry W.	Paid commutation.
Woodbridge, Francis,	Physical disability.
Wood, George,	Out of the country.

The whole number called for by draft was, ... 52
Fifty per cent added for exemptions and contingencies, . . . 25
    Whole number drawn as above, ... 77
Discharged as " physically disabled," 57
Discharged, " dependent widows elect," 4
Discharged, " not liable to draft " in town, ... 5
Discharged on payment of commutation, ... 7
The number that *absented themselves*, ... 3
Held for service (James Ward), ... 1
                                                     — 77

In June and July it appears that the War Department availed itself of the law of Congress, authorizing the raising of troops by draft. A Provost Marshal-General for the State, and Assistant Provost-Marshals for the several Congressional Districts were appointed at Washington to conduct the *draft;* no authority was conferred upon them to accept *Volunteers.* A Board was also established to make an enrolment of all males in the State between the ages of twenty and forty-five years.

It hardly need be stated that the enforcement of this law was obnoxious and distasteful to the people who had so generously responded to all calls of their Governor for Volunteers to sustain the cause of the Union ; to this and the high rate of physical ability required of the conscript was to be attributed the failure of the draft.

The whole number of persons enrolled, exclusive of those in the Army and
    Navy, was 164,178
The whole number drafted, ...   32,078
Exempted for all causes, ...   22,343
Failed to report, . . *   3,044
Paid commutation ($300 each), . . .   3,623
Procured substitutes, ... 2,325
Joined the service, ...   743
                                           ——   3,068
                                                           —— 32,078

A Statement of the proportion of Men that the Town had furnished for the Military Service of the United States, compared with the proportion furnished by the State, to July 1, 1863.

The United States enrolling officers reported the whole number of men enrolled in the State, not including those in the Army and Navy,   164,178
The Mayors of Cities and Selectmen of Towns claimed under oath to have furnished   Three Years' Men, .   . 58,355
                                         Nine Months' Men, .   . 17,747
                                                                                  76,102

The State had in service then 76,102, or 31.67 per cent of   240,280
The same officers reported the number enrolled in Andover,   428
The Selectmen of the Town claimed under oath to have furnished   Three Years' Men, ... 258
                Nine Months' Men, ... 29
                                             287

The Town had in service then 287 or 40.14 per cent of   715
Andover had in service as above, ...   287
The State's average of 31.67 per cent of 715, . .   226

        Surplus furnished by the Town, . .   61

Or, if the number of Nine Months' men is divided by four, to make the *time* equal three years, then the Town's surplus would be about 78, not including some 46 names, heretofore referred to, dropped from the rolls by the Selectmen.

Sept. 10th. The Secretary of the " Soldiers' Aid Society of Andover " made the following Report.

The first public meeting of the " Soldiers' Aid Society " was held in the Town Hall June 24, 1863 ; since which ten meetings have been held. From thirty to sixty ladies have usually been present.

Three hundred and sixty-seven articles have been cut out of cotton cloth, etc., bought for this purpose. And numerous towels, handkerchiefs, caps, slippers, etc., and several dressing-gowns have been cut and made from material not bought, but given to the Society.

Five hundred and seventeen articles have been sent to the Sanitary Commission Rooms in Boston to be forwarded to the Soldiers ; also over fifty bottles and jars of wines, jellies, pickles, etc., and a barrel of dried apples.

Two hundred and seventy dollars and seventy-five cents have been received in monthly subscriptions, eighty-five dollars and forty-eight cents in donations, and one dollar and thirty cents from other sources.

Total from June 10th to Sept. 10th, three hundred and forty-seven dollars and fifty-three cents.

By order of the Society,

E. EDWARDS, SECRETARY.

Since writing this report another closely-packed barrel, and a box of wines and jellies have been forwarded by the Committee to the Sanitary Committee Rooms in Boston.

Oct. 29th. The President of the United States, under date of October 17th, issued a call for 300,000 Volunteers to serve for three years, or the war. The quota assigned to Massachusetts was 15,126. By the Governor's General Order No. 30, this Town's quota was thirty-eight.

Dec. 14th. A Town Meeting was held to act on the following Articles.

Article 2d. — To see what sum of money the Town will appropriate to pay the necessary expenses of recruiting its quota of soldiers under the last call of the President.

Article 3d. — To see if the Town will choose a Committee to aid the Selectmen in securing enlistments.

Took up Article 2d, and

Voted, That the Town Treasurer be authorized to pay, if necessary, for expenses in recruiting, a sum not exceeding fifteen dollars for new recruits, and twenty-five dollars for veterans that shall be accepted as the quota of this town ; it being understood that the above-mentioned sums will be paid by the United States Government for said recruits.

Took up Article 3d, and

Voted, That it be indefinitely postponed. This action was taken in consequence of the good success of the Town in filling up its quota.

Roll of Thirty-eight recruits mustered into service, completing the Town's quota as assigned by General Order No. 30, under the President's call of Oct. 17th.

		State Bounty.
Albee, Freeland N.	Co. H. 1st Regt. Heavy Artilley,	$325 00
Batton, William,	Co. K. 2d Regt. Cavalry,	325 00
Banker, Melvin,	Co. E. 26th Regt. Infantry,	325 00
Chandler, Henry F.	Co. K. 59th Regt. Infantry,	325 00
Colange, Ettienne,	Co. K. 1st Regt. Heavy Artillery,	325 00
Craig, William,	Co. B. 1st Regt. Heavy Artillery,	325 00
Crowther, William,	Co. C. 40th Regt. Infantry,	325 00
Dwine, Daniel, Jr.	Co. D. 2d Regt. Heavy Artillery,	50 00
Eldridge, Hezekiah,	Co. L. 2d Regt. Heavy Artillery,	325 00
Farnham, Moses L.	Co. B. 59th Regt. Infantry,	325 00
Foster, Charles H.	Co. H. 1st Regt. Heavy Artillery,	325 00
Goldsmith, Sanford K. Vet.	2d Lt. 59th Regt. Infantry.	
Goldsmith, Benjamin F.	Co. A. 59th Regt. Infantry,	325 00
Holt, Harrison,*	2d Lt. 55th Regt. Infantry.	
Holt, Harrison,	1st Lt. 1st Regt. Cavalry.	
Mason, Walter B.	Co. H. 1st Regt. Heavy Artillery,	325 00
Mason, Edward,	Co. H. 1st Regt. Heavy Artillery,	325 00
McKenzie, John,	Co. G. 3d Regt. Heavy Artillery,	325 00
Mears, Calvin,	Co. H. 1st Regt. Heavy Artillery,	325 00
Mears, John,	Co. C. 2d Regt. Heavy Artillery,	50 00
O'Malley, Thomas,	Co. F. 19th Regt Infantry,	325 00
Parker, John F.	Co. C. 2d Regt. Heavy Artillery,	50 00
Patrick, Andrew K.	Co. K. 59th Regt. Infantry,	325 00
Raymond, Walter L. Veteran,	Co. L. 1st Regt. Cavalry.	325 00
Roberts, George,	Co. C. 2d Regt. Heavy Artillery,	50 00
Rollins, Robert,	Co. A. 54th Regt. Infantry,	325 00
Ryley, Leonard W.	Co. B. 59th Regt. Infantry,	325 00
Searles, James H.	Co. E. 1st Regt. Cavalry,	325 00
Shattuck, Charles M.	3d U. S. Artillery,	325 00
Skerritt, James,	Co. F. 19th Regt. Infantry,	325 00
Springer, Eugene,	Co. G. 2d Regt. Heavy Artillery.	
Taylor, George H.	2d Lt. 79th Regt. U. S. Volunteers.	
Trainer, John,	Co. G. 3d Regt. Heavy Artillery,	508 00
Vinal, Geo. A. W. Veteran,	Co. D. 59th Regt. Infantry,	325 00
Ward, James,	Co. B. 9th Regt. Infantry.	
Wardman, Thomas,	Co. B. 59th Regt. Infantry,	325 00
White, Charles W.	Co. M. 1st Regt. Cavalry,	325 00
Withey, William H.	Co. E. 1st Regt. Cavalry,	325 00
		$9483 00

* Resigned Oct. 14, 1863.

March 7th, 1864. The Annual Town Meeting was held this day.

Article 16th. — To see if the Town will continue to pay State Aid to the families of Volunteers, as provided for by the Laws of this Commonwealth relating thereto.

Voted, To continue State Aid to the families of Volunteer Soldiers, the same as heretofore.

March 31st. Report of the Andover Soldiers' Aid Society for the six months ending March 9th, 1864.

Meetings for sewing have been held regularly once a fortnight; from twenty to thirty have usually (except in bad weather), been present; many who have not attended the meetings have taken work to be done at home.

During this time the Society has received by monthly subscriptions $327.12; by donations $40.95, in all $368.07. With this money has been purchased cotton cloth and flannel for shirts, sheets, and drawers, delaine for dressing-gowns, bagging for bed-sacks, crash and yarn. The balance in the treasury on the first of March was $29.16.

The Society has made and forwarded to the Sanitary Commission for the Soldiers five hundred articles or more, besides nearly one hundred yards of bandages. In addition, there has been sent numerous second-hand articles of clothing, shirts, sacks, coats, etc.; also several packages of cocoa, farina, corn-starch, coffee, various bottles of tamarinds, catsup, and wine, jars of jelly, pickles, etc., and seventy-three pounds of dried apples.

It is a matter of regret that the uncomfortable weather and walking of the last two or three months have prevented the ladies of the Society from accomplishing nearly as much as they otherwise would have done.

In closing our report we cannot but express a hope that each member, male and female, of the Society will, for the good of the Soldiers, and for the honor of Andover, feel in duty bound to increase its usefulness and success.

We have been warned by the Sanitary Commission that

heavy drafts will be made on it by the opening spring campaigns. It desires to be prepared. It can only be prepared when each Soldiers Aid Society does its best.
"Andover, stir up the gift that is within you."
By order of the Executive Committee.

In accordance with the advice and recommendation of the Adjutant-General, as expressed in his circular letter of March 31, 1864, the Selectmen of this Town made the following return of men enlisted in Sub-District No. 25, in the Naval and Marine service — all inhabitants of Andover.

Names.	Age.	Occupation.	Naval Rendezvous, & when enlisted	Name of Ship.
Smith, David,	29	Civil Engin'r,	Washington,1859,	Sagamon.
Lindsey, William,	23	Seaman,	New York,1861,	Gun-boat G.Gulf.
Robinson, Joseph,	26	Seaman,	Boston,	Minnesota.
Midgley, Joseph,	19	File-cutter,	Boston, 1863,	Hartford.
Welch, Jeremiah,	19	Spinner,	Boston, 1863,	Hartford.
Gibbs, Theodore A.	35	Seaman,	Boston, 1861,	Jacob Bell, Str.
Hayward, Henry A.	22	Farmer,	Boston, June,1861,	Potomac, at Pens.
Butler, William,	34	Seaman,	Boston, 1862,	Pittsburg.
Morse, William H.	23	Mason,	Washington, 1862,	Sch. Para, Fla.
Abbott, William A.	30	Clerk,	Boston,	Portsmouth,N.Yd
Platt, Thomas M.	30	Shoemaker,	Boston, 1861,	Minnesota, Ft. M.
Lovejoy, Wisner,	21	Farmer,	Boston, 1861.	Santiago del Cuba.

The law referred to by General Schouler in his circular of March 31st, was but a partial allowance of the claim which Governor Andrew had been pressing for a long time upon the attention of Congress. By untiring energy and an earnest personal appeal, he was successful in carrying through Congress the Acts of July 4th, 1864, allowing naval credits and recruiting in disloyal States. The substance of the first of these Laws is found in the following letter, a copy of which was addressed to each Commissioner.

WAR DEPARTMENT,
PROVOST MARSHAL-GENERAL'S OFFICE,
WASHINGTON, D.C., July 7, 1864.

His Excellency John A. Andrew, Governor, etc.

SIR, — Section 8 of the Act approved July 4, 1864, " further to regulate and provide for the enrolling and calling out of the National Forces, and for other purposes," is as follows:

"That all persons in the Naval service of the United States, who have entered said service during the present rebellion, who have not been credited to the quota of any town, district, ward, or State, by reason of their being in said service and not enrolled prior to Feb. 24, 1864, shall be enrolled and credited to the quotas of the town, ward, district, or State in which they respectively reside, upon satisfactory proof of their residence made to the Secretary of War."

The Secretary of War hereby appoints your Excellency and Hon. John H. Clifford, a Commission to ascertain what credits the State of Massachusetts and the different sub-divisions of the State are entitled to, under the law given above.

In determining this question, the Secretary thinks it will be fair to presume that the State in which Naval enlistments have been made is entitled to the credit for those enlistments, unless it shall appear by more direct evidence that the credits belong elsewhere; the points of law to be observed in applying the Act quoted will readily be perceived by the Commission.

Major F. N. Clarke, acting Assistant Provost Marshal-General for Massachusetts, will represent the United States.

* * * * * *

JAMES B. FRYE, Prov. Mar. Gen.

July 21st. The Governor issued a second circular-letter requiring the municipal officers of the cities and towns to return to the Adjutant-General's office, on or before the 10th day of August, a sworn list of their residents who have entered the Naval service, as stated in the Act of Congress.

Municipal officers who have already made complete, sufficient, and correct returns of such persons in the Naval service in response to a circular of the Adjutant-General of the 31st of March last, are not required to repeat the same; but those who wish to correct the same can do so.

As Congress did not pass the Law until July 4th, and as a draft was to be made early in September, it became of much importance that the number of Naval credits due to

Massachusetts should be known and properly distributed without delay.

In order to ascertain the number of men who had enlisted for the Navy in Massachusetts it was necessary to copy the rolls on board the receiving ship Ohio, at the Charlestown Navy Yard; when this was done it showed that the total number enlisted from April 13, 1861, to Feb. 24, 1864, was twenty-two thousand three hundred and sixty.

The returns made in response to the above circular, and that of March 31st, showed that the whole number claimed by cities and towns was sixteen thousand one hundred and eighty-one; being six thousand one hundred and seventy-nine less than the number copied from the rolls of the receiving ship.

The instructions given by the Commissioners to their clerks were:

First, To credit only those who had joined the service subsequent to the rebellion.

Second, Only those who had joined the service at some rendezvous in the State.

Third, When a man was claimed by two or more cities or towns, neither city or town was to receive the credit, but the credit in dispute was to be given to the State at large.

The application of these rules reduced the credits claimed by the cities and towns, on the returns made by the Mayors and Selectmen, from sixteen thousand one hundred and eighty-one, to eleven thousand seven hundred and nineteen, 11,719
leaving the number credited to the State at large, and to be distributed, pro rata, to the credit of cities and towns of the State, ten thousand six hundred and forty-one, ... 10,641
Total number of enlistments copied from the rolls of the Ohio, ... 22,360

When the claim of this town for Naval enlistments was subjected to the above rules, it will be seen that Lindsey and Morse were excluded by the 2d, while Midgeley,

Welch, Gibbs, Hayward, Platt, and Lovejoy, all being "claimed by two or more cities or towns," were credited to the State at large. As Smith and Abbott were commissioned officers their names did not appear on the Commissioners' roll. In the case of Abbott, it does appear, however, that there was found an unclaimed man with a similar name, who was allowed to the credit of the town, as a part of its quota.

After these deductions the roll stood as follows:

Roll of Seamen in the Naval Service of the United States to the credit of this Town.

Name.	Age.	Where born.	Naval Rendezvous.	Name of Ship.
Abbott, William,	18	Portland, Me.	Boston, Sept. 30, '62,	Onward.
Butler, William,	33	C. May, N. J.	Boston, Apr. 4, '62,	West Flotilla.
Robinson, Joseph,	21	Maine,	Boston, May 30, '61,	No. Carolina.

Roll of Seamen in the Naval Service of the United States who were assigned to this Town by the Commissioners as a part of its quota.

Names.	Age.	Names.	Age.
*Makin, Samuel,	17	Murphy, Miles,	35
Makin, Joseph,	16	Murphy, Robert,	19
Mason, Aaron W.	17	Murphy, Peter,	23
Mason, Henry G.	18	Murray, Michael,	20
McCann, Jeremiah,	20	Murray, Patrick,	24
McCarty, Jeremiah.	23	Murray, Timothy,	29
McGinness, John,	24	Naughty, Lewis A.	
McGuire, John,	23	Nichols, John S.	28
McHugo, William,	14	Noble, William F.	25
McKenzie, Nicholas,	18	Nolan, Joseph,	21
McLarty, William A.	20	Norris, Thomas K.	24
McLean, James,	19	Nugent, George,	24
McLaughlin, Michael,	23	Paul, David E.	15
McNaughten, John,	22	Perry, James E.	23
Milliken, George E.	18	Phillips, Seth,	22
Minar, Andrew J.	32	Pool, Robert,	21
Moore, John,	18	Potter, William,	22
Morton, Charles,	20		

* Died Jan. 10, 1865.

Roll of Naval Substitutes furnished by men enrolled in the Town of Andover from July 1, 1874 *to Feb.* 1, 1865.

Principal.	Substitute.	Term of Years.	Date of Muster.	Town Bounty.	Subs. Bounty.
Bodwell, Henry A.	George Rogers,	3	July 14, '64,	$125 00	$75 00
Beard, Horace P.	George Taylor,	3	July 19, '64,	125 00	75 00
Chandler, George H.	Thos. Donnelly,	3	Aug. 17, '64,	125 00	75 00
Dodge, James S.	Edwin Sawyer,	3	July 18, '64,	125 00	75 00
Farley, I. Alvin,	Peter Walsh,	3	July 20, '64,	125 00	75 00
Foster, Moses,	William Butler,	2	Aug. 30, '64,	125 00	75 00
Holt, F. Francis,	Lysander Dudley,	3	July 18, '64,	125 00	75 00
Jackson, S. Charles,	Joseph Aurick, or Henriques,	3	July 2, '64,	125 00	75 00
Jefferson, Perry M.	Thos. Roundy,	3	Aug. 20, '64,	125 00	75 00

The total Naval credits to this Town are as follows :

Claimed and allowed on Selectmen's list, ... 3
Assigned to the Town by the Commissioners, ... 35
Substitutes furnished by enrolled citizens, ... 9
                                                                       47

After the thirty-eight men had been mustered into service, the Town had filled all demands upon it by furnishing three hundred and twenty-five men for the army alone, and, following the example of the State authorities, may claim an additional surplus of the seven men who were drafted and paid commutation money in July, 1863.

Before the call of Feb. 11, 1864 was made for twenty-six men from this town, a large number of the veterans whose names follow had re-enlisted in the field to the credit of the town ; taking the whole list of sixty-three veterans and the surpluses before claimed, we have one hundred and thirty-one men to meet the call of Feb. 11, 1864.

Roll of Veterans who re-enlisted in the field to the credit of this Town.

Name.	Regiment.	Date of re-enlistment.	State Bounty.
Abbott, Edward P.	1st Heavy Artillery,	Feb. 29, 1864,	$328 00
Abbott, Lewis F. F.	1st Heavy Artillery,	Dec. 29, 1863,	440 66
Abbott, Noah B.	1st Heavy Artillery,	Feb. 29, 1864,	400 66
Aiken, Samuel,	1st Heavy Artillery,	Feb. 29, 1864,	222 66

1864.] DURING THE REBELLION. 67

Name.	Regiment.	Date of re-enlistment.	State Bounty.	
Anderson, James I.	1st Heavy Artillery,	Dec. 15, 1863,	440	65
Bailey, Thomas R.	1st Heavy Artillery,	Dec. 12, 1863,	423	33
Bailey, George A.	26th Infantry,	Jan. 1, 1864,	325	00
Bell, Joseph,	1st.Heavy Artillery,	Dec. 7, 1863,	463	32
Burnham, Henry O.	1st Heavy Artillery,	Jan. 2, 1864,	395	99
Cheever, Benjamin,	1st Heavy Artillery,	Dec. 29, 1863,	441	99
Chalk, Henry T.	1st Heavy Artillery,	Dec. 11, 1863,	406	66
Clark, John,	1st Heavy Artillery,	Jan. 2, 1864,	259	99
Coulie, John D.	1st Heavy Artillery,	Dec. 31, 1863,	440	66
Conley, Jeremiah,	1st Heavy Artillery,	Feb. 22, 1864,.	250	00
Dane, Elmore,	26th Infantry,	Jan. 5, 1864,	325	00
Dane, George,	1st Heavy Artillery,	Jan. 2, 1864,	427	99
Dearborn, John S.	1st Heavy Artillery,	Feb. 29, 1864,	487	33
Eastes, James H.	1st Heavy Artillery,	Feb. 29, 1864,	325	00
Eagleton, Charles,	24th Infantry,	Jan. 4, 1864,	325	00
Farnham, Samuel P.	1st Heavy Artillery,	Dec. 11, 1863,	443	99
Farmer, Edward,	1st Heavy Artillery,	Dec. 5, 1863,	278	65
Findley, James S.	1st Heavy Artillery,	Dec. 7, 1863,	466	65
Foster, Thomas E.	1st Heavy Artillery,	Jan. 2, 1864,	409	33
Gilcreast. David B.	1st Heavy Artillery,	Jan. 3, 1864,	439	99
Goldsmith, Albert,	1st Heavy Artillery,	Dec. 11, 1863,	453	99
Gooch, John F.	1st Heavy Artillery,	Jan. 2, 1864,	559	99
Green, William H.	1st Heavy Artillery,	Jan. 2, 1864,	429	99
Grant, Farnham P.	1st Heavy Artillery,	Dec. 7, 1863,	456	65 .
Grant, George W.	1st Heavy Artillery,	Jan. 2, 1864,	317	33
Hatch, Andrew J.	1st Heavy Artillery,	Dec. 11, 1863,	423	33
Hatch, George F.	1st Heavy Artillery,	Dec. 22, 1863,	436	65
Hardy, Franklin,	1st Heavy Artillery,	Dec. 7, 1863,	367	32
Hayes, Timothy,	29th Infantry,	Jan. 2, 1864,	325	00
Hervey, Albert G.	4th Cavalry,	April 21, 1864,	325	00
Hovey, John C.	1st Heavy Artillery,	Feb. 22, 1864,	406	65
Jones, Charles E.	1st Heavy Artillery,	Feb. 29, 1864,	448	00
Johnson, Solon,	1st Heavy Artillery,	Dec. 22, 1863,	446	65
Kennedy, John,	1st Heavy Artillery,	Dec. 7, 1863,	325	00
Lovejoy, Benjamin C.	1st Heavy Artillery,	Dec. 7, 1863,	456	65
Lovejoy, Charles W.	7th Battery,	Jan. 10, 1864,	479	99
Logue, John,	1st Heavy Artillery,	Dec. 7, 1863,	456	65
Mahoney, Michael,	1st Heavy Artillery,	Dec. 7, 1863.	425	99
McCabe, Frank,	1st Heavy Artillery,	Jan. 2, 1864,	400	66
McClenna, Chas. W.	1st Heavy Artillery,	Jan. 2, 1864,	439	99
McGurk, Bernard,	1st Heavy Artillery,	Dec. 7, 1863,	287	99
Mears, George,	11th Infantry,	March 26, 1864,	325	00
Melcher, Sylvester C.	1st Heavy Artillery,	Dec. 7, 1863,	446	65

Name.	Regiment.	Date of re-enlistment.	State Bounty.
Nickerson, Ephraim N.	26th Infantry,	Jan. 5, 1864,	325 00
O'Hara, Edward,	1st Heavy Artillery,	Dec. 7, 1863,	383 32
Pasho, William A.	1st Heavy Artillery,	Dec. 4, 1863,	458 65
Porter, Thomas F.	23d Infantry,	Dec. 3, 1863,	325 00
Russell, William,	1st Heavy Artillery,	Dec. 4, 1863,	311 99
Russell, John B. A.	1st Heavy Artillery.	Dec. 7, 1863,	456 65
Russell, Augustine K.	1st Heavy Artillery,	Jan. 4, 1864,	510 66
Sargent, John S.	1st Heavy Artillery,	Dec. 7, 1863,	446 65
Sherman, Henry T.	1st Heavy Artillery,	Dec. 4, 1863,	458 65
Smith, James,	1st Heavy Artillery,	Dec. 4, 1863,	458 65
Stevens, Benjamin F.	1st Heavy Artillery,	Dec. 5, 1863,	456 65
Standing, George,	28th Infantry,	Jan. 2, 1864,	325 00
Townsend, Warren W.	1st Heavy Artillery,	Dec. 11, 1863,	453 99
Trull, Charles,	1st Heavy Artillery,	Feb. 29, 1864,	400 66
Turner, John,	26th Infantry,	Jan. 1, 1864,	325 00
Wardwell, Horace W.	1st Heavy Artillery,	Dec. 29, 1863,	553 99
			$25,259 66

May 16th. Town Meeting was held this day.

Article 2d. — To see if the Town will authorize their Treasurer to pay for recruiting purposes such sums of money as may be necessary to fill the quota of Soldiers which have been, or may be, called for from the Town.

Voted, That the Selectmen be authorized to expend for recruiting purposes a sum not exceeding one hundred and twenty-five dollars for each recruit necessary to fill our quota.

May 21st. A report that the 1st Regiment of Heavy Artillery, of which the Andover Company form a part, had had an engagement with the rebels reached this town this morning. This report naturally caused much anxiety in the town. The Selectmen called a meeting of the citizens in the evening, that such measures might be taken as circumstances should seem to render expedient.

Jonas Holt was chosen President, several Vice-Presidents, and two Secretaries were also chosen.

There was very little information before the meeting beyond the fact of an engagement, and the report that two or three Andover men had been killed or wounded.

The meeting was addressed by the President, Peter Smith, Rev. Mr. Litchfield, and George Foster. It then adjourned to Tuesday evening next.

May 24th. The Citizens' Meeting held this evening by adjournment from Saturday evening last was very large and interesting. Remarks were made by Rev. Dr. Jackson, George Foster, Rev. Mr. Babbitt, Rev. Mr. Merrill, and others.

Rev. Charles Smith, Josiah L. Chapin, and George Foster were appointed a Committee to prepare a letter to the Soldiers, and to report resolutions to the meeting.

The Committee reported the following resolutions which were passed unanimously.

Whereas, The citizens of Andover have heard of the battle of Thursday night, in which Company H. of the 1st Massachusetts Heavy Artillery was conspicuously engaged, and in which they suffered severely in killed and wounded.

Resolved, That we express to the Soldiers of Company H. our admiration of their bravery, and tender them our heartfelt congratulation.

Resolved, That we deeply sympathize with the wounded, and hereby convey to them the expression of our wishes and prayers for their speedy recovery.

Resolved, That we pledge ourselves to assist, to the extent of our ability, our Soldiers who are perilling their persons and lives for the purpose of suppressing this wicked rebellion.

Resolved That we deeply sympathize with those who are called to mourn the death of dear friends who have fallen in battle.

Adjourned to Thursday evening.

May 26th. The Citizens' Meeting met according to the adjournment. Dr. Tracy was called to the chair.

It was voted to send a Commission to Washington to minister to the wounded Andover Soldiers as they might be able. Rev. J. W. Turner and Mr. Joseph Abbott were appointed on this Commission. A subscription to defray the expenses of the Commission was taken up, amounting to one hundred and forty-four dollars and fifty cents, to which one hundred dollars was added from the collection taken in the Episcopal Society.

A Financial Committee was appointed to receive further subscriptions. This Committee consisted of Warren F. Draper, David Howarth, and George Foster.

Another Committee called the "Home Committee," was appointed, to be a medium of communication between the Commission at Washington and the friends of the Soldiers at home.

The meeting was then dissolved.

May 27th. The Commissioners appointed at the Citizens' Meeting on the 26th, left at noon this day for Washington, taking with them the Resolutions passed at the meeting on the 24th, and the following letter:

"ANDOVER, May 26th, 1864.

" *To the Officers and Privates of Company H, and other Soldiers connected with the First Regiment Massachusetts Heavy Artillery :*

" DEAR FRIENDS, — Last Saturday morning the exciting intelligence reached us, that you had been in an engagement with the enemy, even before reaching the main army. And while your bravery and heroism in the deadly conflict were borne to us on every breeze, our admiration of your noble and perilous deeds was mingled with serious apprehensions that casualties had ensued which would bring sadness and mourning to many of our families.

" The Selectmen immediately issued notice for a meeting of the people to be held on the same evening. A large number assembled at the appointed time, all anxious to do whatever could be done to exhibit their sympathy for those in painful suspense, and their friends who might be in great suffering.

As the information then received was meagre, the meeting was adjourned to Tuesday evening.

"The adjourned meeting was a very large one, and the interest manifested was most earnest and sympathetic. Facts gathered from your letters were announced and listened to with intense eagerness. Appropriate addresses were made by several gentlemen, conveying expressions of condolence and tenderness to the afflicted and sorrowful.

"The undersigned were appointed a Committee to address to you a letter, and to prepare and report to the meeting resolutions for adoption. The subjoined resolutions were reported by the Committee, and adopted by a unanimous vote.

"While our attention is at this time more particularly directed to your Company and Regiment on account of the many killed and wounded of your number, we would at the same time make appreciative reference to our other brave friends, scattered throughout the great loyal army, and, like yourselves, perilling all that is dear of earth for the salvation of our beloved country."

CHARLES SMITH,
JOSIAH L. CHAPIN, } COMMITTEE.
GEORGE FOSTER,

The Commissioners did not arrive in Washington until ten o'clock Saturday evening. They started out early Sunday morning to look up the Soldiers in the various hospitals. From the Commissioners letters the following information was received.

In Emery Hospital.

Phillip C. Lavalette, with right leg amputated about six inches below the knee; doing well.

Ziba M. Saunders, detailed, not wounded; comparatively well.

William H. Jenkins, just come in; no particulars.

In Lincoln Hospital.
>Francis W. Edwards, leg amputated about six inches below the knee ; in fine spirits, good appetite, and doing well.
>
>Horatio Johnson, musket-ball entered the hip and passed through the body ; no bones broken ; wound very painful ; every reason to believe he will recover.
>
>George E. Pike, wounded in the neck ; doing well, and may leave for home this week.
>
>James Costello, wounded in the neck ; ball extracted ; doing well.
>
>Edward O'Hara, wounded in the arm ; doing well.
>
>David B. Gilcreast, wounded in the neck, near the jugular vein ; doing well.

In Carver Hospital.
>George E. Hayward, wounded in the right side ; is improving fast ; doing very well.
>
>David S. Morgan, slight wound in the shoulder, and appears to be doing remarkably well.
>
>Andrew J. Hatch, ball through the hip ; says he hopes to be about before many days.
>
>John Hayes, wounded badly in the right hand, among the cords of the thumb ; very painful, but he is hopeful and hearty.
>
>James S. Findley, wounded in the left arm ; appears to be doing as well as the best.
>
>Edward P. Abbott, wounded in the right hand ; third finger amputated ; has bled freely ; also had diarrhoea, but is improving ; no good reason why he will not recover soon.

In Columbia Hospital.
>Charles S. Cummings just received ; suffered very much before reaching the hospital, but is comparatively comfortable now ; wounded in the left wrist ; bled freely ; doing well now.

George W. Stephens, sick, not wounded.

In Fairfax Seminary Hospital.

Lewis G. Hatch, not badly wounded.

At a subsequent date the Commissioners reported as follows:

In Emery Hospital.

Ziba M. Saunders; been sick; well now; detailed.

Charles H. Bell, lost right arm just below the elbow; ball entered below, and passed through the elbow; rather painful still, but is fast improving.

Michael Mahoney, flesh wound through the right thigh; considerable pain in the head, but suffers nowhere else; is all around.

Augustine K. Russell, wounded in the left foot; whole foot amputated; a ball also passed through his left thumb; both wounds quite painful still; no reason why he will not get along well now.

In Fairfax Seminary Hospital.

Lewis G. Hatch, wounded in the left side; ball passing directly through his body and coming out by the side of his back-bone, and yet, strange as it may seem, he is doing well; hearty and cheerful.

In Baptist Church Hospital, Alexandria.

Charles Mears, wounded in the right arm, and this arm has been amputated between the elbow and shoulder.

In Lincoln Hospital.

John Cusick (wounded same as Lewis G. Hatch); ball entering below the heart, and coming out by the back-bone; is apparently doing well.

William Craig, recorded Ward 10, transferred to Baltimore May 18th; slightly wounded (I think).

George F. Hatch, wounded June 3d, at Cold Harbor by the bursting of a shell, striking him near the top of his head ; not a very severe wound ; complains some of pain and occasional dizziness, but is around and doing well ; thinks he shall be able to return before long.

John Hardy, lost the index finger on his right hand, but is all right.

William Russell, wounded in the right leg just below the knee, the ball striking the bone in front, and probably glancing off, and lodging in the flesh below. The surgeon says, in a few days, as soon as Russell gets rested a little, and the inflamation and swelling go down, he shall be able to remove the ball, and he sees no reason why the patient will not get along and do well.

In Third Division Hospital, Cold Harbor.

Lewis G. Holt, slightly wounded, and will doubtless return to the Company soon.

June 20th. The following is a list of the killed, wounded, and missing in the Andover Company from May 19th to June 20th, 1864.

Killed.

Edward Farmer,
James Eastes,
Samuel Aiken,
Granville K. Cutler,

Jonathan A. Holt,
Charles W. Ridley,
James Rothwell,
Bernard McGurk.

Wounded in addition to those reported by the Commissioners.

Lt. Orrin L. Farnham, breast, died.
Enoch M. Hatch, lungs, died.
E. K. Bryant, died.
Leroy S. Brown, knee.
Noah B. Abbott, finger.
George W. Chandler, leg.
William B. Morse, leg amputated.
Charles H. Winchester, leg.

Malachi Nolan.
Joseph Bell.
E. K. Jenkins, shoulder.
John Clark, right side.
William H. Green, foot.
T. P. Allen, hip.
Jeremiah Conley, foot.
John F. Gooch, arm.

DURING THE REBELLION.

Thomas Hastie, hand.
Albert Goldsmith, thumb.
Lieut. Charles Carroll, died.
William E. Jennings.
E. J. Pendleton.
James Cunningham.
H. M. Knox,
Charles E. Jones.

Walter B. Mason.
John McLaughlin, hip.
William Gillespie, wrist.
John S. Sargent.
Henry L. Lovejoy, face.
Samuel P. Farnham.
Charles F. Trull.
Aaron E. Luscomb.

Missing.

George S. Farmer,   Charles P. Barnard,   Samuel Cheever.

The whole amount of money raised and placed in the hands of the Commission in aid of our wounded soldiers, was about five hundred and forty-three dollars and sixty-one cents. An imperfect list of the contributions will be found on file, among the papers deposited in the " Memorial Hall Library."

June 25th. The Report of the Andover Soldiers' Aid Society for the year closing June 9th, 1864, furnishes the following facts.

Total amount received for the year in subscriptions,	$730 87
From donations, etc.	140 66
Total,	$871 53

Paid for sixteen hundred yards of cotton-cloth, one hundred and twenty-five yards of flannel, two hundred and twenty-three yards of delaine for dressing-gowns, two hundred and thirty-one yards of bagging for bed-sacks, one hundred and twenty-four yards crash, thirty-eight pounds yarn, etc., express charges, and cleansing of rooms, $848 12

Leaving a balance in treasury of $23 41

There are also sums due from one or two of the districts, which have not yet paid in their money for the closing month of the year.

During the year there has been forwarded to the Rooms of the Sanitary Commission in Boston nearly sixteen hundred articles made by the ladies of Andover for the soldiers, besides numerous second-hand garments, shirts, coats, pants, etc.; also lint, some three or four hundred yards of bandages, innumerable bundles of soft cotton for dressing wounds, books, pamphlets, papers, etc. In addition, there has been forwarded nearly one hundred bottles and jars of wine, pickles, and jellies, large quantities of dried apples, farina, corn-starch, coffee, sugar, dried berries, etc.

In closing this report we would thank the many friends of the Society and Soldiers, for their constant aid by gifts or labor.

During the coming year the proceeds of the Society will be divided between the Sanitary and Christian Commissions. We trust that all interested in either of these Societies will do what they can for the Soldiers' Aid Society.

Per order of the Executive Committee.

July 5th. Town Meeting was called.

Article 2d. — To see if the Town will authorize their Treasurer to pay for recruiting purposes such sums as may be necessary, not exceeding one hundred and twenty-five dollars, for each recruit required from this town in making up its quota, under all calls hereafter made by the President of the United States.

Voted, To authorize the Treasurer to pay for recruiting purposes such sums of money as may be necessary, at the discretion of the Selectmen, not exceeding one hundred and twenty-five dollars, for each recruit required from the town in making up the quota of the town, under all calls hereafter made by the President of the United States. And whoever shall furnish a recruit, volunteer, or substitute on the quota of the town shall be entitled to receive from the town the sum authorized by the Selectmen as aforesaid, the money to be paid immediately after the call of the President shall be made.

1864.]   DURING THE REBELLION.   77

July 6th. The Governor issued General Order No. 24, calling for five thousand Infantry Volunteers for one hundred days' service, to do garrison duty in the fortifications near the city of Washington. The following is the

Roll of Recruits mustered into Service under this call.

Names.	Organization.	Date Muster.	State B.
Abbott, Alson B.	Co. C. 5th Regt. Infantry,	July 23,	$75 99
Barker, William,	Co. K. 6th Regt. Infantry,	July 14,	69 33
Barnard, Henry F.	Co. K. 6th Regt. Infantry,	July 14,	69 33
Belanger, William F.	Co. K. 6th Regt. Infantry,	July 14,	69 33
Bond, John,	Co. K. 6th Regt. Infantry,	July 14,	69 33
Buchan, George,	Co. K. 6th Regt. Infantry,	July 14,	69 33
Bushfield, John, Jr.,	Co. K. 6th Regt. Infantry,	July 14,	69 33
Dunn, Albert H.	Co. A. 6th Regt. Infantry,	July 15,	68 66
George, Warren,	Co. K. 6th Regt. Infantry,	July 14,	69 33
Gifford, Robert,	Co. D. 60th Regt. Infantry,	July 21,	86 66
Goodwin, Moses F.	Co. K. 6th Regt. Infantry,	July 14,	69 33
Hotchkiss, Arthur E.	Co. B. 42d Regt. Infantry,	July 22,	73 33
Johnston, David, Jr.,	Co. K. 6th Regt. Infantry,	July 14,	69 33
McCullough, John,	Co. K. 6th Regt. Infantry,	July 14,	69 33
Packard, Edward W.	Co. K. 6th Regt. Infantry,	July 14,	69 33
Stevens, Daniel,	Co. K. 6th Regt. Infantry,	July 14,	69 33
Stewart, George,	Co. K. 6th Regt. Infantry,	July 14,	69 33
Stewart, John W.	Co. K. 6th Regt. Infantry,	July 14,	69 33
Total,			$1275 26

COMMONWEALTH OF MASSACHUSETTS.

HEADQUARTERS, BOSTON, July 14, 1864.

GENERAL ORDER No. 27.

By an Act of Congress passed the 4th day of July, 1864, it is enacted that it shall be lawful for the Executive of any of the States to send recruiting agents into any of the States declared to be in rebellion, except Arkansas, Tennessee, and Louisiana, to recruit Volunteers who shall be credited to the State which may procure the enlistment, and to the respective sub-divisions thereof. . . . . .

It is ordered . . . . . That " Representative Recruits " may be obtained through the Provost-Marshall by persons making

the deposit of one hundred and twenty-five dollars for each recruit required. . . . . .
By order of his Excellency, JOHN A. ANDREW, Governor and Commander-in-Chief.

WILLIAM SCHOULER,
ADJUTANT-GENERAL.

Roll of " Representative Recruits" mustered into the U. S. Service, and constituting a part of the quota of this Town, under the Act of Congress referred to above.

Name of Recruit.	Organization.	On whose account procured.	Amount of Deposit.	State Bounty.
Cam Grubbs,*	51st U. S. C. T.	Wm. T. Jackson,	$125 00	$325 00
Isaac Jupiter,*	51st U. S. C. T.	Fred. L. Church,	125 00	325 00
Peter Boston,*	3d U. S. C. Cav.	Francis Cogswell,	125 00	325 00
John Whideman,	20th N. Y. Cav.	William Jenkins,	125 00	325 00
Randal Spradley,*	1st U. S. C. Cav.	Edward Taylor,	125 00	325 00
Henry Jourdan,*	1st U. S. C. Cav.	John L. Taylor,	125 00	325 00
Andrew Stephens,*	103d U. S. C. T.	Town of Andover,	100 00	325 00
Thomas Withsby,*	70th U.S. C. In.	Town of Andover,	100 00	325 00
Minor Bird,*	70th U.S. C. In.	Town of Andover,	100 00	325 00
Nicholas Thomas,*	5th U. S. C. H. A.	Town of Andover,	100 00	325 00
George Jennings,*	103d U. S. C. T.	D. I. C. Hidden,	125 00	325 00
		Total,	$1275 00	$3575 00

NOTE — The sum of one hundred and twenty-five dollars for each recruit was the original deposit; of this twenty-five dollars was subsequently refunded. The amounts coming to individual depositors was generously placed in the hands of Surgeon-General Dale, to aid needy and wounded Soldiers on their return home.

July 21st. The Andover Soldiers whose term of service has expired arrived home from the front this afternoon, and were met at the depot by their friends and a great number of citizens. The members of Phillips Academy with their band of music, and attended by their teachers, led the escort from the depot to the Town Hall. Next followed the Selectmen, ministers of the town, and the Committee of reception. The Soldiers brought home their drummer, George

---

* Colored.

1864.]   DURING THE REBELLION.   79

B. Clark, who beat the accustomed march, and the citizens fell in, in a long line.

At the Town Hall a bountiful collation had been prepared by the ladies, to which the tired and hungry Soldiers were most heartily welcomed, amidst the greetings and sympathies of their friends.

After the collation Francis Cogswell, Chairman of the Committee of Reception addressed the Soldiers.

Roll of Recruits mustered into the army for Three Years' service since the quota of Oct. 17th, 1863 was filled, and before Aug. 1st, 1864.

Name.	Organization.	Date Muster.	State Bounty.	Town Bounty.	Subscrip'n Bounty.
Dane, R. G.	26th Regt. Inf.	April 19,	$325 00	$125 00	
Smith, George,	19th U. S. Inf.	June 2,	325 00	255 00	
Owens, R.	19th U. S. Inf.	June 2,	325 00	255 00	
Comstock, A.	Unas. R. 2d In.	June 2,	325 00	255 00	
Fitzgerald, James,		July 6,		125 00	$95 00
McCusker, James,	1st Regt. H. A.	July 13,	325 00	125 00	75 00
Hill, Emmet C.	Hosp. Steward,	July 29,	325 00	*39 00	100 00
			$1950 00	$1179 00	$270 00

Aug. 19th. A Meeting of the Citizens' " Committee of twenty-five " was duly notified by order of the Executive Committee, and holden at the Town Hall on Friday evening, August 19th, 1864.

The object of the meeting, as stated by the Executive Committee, was to ascertain if the Committee would by vote release the original subscribers to the fund from their subscriptions, so far as they might make payments toward furnishing recruits, under the recent call of the President.

The Treasurer, John Dove, reported that the whole amount of receipts to the present date was, $2837 45
And the amount disbursed was,   2353 10

Leaving in his hands, $484 35

---
* Mr. Draper made this sum up to one hundred and twenty-five dollars.

The Executive Committee were appointed an Auditing Committee to examine the account of the Treasurer and report to the Clerk.

It was then

Voted, That all subscribers to the original fund who may make payments for the purpose of filling the quota of the Town, under the recent call of the President for five hundred thousand men, be released from their subscriptions to the extent of such payment.

Voted, That the Treasurer be directed to invest the balance of funds on hand in the seven and three-tenths United States Government Loan.

Meeting dissolved.

Roll of Substitutes for Enrolled Men, mustered into the army in July and August, 1864.

Name of Principal.	Name of Substitute.	Date Muster.	Town Bounty.	Subscrip'n Bounty.
Morse, Orlando S.	Smith, John,*	July 28,	$125 00	$75 00
Roberts, James A.	Fulmer, Robert,	July 11,	125 00	75 00
Shaw, James,	Becker, Charles,†	Aug. 31,	125 00	75 00
			$375 00	$225 00

Roll of Volunteer Recruits mustered into the army in August and September, 1864.

Name.	Organization.	Date Muster.	State Bounty.	Subscrip'n Bounty.
Abbott, Charles E.	4th H. Art'y,	Aug. 18,	$199 99	$175 00
Allen, Walter B. Vet.	11th Infantry,	Aug. 31,	183 32	175 00
Alderson, James,	4th H. Art'y,	Aug. 17,	193 99	101 00
Bailey, Charles W.	4th H. Art'y,	Aug. 19,	199 33	75 00
Berry, Albert,	11th Infantry,	Aug. 27,	185 32	175 00
Black, Thomas D.	61st Infantry,	Aug. 27,	193 99	175 00
Blunt, J. Milton,	11th Infantry,	Aug. 27,	185 32	175 00
Brown, Charles,	Unas'd rec. 54th In.	Aug. 24,	100 00	175 00
Callahan, Albert J.	11th Infantry,	Aug. 26,	232 66	175 00
Condon Nicholas,	29th Unat. H. A.	Aug. 22,	197 32	275 00
Collins, Timothy,	11th Infantry,	Aug. 30,	183 99	175 00
Collins, Richard,	29th Unat. H. A.	Aug. 22,	197 32	275 00
Chapin, Josiah L.	1st Lt. 11th Inf.	Sept. 24,		175 00

* Co. A. 28th Regt. † Unassigned Recruit, 30th Regt. Inf.

DURING THE REBELLION.

Name.	Organization.	Date of Muster.	State Bounty.	Subscription Bounty.
Clough, William E.	11th Infantry,	Sept. 1,	$182 66	$175 00
Duncan, James,	11th Infantry,	Aug. 24,	100 00	175 00
Dwyer, Michael,	2d H. Art'y,	Sept. 3,	198 66	175 00
Dodge, John A.	11th Infantry,	Sept. 2,	181 99	175 00
Fulton, Joseph W.*	4th H. Art'y,	Aug. 18,	199 99	175 00
Goldsmith, Jeremiah,	11th Infantry,	Aug. 26,	185 99	175 00
Harrington, Barthol.*	4th H. Art'y,	Aug. 22,	197 99	275 00
Higgins, Henry C.	11th Infantry,	Aug. 26,	189 33	175 00
Holt, Ballard, 2d,*	11th Infantry,	Aug. 26,	185 99	175 00
Holt, Samuel M.*	11th Infantry,	Aug. 25,	186 66	175 00
Holloran, Patrick,	29th Unat. H. A.	Aug. 29,	192 66	175 00
Ingalls, John E.	11th Infantry,	Aug. 27,	185 32	175 00
Jenkins, John B.	11th Infantry,	Aug. 26,	185 99	175 00
Jóice, Redmond,*	29th Unat. H. A.	Aug. 26,	194 66	177 00
Melendy, George,	2d H. Art'y,	Aug. 30,	202 00	200 00
Milkins, William,	29th Unat. H. A.	Aug. 26,	194 66	177 00
Moulton, Charles L.	11th Infantry,	Aug. 31,	183 32	175 00
Merrill, John H.	11th Infantry,	Sept. 1,	182 66	175 00
Parker, C. O.*	Vet. Res. Corps,	Aug. 8,	325 00	150 00
Qualey, Patrick,	11th Infantry,	Sept. 3,	181 32	175 00
Russell, Winslow,*	4th H. Art'y,	Aug. 17,	200 66	75 00
Russell, John R.	29th Unat. H. A.	Aug. 22,	197 32	275 00
Stevens, Wendell B.	2d H. Art'y,	Sept. 1,	200 00	175 00
Tomlinson, E. A.	29th Unat. H. A.	Aug. 22,	197 32	225 00
Trask, Elbridge P.	29th Unat. H. A.	Aug. 22,	197 32	225 00
Tucker, William H.	11th Infantry,	Aug. 26,	185 99	175 00
Weston, Frederick,	29th Unat. H. A.	Aug. 24,	195 99	175 00
Wescott, William,	29th Unat. H. A.	Aug. 23,	196 66	175 00
Woodbridge, Francis,	11th Infantry,	Sept. 15,	179 99	
Wardrobe, Fred.	Hosp. St'd.U. S. A.	Oct. 20,	325 00	
			$8165 65	$7405 00

NOTE.— Town Bounty $125 each, amounting to $5375.

Roll of Volunteer Recruits mustered into the Army from September 1864 to the close of the war.

Name.	Organization.	Date of Muster.	State Bounty.	Subscrip'n Bounty.
Blake, John,	26th Infantry,	Feb. 7,	$131 99	$45 00
Bradley, Charles W.	4th Cavalry,	Dec. 31,	210 66	15 00
Cass, Isaac N.	3d Cavalry,	Dec. 30,	179 99	15 00

* Veteran.

82   THE RECORD OF ANDOVER   [1864.

Name.	Organization.	Date of Muster.	State Bounty.	Subscrip'n Bounty.
Carter, Frederick W.	1st Bat. F. Cav.	Jan. 2,	$120 66	$15 00
Clark, Jesse H.	1st Bat. F. Cav.	Jan. 2,	121 33	15 00
Crosby, Alonzo,	26th Infantry,	Feb. 7,	131 99	45 00
Dougherty, James,	1st Bat. F. Cav.	Dec. 30,	122 00	15 00
Downes, Benjamin,	1st Bat. F. Cav.	Jan. 2,	121 33	15 00
Dow, Charles E.	1st Bat. F. Cav.	Jan. 2,	121 33	15 00
Dugan, William,	1st Bat. F. Cav.	Jan. 2,	121 33	15 00
Duncan, Robert,	2d Cavalry,	Feb. 22,	94 66	75 00
English, Charles G.*	1st Bat. F. Cav.	Dec. 30,	122 00	15 00
Fox, William,				15 00
Gibbs, Robert,	1st Bat. F. Cav.	Dec. 30,	122 00	15 00
Gould, Theodore F.	1st Bat. F. Cav.	Dec. 30,	122 00	15 00
Godkins, Stephen F.	4th Cavalry,	Dec. 31,	210 66	15 00
Goodwin, Moses F.	1st Bat. F. Cav.	Jan. 2,	121 33	15 00
Jones, David L.	4th Cavalry,	Dec. 31,	210 66	15 00
Lyman, Edward E.	3d Cavalry,	Dec. 31,	179 32	15 00
Lemon, William H.	1st Bat. F. Cav.	Jan. 2,	121 33	15 00
Mears, John,*	3d Cavalry,	Dec. 30,	141 99	15 00
Morrison, Charles W.	3d Cavalry,	Dec. 31,	179 32	15 00
Mason, Eri,	Unas. Rec. 3d Cav.	Dec. 31,	325 00	55 00
Saunders, James,*	1st Bat. F. Cav.	Dec. 30,	122 00	15 00
Sargent, Herbert N.	3d Cavalry,	Dec. 31,	179 32	15 00
Smith, John,	17th Infantry,	Feb. 20,	325 00	100 00
Smith, Robert,	1st. Bat. F. Cav.	Jan. 2,	122 00	15 00
Stanwood, Lawrence,	1st Bat. H. A.	Feb. 21,	81 33	90 00
Stephenson, Alba,	1st Bat. F. Cav.	Dec. 30,	122 00	
Thomas, Lewis,				15 00
Winthrop, Thos. F.	2d Lt. 62d Inf.	March 11,		
Wescott, Solomon,	3d Cavalry,	Dec. 30,	179 99	15 00
Weeks, Nathaniel,	1st Bat. F. Cav.	Jan. 2,	121 33	15 00
			$4585 85	$785 00

NOTE.— Town Bounty $125 each, except Winthrop, amounting to $4000.

Roll of Commissioned Naval Officers belonging to the Town, not allowed on the quota.

Name.	When Commissioned.	Office.
Abbott, William A.	May, 1861,	Master's Mate.
Dove, George W. W.		3d Assistant Engineer.
Smith, David,	Aug. 26, 1859,	3d Assistant Engineer.

* Veteran.

DURING THE REBELLION.

Roll of Volunteer Recruits omitted in the Selectmen's Return of Aug. 29, 1862, but who were claimed to belong to the Town's quota in the Petition of the Town Committee to Gov. Andrew, dated Nov. 29, 1862.

Name.	Organization.	When Mustered.	Term.
Abbott, Wesley	1st Co. Sharpshooters,	Sept. 2, '61,	3 years.
Bailey, James H.	1st Regt. H. Art'y,	July 5, '61,	3 years.
Barker, Samuel S.	1st Co. Sharpshooters,	Sept. 2, '61,	3 years.
Bentley, Noah,	1st Co. Sharpshooters,	March 24, '62,	3 years.
Beal, William,	1st Regt. H. Artillery,	July 5, '61,	3 years.
Black, James B.	30th Regt. Infantry,	Sept. 24, '61,	3 years.
Barker, Stephen,	Chapl'n 1st Regt. H. A.	July 16, '61,	3 years.
Clark, Edwin L.	Chapl'n 12th Regt. Inf.	June 26, '61,	3 years.
Conley, Jeremiah,	11th Regt. Infantry,	June 13, '61,	3 years.
Collins, Thomas E.	1st Regt. Infantry,	Aug. 21, '61,	3 years.
Craig, David,	15th Regt. Infantry,	July 7, '62,	3 years.
Eels, Frederick S.	32d Regt. Infantry,	Nov. 13, '61,	3 years.
Fleming, John,	16th Regt. Infantry,	July 12, '61,	3 years.
Green, Charles,	1st Regt. H. Artillery,	July 5, '61,	3 years.
Greeley, William,	30th Regt. Infantry,	Oct. 12, '61,	3 years.
Hanson, Charles,	1st Co. Sharpshooters,	Sept. 2, '61,	3 years.
Hayes, Timothy,	29th Regt. Infantry,	Nov. 25, '61,	3 years.
Holt, Joseph F.	1st Regt. Infantry,	May 23, '61,	3 years.
Hunt, Amos,	1st Regt. H. Artillery,	July 5, '61,	3 years.
Jaquith, James,	30th Regt. Infantry,	Nov. 16, '61,	3 years.
Jones, Ambrose,	1st Regt. Minnesota Inf.	Sept. 28, '61,	3 years.
Johnson, Solon,	1st Regt. H. Artillery,	July 5, '61,	3 years.
Kelly, Joseph,	29th Regt. Infantry,	June 30, '61,	3 years.
Kavanagh, Bernard,	20th Regt. Infantry,	July 18, '61,	3 years.
Lovejoy, Henry L.	1st Regt. H. Artillery,	July 5, '61,	3 years.
Lovejoy, Charles W.	7th Light Artillery,	Jan. 16, '62,	3 years.
Logue, Charles,	29th Regt. Infantry,	Nov. 25, '61,	3 years.
Luke, William H.	1st Regt. Infantry,	May 23, '61,	3 years.
Marland, William,	2d Lt. 2d Light Art'y,	Dec. 18, '61,	3 years.
Merrill, Edward C.	4th Light Artillery,	Nov. 7, '61,	3 years.
Messer, Cyrus,	1st Regt. H. Artillery,	July 5, '61,	3 years.
Noonan, Daniel,	Unas'd Rec. 1st Regt. H. A.	March 24, '62,	3 years.
Phillips, Patrick,	3d Regt. Cavalry,	Aug. 6, '62,	3 years.
Parker, Caleb O.	1st Regt. H. Artillery,	July 5, '61,	3 years.
Pray, Seaver,	20th Regt. Infantry,	Aug. 27, '61,	3 years.
Rothwell, James H.	1st Regt. H. Artillery,	July 22, '62,	3 years.
Russell, Joseph, Jr.	1st Regt. H. Artillery,	July 5, '61,	3 years.
Shattuck, Charles W.	1st Regt. H. Artillery,	July 5, '61,	3 years.

Name.	Organization.	When Mustered.	Term.
Smart, George M.	1st Regt. H. Artillery,	July 5, '61,	3 years.
Stevens, James W.	1st Regt. H. Artillery,	July 5, '61,	3 years.
Vinal, George A. W.	1st Regt. H. Artillery,	July 5, '61,	3 years.
Wardwell, Alfred,	1st Regt. H. Artillery,	July 5, '61,	3 years.
Wardwell, George E.	1st Regt. H. Artillery,		
Wardwell, George	19th Regt. Infantry,	Aug. 28, '61,	3 years.
Whittemore, Harrison,	1st Regt. Infantry,	May 24, '61,	3 years.
Whittaker, Amos,	22d Regt. Infantry,	Sept. 16, '61,	3 years.

March 6th, 1865. The Annual Town Meeting was held. The following Articles in the Warrant were acted upon.

Article 15th. — To see if the Town will continue to pay State Aid to the families of Volunteers, as provided for by the Laws of this Commonwealth relating thereto.

Article 17th. — To see if the Town will pay a bounty of one hundred dollars each to certain persons who enlisted in the United States service as Volunteers in 1862, on petition of Charles H. Bell, and others.

Took up the Article 15th, and

Voted, To continue State Aid to the families of Volunteer Soldiers as heretofore.

Took up Article 17th, and

Voted, To refer the subject to the Selectmen to investigate, and report to the Town.

June 7th. The Second Annual Meeting of the Soldiers' Aid Society was this day held in the Town Hall. The Treasurer being prevented by sickness from having her report ready, it was therefore,

Voted, That the Report, together with the action of this meeting, be published in the Andover Advertiser.

Voted, That whereas the work of the Sanitary and Christian Commissions is now nearly done, and as this is the time for our Annual Business Meeting, we do at the close of this meeting disband this Society.

Voted, That the money now in the Treasury, two hundred and twenty-four dollars and thirty-six cents, be kept for the benefit of disabled soldiers, or their families, belonging to this town.

Voted, That Mrs. William Marland, Mrs. David Gray, and Mrs. Jonathan Swift be Committee to hold and disburse this money.

Voted, That the gratitude of this Society is especially due to Mrs. Marland and Mrs. Gray, for their untiring and very efficient labors in behalf of the objects of this Society.

The Report of the Treasurer of the Andover Soldiers' Aid Society from its organization, June 9, 1863, to its disbandment June 7, 1865,

There has been raised during the last two years:

From subscriptions (monthly),	$1190 94
From donations,	303 80
From tea-party,	505 80
From lectures,	65 25
From materials sold,	19 17
Making in all a total of	$2088 82

This money has been expended as follows:

Two thousand six hundred and forty-three yards of cotton-cloth, three hundred and ninety-four yards of flannel, two hundred and thirty-one yards of bagging for bedsacks, four hundred and seventeen yards of print and delaine, three hundred and twenty-seven yards of toweling, and seventy-two pounds of yarn,	$1612 54
Society expenses: Tea-party and lecture,	81 92
Handkerchiefs,	28 44
Tape, needles, and buttons,	27 10
Express,	7 21
Janitor,	7 25
Sanitary Commission,	'50 00
Christian Commission,	50 00
Balance on hand,	224 36
	$2088 82

The money raised from the several districts by subscription is as follows:

District.	Amount.	District.	Amount.
Centre,	$421 12	Ballard Vale,	$19 00
Phillips,	305 52	North,	15 90
Frye Village,	165 89	Bailey,	7 45
West Centre,	95 42	Abbott (West Parish),	5 70
Abbott Village,	48 63	Holt,	4 20
Osgood,	43 00		
Scotland,	41 60	Total,	$1173 43

Articles made by the Society and sent to the Sanitary and Christian Commissions: sheets, three hundred and thirty-two; towels, four hundred and thirty-five; drawers, five hundred and forty pairs; handkerchiefs, five hundred and fifty-eight; quilts, eight; pillows, six; pillow-cases, thirteen; hop-pillows, twelve; dressing-gowns, fifty-two; comfort-bags, thirty-four; bandages, sixty rolls; socks, one hundred and eighty-seven pairs; shirts, one hundred and twenty-one; caps, one hundred and one; bed-sacks, fifty-one; shoes, four pairs; corn-starch, papers, and numerous articles of clothing and hospital stores.

March 5th, 1866. The Annual Town Meeting was held. The following Article in the Warrant was acted upon.

Article 16th. — To see if the Town will continue to pay State Aid to the families of Volunteers, as provided by the Laws of this Commonwealth relating thereto.

Took up Article 16th, and

Voted, To continue State Aid to the families of Volunteer Soldiers as heretofore.

Oct. 29th. Town Meeting was held. The following Articles in the Warrant were acted upon.

Article 2d. — To see if the Town will pay to each Volunteer who was a resident, or who enlisted to the credit of said Town, and who at the time of his enlistment had a family dependent upon him for support, the sum of eight dollars per month during the time of such Volunteer, providing such sum has not been paid to such Volunteer, or his family, in addition to State Aid.

Article 3d. — To see if the Town will pay to each Volunteer who enlisted to the credit of said Town, and was sworn into the service of the United States, the bounty of one hundred dollars, according to a vote of the Town at a meeting held September 15, 1862, provided the same has not been paid.

Article 4th. — To see if the Town will pay all persons who enlisted to the credit of Andover, all sums of money that in right and equity are due to such Volunteer, or their families, under any vote of said Town, or by virtue of any promise or contract made to or with such Volunteers by the Selectmen or recruiting agents of said Town, for the purpose of procuring enlistments to the credit of said Town, in addition to State Aid.

Article 5th. — To take measures to raise such an amount of money as may be necessary for the payment of the same, on the petition of Thomas Smith and others.

Took up Articles 2d, 3d, 4th, and 5th, and

Voted, Unanimously, That all claims against the Town arising under or affected by any of its votes, the Statutes of the Commonwealth, or Acts of Congress, or arising in any other way on account of enlistment or service in the Army and Navy of the United States, during the late civil war, be referred to Jarius W. Perry of Salem, Hon. Charles Kimball of Salem, Frederick J. Coffin of Newburyport, George H. Poor and Nathan W. Hazen of Andover. And that the Selectmen be authorized and directed to execute, in the name of the inhabitants, proper writings of arbitration between them and said claimants, or any of them.

Voted, That the Treasurer, under the direction of the Selectmen, be instructed to pay out of the funds of the Town, not otherwise apportioned, all such claims and costs as said arbitrators, or a majority of them, shall award to be due in the premises.

Voted, That the Treasurer under the direction of the Selectmen, be empowered to hire such sum or sums of money as shall be needed to make such payments.

Voted, That the Selectmen be authorized to select and retain counsel in all matters arising under the above votes, and cause a suitable number of awards to be printed.

Nov. 26th. Town Meeting was held. The following Articles in the Warrant were acted upon.

Article 2d. — To see if the Town will reconsider the votes passed at a meeting held on Monday, October 29, 1866, in reference to Articles 2d, 3d, 4th and 5th, in warrant for said meeting, dated Oct. 20, 1866.

Article 3d. — To see what action the Town will take in reference to any and all claims alleged to be due from said town to the Volunteers, or to the families of the Volunteers, who enlisted to the credit of said town in the late war for the suppression of the rebellion, on petition of William Chickering, and one hundred and fifty-six others.

Took up Articles 2d and 3d, and

Voted, To reconsider the vote passed at a meeting held on Monday, Oct. 29, 1866, in reference to Articles 2d, 3d, 4th, and 5th, in warrant for said meeting.

Voted, That the subject-matter in the 3d Article in the warrant be referred to a Committee [consisting of George Foster, Edward Taylor, Asa A. Abbott, Benjamin Boynton, William S. Jenkins, John B. Abbott, and Hermon Phelps], whose duty it shall be to examine all the records and files in possession of the Town, or which may be presented to them for examination, relating to the subject, and report hereafter to the Town, in town meeting assembled, the results of said investigation ; and that the Committee heretofore appointed to act upon the subject-matter of the 3d Article be requested to prepare, print, and circulate a pamphlet containing the name of every Volunteer who has heretofore received from the Town, or by its agency, any sum of money as bounty, or otherwise, stating the sum paid to each, and on what account it was paid, distinguishing whether it was paid to the Volunteer or his family; and also the amount repaid on account of each ; also the amounts the Soldiers now claim, and the amounts in their opinion due ; and report the same at a subsequent meeting.

Voted, That the Committee be authorized to employ counsel, if necessary.

Voted, That the Committee be authorized to print, and circulate one thousand copies of their investigations.

March 4th, 1867. The Annual Town Meeting was held this day.

Voted, To accept the following :

Resolved, That a Committee of seven be appointed by this town meeting, whose duty it shall be to investigate the claims of Soldiers, and report in writing or otherwise, what equitable claims said Soldiers may have against the Town, and in what manner they can best be met if found to exist.

Resolved, That this Committee consist of George Foster, Edward Taylor, Asa A. Abbott, Benjamin Boynton, William S. Jenkins, John B. Abbott, and Hermon Phelps.

Resolved, That this Committee report at the adjournment of this meeting, three weeks from to-day.

March 25th. Adjourned Town Meeting. The following opinion from the Attorney-General was submitted by the Committee.

BOSTON, Jan. 25, 1867.

HON. GEO. FOSTER,
Chairman of a Committee of the Town of Andover.

DEAR SIR, — My opinion is asked respecting three classes of claims made upon the Town of Andover by men, or by the families of men, who served from Andover, or on the quota of Andover, during a portion of the time covered by the late rebellion.

As I understand it, the claims are these :

First, At Town Meetings held in Andover on the sixth of

May, and on the eighth of July, A.D. 1861, the Town, among other things, voted to pay the family of each Volunteer the sum of eight dollars per month, as long as such Volunteer continued in service. [This is the substance, though not the exact language, of the vote passed at the meeting in May, and ratified in July].

It is claimed that, by virtue of this vote, the town is bound in law or equity, or both, to pay this sum to such families from the sixth of August, A.D. 1861 (at which time payments under the vote ceased to be made), to the time when the service of each Volunteer was ended.

Second, There was distributed and posted up in the town, by authority of the Selectmen, as it is said, and as I shall assume to be true, a hand-bill, the material portions of which are as follows:

The bounties now offered to recruits to fill up the quota of Andover, amount to $210.

The Government pays in advance, ...	$25 00
The Government pays at the end of the service, .	75 00
The Town pays, ...	100 00
Messrs. Smith and Dove, ...	10 00
Amounting to	$210 00

[Dated] ANDOVER, July 19th, 1862.

In fact the bounty offered by the Government was to those only who served two years. Some, or all of the men, enlisting at this time from Andover, served less than two years (having been discharged by the Government, because of the substantial cessation of hostilities), and received none, or but a portion, of the Government bounty.

These men now claim that the Town shall make their bounty up to $210.

Third, Volunteers from Andover re-enlisted in the field in the latter part of the year 1863, and in the year 1864, prior to the sixteenth of May of that year. On the sixteenth of May, 1864, the Town voted (in substance), to authorize the Selectmen to expend $125 for each recruit necessary to fill the Town's quota. Before this vote was passed, many of the towns in the State had been paying the same sum to re-enlisting men. It is said that citizens of Andover, both private and official, expressed the opinion, and, perhaps, promised persons who had re-enlisted, and who afterwards re-enlisted, that Andover would do as well by such persons as other Towns did.

The claim is that these persons, so re-enlisting as I have described, are now entitled to receive from the Town the bounty of $125.

The hand-bill which I have alluded to, and the votes of the Town upon these subjects, have been put into my hands, in addition to the facts above stated.

It is on this case, and these facts, that my opinion is asked.

I may say in the outset upon the general question involved in these claims, that the power of Towns to raise and appropriate money is to be exercised only within the limits prescribed by the Statutes of the Commonwealth. And it was long ago determined by the Supreme Court of this Commonwealth in the case, Stetson vs. Kempton, 13 Mass. 272, that Towns have no authority in times of war and danger of hostile invasion to raise money for additional wages to soldiers or for other purposes of defence.

This decision, except as it has been modified by subsequent acts of legislation, is the law.

As to the first class of cases.

In the light of the decision which I have just referred to, the vote of the Town passed on the sixth of May, 1861, was undoubtedly illegal.

The Legislature, however, on the twenty-second of May, 1861, by an Act then passed (chap. 222 of the Acts of 1861), ratified the contract made by the Town by this vote, so far as to authorize payments under it to a certain limited extent. This Act provided that the contract so made should terminate at the end of ninety days from its date, or from the date of a subsequent enlistment made under the contract.

I understand that all such contracts made by the Town of Andover expired by virtue of this Act as early as August 6th, 1861.

I think the Town is not only not bound to make any payments under this vote for a service subsequent to August 6th, but that no such payment can legally be made.

The vote of the Town on the eighth of July, 1861, passed as it was after the before-named Act of the Legislature, which (by section 3) expressly forbade such payments to Soldiers, is merely void. It enacted no contract and would authorize no payment.

So I am of opinion that the first class of claims is unfounded.

As to the claims of the second class.

In my judgment the hand-bill, even if it had been signed by the Selectmen, and even if they had authority to bind the Town, cannot be construed as a promise or agreement by the Town to pay the Government bounty. The whole effect of it is, that the Town agree to pay a certain sum; and it contains the statement that the Government have agreed to pay a certain sum, and Smith and Dove a certain sum. These sums, together, make up the $210, which is the amount which the hand-bill states is now offered to Andover recruits.

The hand-bill contains no contract that the Town will pay the bounties offered by the Government, or by Smith and Dove, if they should fail to pay. The only ground on which it can be pretended that the Town is either equitably or legally bound, is that the hand-bill (still supposing it to have been authorized or signed by the Selectmen), does not state things truly, and that men enlisting were misled by it.

The hand-bill states, in substance, that the Government will pay to recruits a bounty of $100. In fact, this bounty was payable only to those who served two years. This was not so stated in the hand-bill. If any persons were misled by this, and I shall assume that there were such, then the case would stand somewhat as it would if Smith and Dove had never promised to pay the sum stated in the hand-bill, and persons misled by such statement, and because of such statement, had enlisted. If the Selectmen, knowing that Smith and Dove had made no such promise, had falsely stated in such a hand-bill that they had so promised, and persons had been misled by this statement, and had enlisted in consequence of it, the Town would not have been in any way liable. It would have been fraud on the part of the Selectmen, but the Town would not be responsible.

In the actual case before us, no one will contend or pretend that any fraud was intended. Everybody reading the hand-bill knew that whatever the Government had promised was by virtue of some Act of Congress, or by some Proclamation from the President or the War Department. No one reading the hand-bill would suppose that it stated anything but a very brief epitome of such Act or Proclamation ; and every one would suppose that for particulars, for modifications, for qualifications, for modes, and times, and conditions of payment, he must go to the document itself.

With the views that were then entertained by the community as to the duration of the war, no one issuing such a hand-bill would have supposed that the fact that the bounty was payable only in the event of two years service was of any consequence. Every one then supposed that the rebellion would last a longer time than that, and the Government itself indicated the same belief by calling for enlistments for three years.

Even if there had been knowingly made by the Selectmen a false statement, with the intention to deceive, and if persons had been deceived, as I have before said, the Town would not be responsible. How much less, then, is the Town responsible when there was no intention to deceive, and when no one could be deceived unless grossly negligent himself ?

I have assumed that persons were misled by the hand-bill. It would probably be found, however, that no person enlisted without well-knowing that the Government bounty was only payable on two years' service.

I am of opinion that the Town is no way liable for, and, moreover, cannot legally pay the claims of the second class. Even if the Town should now vote to pay these claims, I think such vote would be illegal, and that the money could not lawfully be paid in virtue of it.

As to the claims of the third class.·

The only authority which Towns have or had to pay the bounties asked for by these claimants, is derived from the Act of March 18th, 1864 (Chap. 103, 1864).

That Act, Sec. 1, authorizes a Town to raise money for the purpose of procuring its quota called for under the Orders of the President, dated October 17th, 1863, and February 1st, 1864, and that the amount raised shall not exceed $125 for each person enlisted after the passage of this Act. Section 2, of the same Act, provides that all sums raised under this Act shall be assessed at the next annual assessment, which would be the assessment of 1865.

Under this Act the Town might have raised sufficient money to pay $125 to each person enlisting after March 18th, 1864, and no more. The Town, however, passed no vote to raise any money or make any payment under this Act until May 16th, 1864, and this vote authorized the expenditure only of $125 for " each recruit necessary to fill our quota."

Persons enlisting after that date, and to whom the promise was made of this sum, even by the Selectmen, are entitled to it, undoubtedly.

Persons enlisting before that time, and especially persons enlisting before the Act of March 18th, 1864, can have no possible claim under any vote of the Town submitted to me. And I do not think it would be possible for the Town now to pass any vote which would enable it, legally, to pay this bounty to those men, if any, who enlisted between March 18th, 1864, and May 16th, 1864.

The year 1865, in which any money raised under this Act must have been assessed, is past, and the power of the Towns to proceed under it is ended. It may be said that the terms

" at the next annual assessment," used in the second section, means the next annual assessment after the appropriation of such money, and that money may now be appropriated and assessed at the next annual assessment now coming. The only effect of such a construction, and a vote now passed by the Town, would be to authorize the payment of this bounty to such as enlisted between March 18th and May 16th, 1864.

But, as I have said, I do not think this the correct construction of the Act. I think the assessment intended was the assessment of 1865.

This Act was designed as a temporary and war measure, and to enable the Towns to meet the then pressing exigency, and to enable Towns then to procure their quotas.

I am, therefore, of opinion that the Town of Andover cannot legally pay the claims of the third class.

I have discussed these questions with more detail and at greater length than I intended, or than was perhaps necessary. But as I went on, and remembered that it was the people of the Town, and not a single individual, to whom the opinion is addressed, and who are to be satisfied and convinced, if possible, I thought this full consideration of the questions would possibly be more acceptable than a much briefer one. Yours, truly,

CHESTER I. REED.

The Committee desire to say that they have endeavored to consider the Soldiers' claims with fairness and impartiality. Finding them in the aggregate to amount to about thirty thousand dollars, it seemed important to obtain a legal opinion on these questions of the highest authority. They therefore submitted all the facts in the case to the Attorney-General of the State. His very able and elaborate opinion upon these claims will be read with interest; and the distinguished source from whence it emanated will give it much weight and importance.

All of which is respectfully submitted to the citizens of Andover.

GEORGE FOSTER,
EDWARD TAYLOR,
ASA A. ABBOTT,
BENJAMIN BOYNTON, } COMMITTEE.
WILLIAM S. JENKINS,
JOHN B. ABBOTT,
HERMAN PHELPS,

ANDOVER, Feb. 1, 1867.

After reading the Report of the Committee on Soldiers' claims in equity due, it was

Voted, To accept said Report.

TABULAR STATEMENTS.

A Statement showing the Whole Number of Men furnished by the Town for service in the Army and Navy of the United States during the Rebellion.

ARMY ROLLS.

	No. of Men.	Page.
Selectmen's return of men in service,	222	34
Nine months' men,	23	38
Three years' men enlisted in Boston,	34	50
Three years' men enlisted by A. A. Lawrence,	2	51
Nine months' men allowed on petition,	6	51
Three years' men,	38	60
Re-enlisted Veterans,	63	66
One hundred days' men,	18	77
" Representative Recruits,"	11	78
Three years' men,	7	79
Substitutes for enrolled men,	3	80
Recruits, principally for three years,	43	80
Frontier Cavalry, etc.,	33	81
Total on Army quotas,	503	
Recruits omitted by Selectmen,	46	83
Total furnished for the Army,	549	

NAVY ROLLS.

	No. of Men.	Page.
Seamen allowed on Selectmen's list,	3	65
Seamen assigned by Commissioners,	35	65
Substitutes for enrolled men,	9	66
Total on Naval quotas,	47	
Commissioned officers,	3	82
Total furnished for the Navy,	50	
Total number in Army and Navy on quotas	550	
Total number in Army and Navy not allowed on quotas,	49	
Whole number furnished,	599	

13

THE RECORD OF ANDOVER

A Statement showing the Proportion of Men that this Town furnished for the Military and Naval service of the United States during the Rebellion, as compared with the number furnished by the State at large.

As has been before stated, the whole number of enrolled militia in the State as returned by the United States enrolling officers in July, 1863, not including those in the Army and Navy, was	164,178
The Mayors and Aldermen of cities and Selectmen of Towns claimed under oath to have furnished to that date for the Army,	76,102
The Commissioners reported the number of enlistments in the Navy at Charlestown from the commencement of the war to Feb. 24, 1864, to have been	22,360
	262,640

The Adjutant-General reported that the whole number of men furnished by the State to both Army and Navy was 159,165 or 60.60 per cent of 262,640.	
The number of enrolled militia in Andover in July, 1863, was	428
The Town had furnished to that date for the Army,	287
And to the Navy, three commissioned officers and two seamen,	5
	720

By the statement that immediately precedes this, it will be noticed that the Town had furnished on her quotas,	550
The Town's proportion according to the average would have been 60.60 per cent of 720, or,	436
An excess on quotas of	114
Add the number of men furnished, but not counted on quotas,	49
A total surplus of	163

Bounties paid by the State, by the Town, and by subscription, with a reference to the page for detail, and the number of recruits.

ARMY.

	Page.	No. of Men.	State Bounty.	Town Bounty.	Subsc'n Bounty.
Recruits mustered July 22, '62,	26	52		$5200 00	[1]$520 00
Nine months' recruits,	38	23		2200 00	[2]
"Bounty Jumpers," (Boston),	50	34		3740 00	
"Bounty Jumpers" (A. A. L.),	51	2		220 00	
Recruits to fill quota Oct. 17, '63,	60	38	$9483 00		
Veterans re-enlisted in the field,	66	63	25259 66		
One hundred days' recruits,	77	18	1275 66		
"Representative Recruits,"	78	11	3575 00	400 00	[3]875 00
Three years' recruits,	79	7	1950 00	1179 00	[4]357 28
Substitutes for enrolled citizens,	80	3		375 00	[5]1725 00
Recruits, principally for 1 year,	80	43	8165 65	5375 00	7405 00
Frontier Cavalry, etc.,	81	33	4585 85	4000 00	785 00
Draft'd militia paid commutation,	55	7			[6]2100 00
			$54294 92	$22689 00	$13767 28

NAVY.

	Page.	No. of Men.	State Bounty.	Town Bounty.	Subsc'n Bounty.
Substitutes for enrolled citizens,	66	9		1125 00	[7]5175 00
			$54294 92	$23814 00	$18942 28

---

[1] Paid by Smith and Dove.
[2] Bowen's bounty paid by F. L. Church, amount unknown.
[3] Paid by the Principals.
[4] $87.28 paid by Warren F. Draper to Hill. $270.00 from Subscription Fund.
[5] $225.00 from Subscription Fund, and about $1500.00 by Principals.
[6] Paid by the conscript.
[7] $675.00 from Subscription Fund, and about $4500.00 by Principals.

Total Receipts and Expenditures of the Town's " Committee of

RECEIPTS.

Collectors.	Districts.			
William Chickering	No. 1,	$99 80		
Nathan Frye,	No. 1,	37 90		
			$137 70	
William S. Foster,	No. 2,	$36 00		
John Abbott,	No. 2,	191 60		
			227 60	
Calvin E. Stowe,	No. 3 and 5,	$92 50		
Warren F. Draper,	No. 3 and 5,	80 50		
			173 00	
Stephen D. Abbott,	No. 4 and 7,		61 00	
William Jenkins,	No. 8 and 9,		58 00	
Benjamin F. Wardwell,	No. 10,		19 25	
John Dove,	No. 11 and 12,		709 15	
Peter Smith,	No. 13,	$19 00		
Francis Cogswell,	No. 13,	106 00		
			125 00	
Benjamin Boynton,	No. 14, 15, and 18,		36 20	
Jedediah Burtt,	No. 16 and 17,		41 80	
James Bailey,	No. 19 and 24,		14 40	
Nathan Shattuck,	No. 20,		8 25	
William Abbott,	No. 21,		7 00	
Isaac O. Blunt,	No. 22 and 23,		47 00	
Joseph Holt,	No. 6 and 25,		36 00	
Willard Pike,	No. 26,		285 00	
George Foster,	No. 27,		52 60	
James Shaw,	No. 28,		27 00	
From sale of Pistols,			771 50	
			$2837 45	

Balance on hand, old account, $484 35

$484 35

DURING THE REBELLION.

Twenty-five," on account of the War of the Rebellion.

EXPENDITURES.

For Pistols,	$1382 50
Braid and Handkerchiefs,	5 45
Sashes,	32 00
Belts, Gloves, etc.,	37 50
Belts,	3 75
Swords, etc.,	109 50
Drums, etc.,	18 00
Belts,	40 00
Blunt's bill,	5 38
Chandler and Company's bill,	9 55
Dean's bill,	7 53
Dodge and Beard's bill,	7 54
Earl's bill,	164 75
Abbott and Holt's bill,	94 91
Walton's bill,	2 19
Cornell's bill,	25 00
Bodwell's bill,	3 00
George Foster's bill,	2 71
Stearn's bill,	158 06
Gilt braid,	3 20
Walton's bill,	1 08
Pistol's for officers,	52 50
Bounty to 11 recruits at $17 each,	187 00
Balance, new account,	484 35
	$2837 45

Charles H. Bell, loss of arm,	$50 00
Charles Mears, loss of arm,	50 00
Mrs. Bryant, widow of E. K. Bryant,	50 00
John Dearborn, loss of arm,	50 00
William B. Morse, loss of leg,	50 00
Horatio Johnson, wounded,	50 00
Charles H. Bell,	67 18
Charles Mears,	67 17
John Dearborn,	50 00
	$484 35

Town Expenditures from 1861 *to* 1865, *on account of her Soldiers and Seamen,—bounties included.*

Clement, Coburn, and Company, shoes,	$102 50	
Freeland, and Company, uniforms,	858 00	
C. Rice and Cook, hats,	62 25	
Marland Manufacturing Company, flannel,	188 92	
Houghton, Sawyer, and Company, blankets,	355 50	
J. W. Barnard, shoes,	2 42	
William Chickering, fitting armory,	10 11	
H. G. Kimball, returning drums,	4 00	
S. G. Bean, returning uniforms,	1 75	
Andover Company, fitting recruits,	122 43	
Paid Andover Company, for drilling,	2169 00	
John Dean, goods,	7 34	
H. G. Kimball, recruits,	20 00	
Geo. Stewart, band,	7 00	
Dr. W. H. Kimball, examining recruits,	5 00	
John Cornell, expenses to Boston,	3 00	
W. F. Draper, expenses to Boston,	2 80	
S. G. Bean, expenses to Boston,	4 00	
Dr. S. Tracy, attending on Soldier,	75	
		$3926 77
Gratuity of $17 each, to 86 members Andover Co.		$1462 00
Paid for recruiting,	$493 82	
Reimbursed by the State,	209 37	
		$284 45
Benjamin Boynton, for recruiting,		$25 00
State Aid,—paid 1862 to 1866, inclusive,	$48203 75	
Reimbursed by State,	42092 12	
		$6111 63
Bounties paid,		$23814 00
Total,		$35623 85

DURING THE REBELLION. 103

List of Subscriptions received, and Payments made by George Foster, one of the Selectmen and Recruiting Officers of the Town, for recruiting purposes.

RECEIPTS.

Abbott, George L.	$100	00
Abbott, John L.	50	00
Abbott, Nathan F.	25	00
Abbott, Richard M.	25	00
Abbott, Joseph A.	50	00
Abbott, Henry R.	10	00
Abbott, Henry W.	20	00
Abbott, Nathan G.	30	00
Allen, William,	25	00
Abbott, Timothy,	20	00
Abbott, Hartwell B.	5	00
Aiken, John,	50	00
Abbott, Nathaniel B.	10	00
Abbott, Stephen D.	10	00
Bridgeman, Isaac,	40	00
Blanchard, Joshua,	10	00
Bailey, T. B.	30	00
Bailey, M. A.	30	00
Bean, Samuel G.	15	00
Barnard, Edwin H.	25	00
Barnard, Jacob W.	35	00
Bodwell, Horace,	10	00
Blunt, Isaac O.	90	00
Byers, James,	20	00
Butterfield, James P.	20	00
Berry, Samuel,	10	00
Boutwell, S. G.	20	00
Boynton, F. H.	5	00
Baldwin, Curtis M.	10	00
Babbitt, Benjamin B.	10	00
Berry, Jacob W.	5	00
Bodwell, Henry A.	40	00
Boynton, Benjamin, balance,	153	83
Cornell, John, collected,	2881	50
Chandler, George H.	90	00
Cogswell, Joseph B.	50	00
Cogswell, Francis,	50	00

EXPENDITURES.

Bounties to Principals of Naval Recruits.

Bodwell, Henry A.	$75	00
Beard, Horace P.	75	00
Chandler, George H.	75	00
Dodge, James S.	75	00
Farley, I. Alvin,	75	00
Foster, Moses,	75	00
Holt, E. Francis,	75	00
Jackson, S. Charles,	75	00
Jefferson, Perry M.	75	00
		$675 00

Bounties to Principals of Army Substitutes.

Morse, Orlando S.	$75	00
Roberts, James A.	75	00
Shaw, James,	75	00
		$225 00

Bounties to Volunteers.

Abbott, Charles E.	$175	00
Allen, Walter B.	175	00

THE RECORD OF ANDOVER

Cornell, John,	$80 00	Anderson, James,	$101 00
Clarke, Amasa,	50 00	Bailey, Charles W.	75 00
Chandler, Holbrook,	15 00	Berry, Albert,	175 00
Clark, Lewis,	10 00	Black, Thomas D.	175 00
Chandler, Joshua H.	15 00	Blunt, J. Milton,	175 00
Chickering, William,	20 00	Brown, Charles,	175 00
Chickering, Jacob,	20 00	Callahan, Albert J.	175 00
Cornell, John, collected,	40 00	Condon, Nicholas,	275 00
Corse, William,	50 00	Collins, Timothy,	175 00
Cheever, James O.	40 00	Collins, Richard,	275 00
Carruth, Isaac S.	15 00	Chapin, Josiah L.	175 00
Carleton, Benjamin F.	10 00	Clough, Wm. E.	175 00
Cummings, Charles O.	10 00	Duncan, James,	175 00
Corse, William,	50 00	Dwyer, Michael,	175 00
Cochran, James H.	5 00	Dodge, John A.	175 00
Carruth, Isaac,	20 00	Fulton, Joseph W.	175 00
Dean, John H.	85 00	Goldsmith, Jere.	175 00
Doran, Andrew,	25 00	Harrigan, Bart.	275 00
Dane, Henry,	10 00	Higgins, Henry C.	175 00
Duncan, John,	25 00	Hill,E.C.pd.W.F.D.	50 00
Dearborn, A. J.	25 00	Holt, Ballard, 2d,	175 00
Dearborn, J. W.	15 00	Holt, Samuel M.	175 00
Drew, C. C.	50 00	Holloran, Patrick,	175 00
De Bevoise, George H.	100 00	Ingalls, John E.	175 00
Draper, Warren F.	10 00	Jenkins, John B.	175 00
Dane, Hermon,	20 00	Joice, Redmond,	177 00
Eaton, James S.	40 00	McCusker, James,	75 00
Edgell, J. Q. A.	10 00	Melendy, George,	200 00
Emerson, Hovey,	5 00	Milkins, William,	177 00
Farnham, Ezra,	5 00	Moulton, Charles,	175 00
Foster, William P.	300 00	Merrill, John H.	175 00
Fessenden, James M.	50 00	Parker, Caleb O.	150 00
French, S. F.	15 00	Qualey, Patrick,	175 00
Giddings, Isaac E.	25 00	Russell, Winslow,	75 00
Gutterson, George,	15 00	Russell, John R.	275 00
Gould, Henry E.	15 00	Stevens,Wendell B.	175 00
Grover, Lyman,	30 00	Tomlinson, E. A.	225 00
Grosvenor, James Mrs.	20 00	Trask, Elbridge P.	225 00
Higgins, William,	10 00	Tucker, Wm. H.	175 00
Higgins, Charles W. for fund,	30 00	Weston, Frederick,	175 00
Hussey, Elijah,	25 00	Wescott, William,	175 00
Higgins, Charles W.	50 00		———$7530 00
Howarth, David,	25 00		
Harding, John,	7 00		

DURING THE REBELLION.

Hill, George O.	$10 00	
Hardy, Stephen,	10 00	
Holt, Samuel B.	10 00	
Hidden, David I. C.	80 00	
Harnden, Jesse,	10 00	
Jameson, David,	20 00	
Jenkins, William S.	35 00	
Kirk, James,	5 00	
Lovejoy, Joseph T.	15 00	
Merrill, William,	30 00	
Mason, George F.	40 00	
Macomber, Norman M.	15 00	
Mears, Moses,	25 00	
Middleton, James,	10 00	
Mears, Albert F.	5 00	
Marland, Charles H.	15 00	
Morris, Benjamin G.	5 00	
Marshall, Alvin,	40 00	
Merrill, Samuel,	5 00	
Marland, Abraham,	25 00	
McDonald, John,	10 00	
Newman, Samuel H.	10 00	
Newman, Henry J.	15 00	
Noyes, Henry A.	15 00	
O'Connell, John,	10 00	
Oliphant, David,	30 00	
Pasho, Henry F. Jr.	25 00	
Pearson, J. B.	20 00	
Rogers, Benjamin,	10 00	
Raymond, Samuel,	50 00	
Ryley, George W.	100 00	
Rea, John H.	15 00	
Smith, W. H.	15 00	
Shattuck, John T.	40 00	
Smith, Dove, and Co.	2400 00	
Simpson, S. W.	5 00	
Southwick, A. B.	5 00	
Shattuck, Jane, Miss	5 00	
Scrimegour, W. D.	10 00	
Tebbetts, William,	20 00	
Tilton, George F.	10 00	
Towle, Jonathan,	20 00	
Thompson, B. F.	15 00	
Tyer, Henry G.	25 00	

Subscriptions Refunded.

Busfield, John, Jr.	$15 00
Buchan, George,	12 00
Chandler, Geo. H.	100 00
Duncan, John,	10 00
Gorman, Patrick,	10 00
Higgins, William,	10 00
Jefferson, Perry M.	25 00
McCullough, John,	10 00
McDonald, John,	10 00
Roberts, John,	6 00
Stewart, George,	15 00
	$223 00

Expenses of Recruiting.

Allen, Fred. L.	$10 00
Abbott, Milton,	30 00
Allen, Walter B.	10 00
Burtt, Henry,	11 00
Chapin, Josiah L.	175 00
Casey, John,	21 00
Cornell, John,	59 63
Foster, George,	39 70
Goldsmith, Jeremiah,	10 00
Ingalls, John E.	25 00
J. C. S.	10 00

Taylor, Edward,	$50 00	Jefferson, Perry M.	$15 00
Tracy, Stephen,	15 00	Logue, Charles,	25 00
Upton, E. W.	50 00	Murray, Patrick,	4 00
Wilson, George,	15 00	O'Donnell, Hugh,	5 00
Wilson, Horace,	10 00	Stevens, S. H.	5 00
Woodbridge, Francis,	10 00	Woodbridge, Francis,	10 00
Warren, Charles G.	20 00		——— $465 33
Wardwell, Edward T.	50 00		
Whittier, Nathaniel,	15 00		
Wardwell, Simon,	6 00		
Worthley, Lewis T.	10 00		
Wood, William,	5 00		
	$9118 33		$9118 33

Subscription Expenditures from 1861 to 1865, on account of the Soldiers and Seamen of Andover, — bounties included.

" Committee of Twenty-five " disbursed as per account, $2837 45

Bounties disbursed by George Foster, $8430 00
Bounties disbursed by Benjamin Boynton, 930 00
——— $9360 00

Expenses of recruiting disbursed by George Foster, $465 33
Expenses of recruiting disbursed by Benj'n Boynton, 28 95
——— $494 28

Smith and Dove, to fifty-two recruits, $520 00
Warren F. Draper, to E. C. Hill, 87 28
Principals, for " Representative " recruits, 875 00
Citizens drafted, paid Commutation, 2100 00
Principals of substitutes in Army and Navy, about 6000 00
——— $9582 28

Ladies Soldiers' Aid Society, as per final report, $2088 82
Rev. J. W. Turner, disbursed in aid of the wounded, 543 60
Churches, and associations connected therewith, 2178 96
Collections for " Meeting Tent " for 1st H. A. 141 25

Total, $27226 64

DURING THE REBELLION.

List of Subscriptions received and Payments made by Benjamin Boynton, one of the Selectmen and Recruiting Officers of the Town for Recruiting purposes.

RECEIPTS.

Abbott, Nathan G. collected,	$15 00
Abbott, Charles M. col.	55 00
Abbott, Asa A.	5 00
Abbott, Nathan C. col.	20 00
Abbott, John B. col.	9 00
Boutwell, Edward H. col.	68 00
Buchan, George, col.	30 00
Burtt, Henry, col.	20 00
Bridgman, Isaac N.	5 00
Byers, James,	10 00
Blood, Marshall,	20 00
Cummings, Daniel, col.	151 00
Chandler, Joshua H. col.	79 00
Cornell, John, col.	224 00
Chandler, Holbrook,	3 00
Cogswell, Thomas M. col.	10 00
Dearborn, A. J. col.	100 50
Dearborn, James W. col.	121 00
Draper, Warren F.	1 28
Gray, Henry J. and others, col.	33 00
Jenkins, William S.	10 00
Jenkins, William, col.	35 00
Jefferson, Perry M.	20 00
Logue, Charles,	10 00
Merrill, Charles H.	15 00
Mason, George, col.	40 00
Walker, Abel B.	3 00
	$1112 78

BOUNTIES TO VOLUNTEES.

Bradley, Chas. W.	$15 00
Blake, John,	45 00
Cass, Isaac N.	15 00
Carter, Frederick W.	15 00
Clark, Jesse H.	15 00
Crosby, Alonzo,	45 00
Dougherty, James,	15 00
Downes, Benjamin,	15 00
Dow, Charles E.	15 00
Dugan, William,	15 00
Duncan, Robert,	75 00
English, Charles G.	15 00
Fitsgerald, James,	95 00
Fox, William,	15 00
Gibbs, Robert,	15 00
Gould, Theodore F.	15 00
Godkins, Stephen F.	15 00
Goodwin, Moses F.	15 00
Hill, Emmett C	50 00
Jones, David L.	15 00
Lyman, Edward E.	15 00
Lemon, William H.	15 00
Mears, John,	15 00
Morrison, Chas. W.	15 00
Mason, Eri,	55 00
Saunders, James, Jr.	15 00
Sargent, Herbert N.	15 00
Smith, John,	100 00
Smith, Robert,	15 00
Stanwood, Lawrence,	90 00
Thomas, Lewis,	15 00
Wescott, Solomon,	15 00
Weeks, Nathaniel,	15 00
Total,	$930 00

EXPENSES OF RECRUITING.

Boynton, Benj'n,	$16 45
Chandler, Henry F.	5 00
Hatch, Andrew J.	5 00
Telegraphing,	2 50
Total Expenses,	$28 95
Balance paid Geo. Foster,	$153 83
	$1112 78

First Regiment Infantry (3 Years).

Mustered in, June 15, 1861.   Mustered out, May 25, 1864.

ENGAGEMENTS. — Bull Run, Williamsburg, Fair Oaks, Glendale, and other Battles on the Peninsula, Kettle Run, second Bull Run, Chantilly, Fredericksburg, Chancellorsville, Gettysburg, Locust Grove, Wilderness, and Spottsylvania.

Killed in action,	93	Discharged: promoted,	59
Died of wounds and disease,	88	Discharged, honorably,	175
Deserted,	155	Discharged, dishonorably,	6
Missing,	6	Discharged for disability,	580
Transferred,	53	Discharged, expiration service,	528
Unaccounted for,	238	Total,	1981

ANDOVER SOLDIERS BELONGING TO THE REGIMENT.

Collins, Thomas E.
Holt, Joseph F.
Lovejoy George W.

Luke, Wm. H.
Stowe, Frederick W.
Whittemore, Harrison,

Second Regiment Infantry (3 Years).

Mustered in, May 25, 1861.   Mustered out, July 14, 1865.

ENGAGEMENTS. — Jackson, Front Royal, Winchester, Antietam, Cedar Mountain, Fredericksburg, Chancellorsville, Gettysburg, Resaca, Kenesaw Mountain, Peach-Tree Creek, Atlanta, Raleigh, Averysboro, etc.

Killed in action,	116	Discharged: promoted,	137
Died of wounds and disease,	156	Discharged, honorably,	361
Deserted,	276	Discharged, dishonorably,	1
Missing,	4	Discharged for disability,	376
Transferred,	1	Discharged, expiration service,	751
Unaccounted for,	588	Total,	2767

ANDOVER SOLDIERS BELONGING TO THE REGIMENT.

Comstock, Alfred, | French, Henry P.
Lovejoy, William W.

Fourth Regiment Infantry (3 Months).

Mustered in, April 22, 1861. Mustered out, July 22, 1861.

This Regiment was on service at Fortress Munroe, Va.

Killed in action,		Discharged: promoted,	
Died of wounds and disease,	1	Discharged, honorably,	
Deserted,		Discharged, dishonorably,	
Missing,		Discharged for disability,	5
Transferred,		Discharged, expiration service.	629
Unaccounted for		Total,	635

ANDOVER SOLDIER BELONGING TO THE REGIMENT.

Hanson, Charles.

Fifth Regiment Infantry (3 Months).

Mustered in, May 1, 1861. Mustered out, July 31, 1861.

ENGAGEMENTS. — First Bull Run Battle.

Killed in action,	8	Discharged: promoted,	8
Died of wounds and disease,	2	Discharged, honorably,	4
Deserted,		Discharged, dishonorably,	1
Missing,	1	Discharged for disability,	28
Transferred,		Discharged, expiration service,	777
Unaccounted for,		Total,	829

ANDOVER SOLDIERS BELONGING TO THE REGIMENT.

Barker, Samuel S. | Grandy, Henry E.

Fifth Regiment Infantry (100 Days).

Mustered in, July 23, 1864. Mustered out, Nov. 16, 1864.

This Regiment was stationed at Fort Marshall, in the vicinity of Baltimore, Md.

Killed in action,		Discharged : promoted,	5
Died of wounds and disease,	7	Discharged, honorably,	10
Deserted,		Discharged, dishonorably,	
Missing,		Discharged for disability,	
Transferred,		Discharged, expiration service,	921
Unaccounted for,		Total,	943

ANDOVER SOLDIER BELONGING TO THE REGIMENT.

Abbott, Alson B.

Sixth Regiment Infantry (3 Months).

Mustered in, April 22, 1861. Mustered out, Aug. 2, 1861.

This Regiment was assaulted by a mob in the streets of Baltimore, April 19, 1861.

Killed in action,	4	Discharged : promoted,	11
Died of wounds and disease,		Discharged, honorably,	2
Deserted,		Discharged, dishonorably,	
Missing,		Discharged for disability,	10
Transferred,		Discharged, expiration service,	720
Unaccounted for,		Total,	747

ANDOVER SOLDIERS BELONGING TO THE REGIMENT.

Carter, William S.
Cooper, Thomas H.
Dane, Albert L.
Marland, William,
Merrill, Frank H.
Sanborn, Frank,
Turkington, Henry.

Sixth Regiment Infantry (9 Months).

Mustered in, Aug. 31, 1862.   Mustered out, June 3, 1863.

This Regiment was on duty near Suffolk, Va., during its whole term of service.

Killed in action,	8	Discharged: promoted,	12
Died of wounds and disease,	19	Discharged, honorably,	6
Deserted,	9	Discharged, dishonorably,	
Missing,		Discharged for disability,	23
Transferred,	2	Discharged, expiration service,	859
Unaccounted for,		Total,	938

ANDOVER SOLDIERS BELONGING TO THE REGIMENT.

Noyes, Aaron,   Vinal, George A. W.

Sixth Regiment Infantry (100 Days).

Mustered in, July 14, 1864.   Mustered out, Oct. 27, 1864.

This Regiment was stationed at Fort Delaware, Md., a Depot for Rebel Prisoners.

Killed in action,		Discharged: promoted,	3
Died of wounds and disease,	6	Discharged, honorably,	•3
Deserted,	1	Discharged, dishonorably,	
Missing,		Discharged for disability,	1
Transferred,		Discharged, expiration service,	957
Unaccounted for,		Total,	971

ANDOVER SOLDIERS BELONGING TO THE REGIMENT.

Barker, William,   George, Warren,
Barnard, Henry F.   Goodwin, Moses F.
Belanger, William F.   Johnston, David, Jr.
Bond, John,   McCullough, John,
Buchan, George,   Packard, Edward W.
Busfield, John, Jr.   Stevens, Daniel,
Dunn, Albert H.   Stewart, George,
              Stewart, John W.

Ninth Regiment Infantry (3 Years).

Mustered in, June 11, 1861. Mustered out, June 21, 1864.

ENGAGEMENTS. — Battles on the Peninsula, Fredericksburg, Chancellorsville, Mine Run, Wilderness, Spottsylvania, Po River, North Anna River, Bethesda Church, Shady Grove, and Cold Harbor.

Killed in action,	153	Discharged : promoted,	90
Died of wounds and disease,	105	Discharged, honorably,	143
Deserted,	241	Discharged, dishonorably,	12
Missing,	8	Discharged for disability,	407
Transferred,	218	Discharged, expiration service,	449
Unaccounted for,	96	Total,	1922

ANDOVER SOLDIER BELONGING TO THE REGIMENT.

Ward, James.

Eleventh Regiment Infantry (3 Years).

Mustered in, June 13, 1861. Mustered out, June 12, 1864.

ENGAGEMENTS. — First Bull Run, Yorktown, Williamsburg, Fair Oaks, Savage Station, Glendale, Malvern Hill, Bristow Station, 2d Bull Run, Chantilly, Fredericksburg, Chancellorsville, Gettysburg, Kelley's Ford, Locust Grove, Wilderness, Spottsylvania, North Anna, Tolopotomy, Cold Harbor, Petersburg, Strawberry Plains, Deep Bottom, Poplar Spring Church, Boydton Road.

Killed in action,	85	Discharged : promoted,	123
Died of wounds and disease,	147	Discharged, honorably,	275
Deserted,	328	Discharged, dishonorably,	13
Missing,	32	Discharged for disability,	338
Transferred,	4	Discharged, expiration service,	847
Unaccounted for,	231	Total,	2423

ANDOVER SOLDIERS BELONGING TO THE REGIMENT.

Allen, Walter B.
Berry, Albert,
Blunt. J. Milton,
Bolton, William A.
Chapin, Josiah L.
Callahan, Albert J.
Clough, William E.
Collins, Timothy,
Conley, Jeremiah,
Duncan, James,
Dodge, John A.
Goldsmith, Jeremiah,
Gallon, James,
Holt, Ballard, 2d,
Holt, Samuel M.

Higgins, Henry C.
Ingalls, John E.
Jenkins, John B.
Keating, John,
Moulton, Charles L.
Mears, Daniel, Jr.
Mears, George,
Merrill, John H.
Qualey, Patrick,
Shannon, John,
Tucker, William H.
Vaux, Walter R.
Woodbridge, Francis,
Wallace, Alexander,
Woodlin, Elgin.

Twelfth Regiment Infantry (3 Years).

Mustered in, June 26, 1861.   Mustered out, July 8, 1864.

ENGAGEMENTS. — Cedar Mountain, 2d Bull Run, Antietam, Fredericksburg, Chancellorsville, Gettysburg, Wilderness, Spottsylvania, North Anna River, Cold Harbor, and Petersburg.

Killed in action,	128	Discharged : promoted,	86
Died of wounds and disease,	126	Discharged, honorably,	253
Deserted,	191	Discharged, dishonorably,	2
Missing,	12	Discharged for disability,	318
Transferred,	241	Discharged, expiration service,	314
Unaccounted for,	87	Total,	1758

ANDOVER SOLDIERS BELONGING TO THE REGIMENT.

Clark, Edwin L.   Townley, John J.

Thirteenth Regiment Infantry (3 Years).

Mustered in, July 16, 1861. Mustered out, August 1, 1864.

ENGAGEMENTS. — Second Bull Run, Antietam, Fredericksburg, Chancellorsville, Gettysburg, Wilderness, Spottsylvania, North Anna River, Cold Harbor, and Petersburg.

Killed in action,	71	Discharged : promoted,	93
Died of wounds and disease,	75	Discharged, honorably,	261
Deserted,	171	Discharged, dishonorably,	6
Missing,	9	Discharged for disability,	418
Transferred,	100	Discharged, expiration service,	360
Unaccounted for,	20	Total,	1584

ANDOVER SOLDIER BELONGING TO THE REGIMENT.

Clement, Charles A.

Fifteenth Regiment Infantry (3 Years.)

Mustered in, July 12, 1861. Mustered out, July 28, 1864.

ENGAGEMENTS. — Balls Bluff, Battles on the Peninsula, Antietam, Fredericksburg, Chancellorsville, Gettysburg, Bristow Station, Robertson's Tavern, Wilderness, and in all the battles from the Rapidan to Petersburg in which the Second Army Corps was engaged.

Killed in action,	151	Discharged : promoted,	122
Died of wounds and disease,	186	Discharged, honorably,	357
Deserted,	125	Discharged, dishonorably,	6
Missing,	16	Discharged for disability,	472
Transferred,	242	Discharged, expiration service,	214
Unaccounted for,	84	Total,	1975

ANDOVER SOLDIERS BELONGING TO THE REGIMENT.

Craig, David, | Critchett, George D.

Sixteenth Regiment Infantry (3 Years).

Mustered in August 5, 1861. Mustered out, July 27, 1864.

ENGAGEMENTS. — Fair Oaks, Glendale, Malvern Hill, Kettle Run, Chantilly, Fredericksburg, Chancellorsville, Gettysburg, Locust Grove, Wilderness, Spottsylvania, North Anna River, Cold Harbor, Petersburg.

Killed in action,	105	Discharged: promoted,	83
Died of wounds and disease,	128	Discharged, honorably,	275
Deserted,	141	Discharged, dishonorably,	4
Missing,	9	Discharged for disability,	339
Transferred,	192	Discharged, expiration service,	267
Unaccounted for,	20	Total,	1563

ANDOVER SOLDIER BELONGING TO THE REGIMENT.

Flemming, John.

Seventeenth Regiment Infantry (3 Years).

Mustered in, July 22, 1861. Mustered out, July 11, 1865.

ENGAGEMENTS. — Kinston, Goldsboro', Bachelder's Creek.

Killed in action,	11	Discharged: promoted,	96
Died of wounds and disease,	142	Discharged, honorably,	700
Deserted,	80	Discharged, dishonorably,	4
Missing,		Discharged for disability,	404
Transferred,		Discharged, expiration service,	769
Unaccounted for,	93	Total,	2299

ANDOVER SOLDIERS BELONGING TO THE REGIMENT.

Condon, Nicholas,
Dwyer, Michael,

Melendy, George E.
Smith, John.

Eighteenth Regiment Infantry (3 Years).

Mustered in, Aug. 24, 1861. Mustered out, Sept. 2, 1864.

ENGAGEMENTS. — Battles on the Peninsula, 2d Bull Run, Shepardstown, Fredericksburg, Chancellorsville, Gettysburg, Rappahannock Station, Wilderness, Spottsylvania, Weldon Railroad, Cold Harbor, Petersburg.

Killed in action,	84	Discharged: promoted,	72
Died of wounds and disease,	148	Discharged, honorably,	309
Deserted,	92	Discharged, dishonorably,	5
Missing,		Discharged for disability,	405
Transferred,	241	Discharged, expiration service,	219
Unaccounted for,	58	Total,	1633

ANDOVER SOLDIER BELONGING TO THE REGIMENT.

Abbott, Moses B.

Nineteenth Regiment Infantry (3 Years).

Mustered in, Aug. 3, 1861. Mustered out, June 30, 1865.

ENGAGEMENTS. — Balls Bluff, Yorktown, West Point, Fair Oaks, Peach Orchard, Savage Station, White Oak Swamp, Malvern Hill, 2d Bull Run, Antietam, Fredericksburg, Chancellorsville, Gettysburg, Bristow Station, Mine Run, Wilderness, Spottsylvania, Tolopotomy, Cold Harbor, Petersburg, Deep Bottom, Ream's Station, Boydton Road, Vaughn Road, and Farmville.

Killed in action,	104	Discharged: promoted,	144
Died of wounds and disease,	160	Discharged, honorably,	408
Deserted,	174	Discharged, dishonorably,	6
Missing,	4	Discharged for disability,	449
Transferred,	91	Discharged, expiration service,	640
Unaccounted for,	289	Total,	2469

ANDOVER SOLDIERS BELONGING TO THE REGIMENT.

Barrows, William E.
Bentley, Noah,
Higgins, Archibald,
O'Malley, Thomas,
Skerritt, James,
Wardwell, George E.
Winthrop, Thomas F.

DURING THE REBELLION. 117

Twentieth Regiment Infantry (3 Years).

Mustered in, Aug. 28, 1861. Mustered out, July 16, 1865.

ENGAGEMENTS. — Balls Bluff, Yorktown, West Point, Fair Oaks, Peach Orchard, Savage Station, Glendale, Malvern Hill, Chantilly, Antietam, Fredericksburg, Chancellorsville, Gettysburg, Bristow Station, Mine Run, Wilderness, Po River, Spottsylvania, Tolopotomy, Cold Harbor, Petersburg, Strawberry Plains, Deep Bottom, Ream's Station, Boydton Road, Vaughn Road, and Farmville.

Killed in action,	192	Discharged : promoted,	122
Died of wounds and disease,	192	Discharged, honorably,	441
Deserted,	229	Discharged, dishonorably,	13
Missing,	13	Discharged for disability,	576
Transferred,	14	Discharged, expiration service.	905
Unaccounted for	533	Total,	3230

ANDOVER SOLDIERS BELONGING TO THE REGIMENT.

Armstrong, Thomas,
Buguay, George A.
Callahan, Charles H.

* Craig, David,
Gray, Nathan H.
Kavanagh, Bernard,

Pray, Seaver.

Twenty-Second Regiment Infantry (3 Years).

Mustered in, Oct. 5, 1861. Mustered out, Oct. 17, 1864.

ENGAGEMENTS. — Battles before Richmond, Antietam, Fredericksburg, Chancellorsville, Gettysburg, Rappahannock Station, Wilderness, Laurel Hill, Spottsylvania, Jericho Ford, Little River, Tolopotomy, Bethesda Church, Shady Grove Church, and Petersburg.

Killed in action,	141	Discharged : promoted,	87
Died of wounds and disease,	143	Discharged, honorably,	244
Deserted,	124	Discharged, dishonorably,	6
Missing,	3	Discharged for disability,	464
Transferred,	179	Discharged, expiration service,	195
Unaccounted for,	272	Total,	1858

ANDOVER SOLDIERS BELONGING TO THE REGIMENT.

Hunter, William,
Hayes, Patrick,
Whittaker, Amos.
Johnson, John,
Trulan, William,

The following is a Roll of "Bounty Jumpers" who were recruited in Boston for, but who never joined, the Regiment; most of their names are to be found among the "unassigned recruits," on the Regimental Roll.

Boyden, James,
Boyle, John,
Boyd, Patrick,
Boyce, Thomas,
Clark, John,
Clarkson, John,
Collins, James,
Coombs, James,
Delany, Edward,
Durant, George,
Flood, Thomas,
Gorman, Joseph E.
Gorman, William B.
Green, Joseph,
Jameson, John,
Johnson, James,
Lyon, John,

Malone, John,
McAndrews, John,
McCarty, Charles,
Murphy, William,
Morton, Charles H.
Morrison, John,
O'Brien, John,
Riley, John,
Smith, Charles,
Stanton, Michael,
Sylvester, William,
Thompson, William,
Tumey, Peter,
Walsh, William,
Wilson, Charles,
Woods, William,
Young, Samuel.

Twenty-Third Regiment Infantry (3 Years).

Mustered in, Sept. 28, 1861.   Mustered out, Sept. 28, 1864.

ENGAGEMENTS. — Roanoke, Newbern, Rawles Mills, Kinston, Goldsboro', Wilcox Bridge, Winton, Smithfield, Heckman's Farm, Arrowfield Church, Drury's Bluff, Cold Harbor, and other battles before Richmond, and Kinston, 2d.

DURING THE REBELLION.   119

Killed in action,	40	Discharged: promoted,	96
Died of wounds and disease,	144	Discharged, honorably,	396
Deserted,	27	Discharged, dishonorably,	8
Missing,	23	Discharged for disability,	377
Transferred,	1	Discharged, expiration service,	563
Unaccounted for,	36	Total,	1710

ANDOVER SOLDIERS BELONGING TO THE REGIMENT.

Christian, William T. | Porter, Thomas F.

Twenty-Fourth Regiment Infantry (3 Years).

Mustered in, Dec. 6, 1861.　　　Mustered out, Jan. 20, 1866.

ENGAGEMENTS. — Roanoke Island, Kinston, Whitehall, Goldsboro', Tranter's Creek, Newbern, James Island, Morris Island, Fort Wagner, Green Valley, Drury's Bluff, Richmond and Petersburg Railroad, Weir Bottom Church, Deep Bottom, Deep Run, Fussell's Mills, Siege of Petersburg, Four Mile Run Church, Darby Town Road.

Killed in action,	63	Discharged: promoted,	124
Died of wounds and disease,	147	Discharged, honorably,	535
Deserted,	112	Discharged, dishonorably,	2
Missing,	1	Discharged for disability,	262
Transferred,	1	Discharged, expiration service,	839
Unaccounted for,	29	Total,	2116

ANDOVER SOLDIERS BELONGING TO THE REGIMENT.

Crowther, William, | Parker, George W.
Eagleton, Charles, | Saunders, Thomas.

Twenty-Sixth Regiment Infantry (3 Years).

Mustered in, Oct. 18, 1861.　　　Mustered out, Aug. 26, 1865.

ENGAGEMENTS. — Winchester, Cedar Creek, and Fisher's Hill.

120 THE RECORD OF ANDOVER

Killed in action,	43	Discharged : promoted,	91
Died of wounds and disease,	194	Discharged, honorably,	648
Deserted,	160	Discharged, dishonorably,	2
Missing,	2	Discharged for disability,	263
Transferred,	1	Discharged, expiration service,	644
Unaccounted for,	53	Total,	2101

ANDOVER SOLDIERS BELONGING TO THE REGIMENT.

Bailey, George A.
Banker, Melvin,
Blake, John,
Chandler, Joseph, Jr.
Crosby, Alonzo,
Dane, Elmore,

Dane, Richard G.
Mason, Warren,
Nickerson, Ephraim N.
Raymond, Jefferson N.
Turner, John,
Worthley, Daniel E.

Twenty-Eighth Regiment Infantry (3 Years).

Mustered in, latter part 1861. Mustered out, June 30, 1865.

ENGAGEMENTS. — James Island, 2d Bull Run, Chantilly, South Mountain, Antietam, Fredericksburg, Chancellorsville, Gettysburg, Bristow Station, Mine Run, Wilderness, Po River, Spottsylvania, Tolopotomy, Cold Harbor, Petersburg, Strawberry Plains, Deep Bottom, Ream's Station, South Side Railroad.

Killed in action,	161	Discharged : promoted,	115
Died of wounds and disease,	203	Discharged, honorably,	488
Deserted,	288	Discharged, dishonorably,	4
Missing,	32	Discharged for disability,	411
Transferred,	1	Discharged, expiration service,	424
Unaccounted for,	377	Total,	2504

ANDOVER SOLDIERS BELONGING TO THE REGIMENT.

Standing, George, | Smith, John.

Twenty-Ninth Regiment Infantry (3 Years).

Mustered in, 1861. Mustered out, July 29, 1865.

ENGAGEMENTS. — Hampton Roads, Gaines' Mills, Savage Station, White Oak Swamp, Malvern Hill, 2d Bull Run, Antietam, Fredericksburg, Vicksburg, Jackson, Blue Springs, Campbell Station, Siege of Knoxville, Cold Harbor, Petersburg, Weldon Railroad, Fort Stedman.

Killed in action,	47	Discharged: promoted,	103
Died of wounds and disease,	107	Discharged, honorably,	262
Deserted,	88	Discharged, dishonorably,	4
Missing,	5	Discharged for disability,	304
Transferred,	6	Discharged, expiration service,	711
Unaccounted for,	183	Total,	1820

ANDOVER SOLDIERS BELONGING TO THE REGIMENT.

Carlton, Oscar F. Kelly, Joseph,
Hayes, Timothy, Logue, Charles.

Thirtieth Regiment Infantry (3 Years).

Mustered in, Jan. 4, 1862. Mustered out, July 10, 1866.

ENGAGEMENTS. — Vicksburg, Baton Rouge, Plains Store, Port Hudson, Donaldsonville, Winchester, Cedar Creek, and Fisher's Hill.

Killed in action,	27	Discharged: promoted,	109
Died of wounds and disease,	344	Discharged, honorably,	420
Deserted,	195	Discharged, dishonorably,	6
Missing,	36	Discharged for disability,	308
Transferred,		Discharged, expiration service,	514
Unaccounted for,	105	Total,	2064

ANDOVER SOLDIERS BELONGING TO THE REGIMENT.

Becker, Charles, Greeley, William,
Black, James B. Jaquith, James.

Thirty-Second Regiment Infantry (3 Years).

Mustered in, 1862. Mustered out, June 29, 1865.

ENGAGEMENTS. — Malvern Hill, Gainesville, 2d Bull Run, Chantilly, Antietam, Fredericksburg, Chancellorsville, Gettysburg, Rappahannock Station, Mine Run, Wilderness, Spottsylvania, North Anna, Tolopotomy, Bethesda Church, Petersburg, Weldon Railroad, Vaughn Road, Dabney's Mills, Boydton Road, and White Oak Road.

Killed in action,	79	Discharged: promoted,	148
Died of wounds and disease,	198	Discharged, honorably,	777
Deserted,	163	Discharged, dishonorably,	2
Missing,	11	Discharged for disability,	392
Transferred,	2	Discharged, expiration service,	1133
Unaccounted for,	64	Total,	2969

ANDOVER SOLDIERS BELONGING TO THE REGIMENT.

Eeles, Frederick S. | Ward, James.

Thirty-Third Regiment Infantry (3 Years.)

Mustered in, Aug. 13, 1862. Mustered out, June 11, 1865.

ENGAGEMENTS. — Fredericksburg, Chancellorsville, Beverly Ford, Gettysburg, Lookout Mountain, Missionary Ridge, and the battles of Sherman's Grand Army.

Killed in action,	69	Discharged: promoted,	97
Died of wounds and disease,	107	Discharged, honorably,	234
Deserted,	79	Discharged, dishonorably,	3
Missing,		Discharged for disability,	201
Transferred,	94	Discharged, expiration service,	402
Unaccounted for,	126	Total,	1412

ANDOVER SOLDIER BELONGING TO THE REGIMENT.

Smith, James B.

Thirty-Fifth Regiment Infantry (3 Years).

Mustered in Aug. 21, 1862.   Mustered out, June 9, 1865.

ENGAGEMENTS. — Antietam, Fredericksburg, Jackson, Campbell Station, Siege of Knoxville, Spottsylvania, North Anna, Cold Harbor, Weldon Railroad, South Mountain, Vicksburg, Poplar Spring Church, Hatcher's Run, Fort Sedgwick, Fort Mahone, and Petersburg.

Killed in action,	91	Discharged : promoted,	125
Died of wounds and disease,	134	Discharged, honorably,	163
Deserted,	40	Discharged, dishonorably,	2
Missing,	6	Discharged for disability,	322
Transferred,	418	Discharged, expiration service,	356
Unaccounted for,	8	Total,	1665

ANDOVER SOLDIERS BELONGING TO THE REGIMENT.

Shattuck, Charles William, | Wardwell, Joseph W.

Thirty-Sixth Regiment Infantry (3 Years).

Mustered in, Aug. 30, 1862.   Mustered out, June 8, 1865.

ENGAGEMENTS. — Fredericksburg, Vicksburg, Jackson, Blue Springs, Campbell Station, Siege of Knoxville, Wilderness, Spottsylvania, North Anna, Cold Harbor, Petersburg, Poplar Spring Church, and Hatcher's Run.

Killed in action,	56	Discharged : promoted,	90
Died of wounds and disease,	193	Discharged, honorably,	244
Deserted,	42	Discharged, dishonorably,	
Missing,	3	Discharged for disability,	189
Transferred,	229	Discharged, expiration service,	355
Unaccounted for,	15	Total,	1416

ANDOVER SOLDIER BELONGING TO THE REGIMENT.

Kelly, Joseph.

Thirty-Seventh Regiment Infantry (3 Years).

Mustered in, Sept. 4, 1862.   Mustered out, June 21, 1865.

ENGAGEMENTS. — Fredericksburg, Mayre's Heights, Salem Heights, Gettysburg, Rappahannock Station, Wilderness, Spottsylvania, Cold Harbor, Petersburg, Fort Stedman, and Opequan.

Killed in action,	110	Discharged : promoted,	107
Died of wounds and disease,	138	Discharged, honorably,	184
Deserted,	88	Discharged, dishonorably,	6
Missing,	2	Discharged for disability,	187
Transferred,	213	Discharged, expiration service,	410
Unaccounted for,	38	Total,	1483

ANDOVER SOLDIER BELONGING TO THE REGIMENT.

Abbott, George B.

Fortieth Regiment Infantry (3 Years).

Mustered in, Sept. 5, 1862.   Mustered out, June 16, 1865.

ENGAGEMENTS. — Battles on the Blackwater, Bombardments of Forts Sumter and Wagner, Siege of Charleston, Olustee, Cedar Creek, Ten Mile Run, Jacksonville, Drury's Bluff, Cold Harbor, Fort Harrison, Fair Oaks, and the several battles before Petersburg and Richmond.

Killed in action,	46	Discharged : promoted,	113
Died of wounds and disease,	146	Discharged, honorably,	258
Deserted,	13	Discharged, dishonorably,	
Missing,	4	Discharged for disability,	204
Transferred,	19	Discharged, expiration service,	361
Unaccounted for,	3	Total,	1167

ANDOVER SOLDIER BELONGING TO THE REGIMENT.

Crowther, William.

Forty-Second Regiment Infantry (100 Days).

Mustered in, July 22, 1864. Mustered out, Nov. 11, 1864.

This Regiment was stationed at or near Alexandria, Va.

Killed in action,		Discharged : promoted,	4
Died of wounds and disease,	14	Discharged, honorably,	1
Deserted,	2	Discharged, dishonorably,	
Missing,		Discharged for disability,	6
Transferred,		Discharged, expiration service.	926
Unaccounted for		Total,	953

ANDOVER SOLDIER BELONGING TO THE REGIMENT.

Hotchkiss, Arthur E.

Forty-Third Regiment Infantry (9 Months).

Mustered in, Sept. 20, 1862. Mustered out, July 30, 1863.

ENGAGEMENTS. — Goldsboro', Kinston, and Whitehall, N. C.

Killed in action,	2	Discharged : promoted,	12
Died of wounds and disease,	13	Discharged, honorably,	28
Deserted,	109	Discharged, dishonorably,	
Missing,		Discharged for disability,	35
Transferred,	1	Discharged, expiration service,	876
Unaccounted for,		Total,	1076

ANDOVER SOLDIERS BELONGING TO THE REGIMENT.

Burtt, Joseph A. Carruth, Isaac S.
Lovejoy, Joseph T.

126   THE RECORD OF ANDOVER

Forty-Fourth Regiment Infantry (9 Months).

Mustered in, Sept. 12, 1862.   Mustered out, June 18, 1863.

ENGAGEMENTS. — Kinston, Whitehall, Goldsboro' and the Siege of Washington, N. C.

Killed in action,	8	Discharged : promoted,	15
Died of wounds and disease,	28	Discharged, honorably,	11
Deserted,	3	Discharged, dishonorably,	
Missing,		Discharged for disability,	66
Transferred,	2	Discharged, expiration service,	914
Unaccounted for,		Total,	1047

ANDOVER SOLDIERS BELONGING TO THE REGIMENT.

Allen, Walter B.
Clarke, Amasa,
Cogswell, Thomas M.
Holt, Ballard, 2d,
Kimball, Henry G.
Lovejoy, George W.
Marland, Charles H.

Moar, Charles J.
Raymond, Edward G.
Raymond, Walter L.
Rogers, L. Waldo,
Tyler, Herbert,
Young, Francis C.
Young, George W.

Forty-Fifth Regiment Infantry (9 Months).

Mustered in, Sept. 26, 1862.   Mustered out, July 8, 1863.

ENGAGEMENTS. — Kinston, Whitehall, and Goldsboro'.

Killed in action,	10	Discharged : promoted,	
Died of wounds and disease,	36	Discharged, honorably,	12
Deserted,	48	Discharged, dishonorably,	
Missing,		Discharged for disability,	51
Transferred,		Discharged, expiration service,	868
Unaccounted for,		Total,	1025

ANDOVER SOLDIERS BELONGING TO THE REGIMENT.

Bowen, Albert L.
Holt, Samuel M.

Merrill, James W.
Tracy, William W.

Forty-Seventh Regiment Infantry (9 Months).

Mustered in, 1862. Mustered out, Sept. 1, 1863.

This Regiment was stationed in and around New Orleans, La.

Killed in action,	1	Discharged: promoted,	18
Died of wounds and disease,	33	Discharged, honorably,	39
Deserted,	225	Discharged, dishonorably,	
Missing,		Discharged for disability,	57
Transferred,	1	Discharged, expiration service,	781
Unaccounted for,	3	Total,	1158

ANDOVER SOLDIERS BELONGING TO THE REGIMENT.

Farnham, David T.   Hunt, William.

Forty-Eighth Regiment Infantry (9 Months).

Mustered in, 1862. Mustered out, Sept. 3, 1863.

This Regiment was in service at New Orleans, and in the Siege of Port Hudson.

Killed in action,	11	Discharged: promoted,	29
Died of wounds and disease,	53	Discharged, honorably,	43
Deserted,	154	Discharged, dishonorably,	1
Missing,		Discharged for disability,	24
Transferred,	1	Discharged, expiration service,	708
Unaccounted for,	1	Total,	1025

ANDOVER SOLDIER BELONGING TO THE REGIMENT.

Logue, James.

Fiftieth Regiment Infantry (9 Months).

Mustered in, Sept. 19, 1862.   Mustered out, Aug. 24, 1863.

This Regiment was engaged in the Siege and capture of Port Hudson.

Killed in action,		Discharged : promoted,	3
Died of wounds and disease,	89	Discharged, honorably,	11
Deserted,	27	Discharged, dishonorably,	2
Missing,		Discharged for disability,	25
Transferred,		Discharged, expiration service,	831
Unaccounted for,	6	Total,	994

ANDOVER SOLDIERS BELONGING TO THE REGIMENT.

Fulton, Joseph W. | Harnden, George W.
                  Holt, Joseph F.

Fifty-Fourth Regiment Infantry (3 Years).

Mustered in, May 13, 1863.   Mustered out, Aug. 20, 1865.

ENGAGEMENTS. — Fort Wagner, and the several engagements before Charleston, Olustee, James Island, Honey Hill, and Boykin's Mills.

Killed in action,	54	Discharged : promoted,	77
Died of wounds and disease,	154	Discharged, honorably,	64
Deserted,	40	Discharged, dishonorably,	1
Missing,	51	Discharged for disability,	140
Transferred,	94	Discharged, expiration service,	860
Unaccounted for,	39	Total,	1574

ANDOVER SOLDIERS BELONGING TO THE REGIMENT.

Brown, Charles, | Rollins, Robert.

Fifty-Fifth Regiment Infantry (3 Years).

Mustered in, June 22, 1863.   Mustered out, Aug. 29, 1865.

ENGAGEMENTS. — Siege of Charleston, James Island, and Honey Hill.

Killed in action,	52	Discharged: promoted,	64
Died of wounds and disease,	132	Discharged, honorably,	34
Deserted,	27	Discharged, dishonorably,	10
Missing,		Discharged for disability,	116
Transferred,		Discharged, expiration service,	856
Unaccounted for,	4	Total,	1295

ANDOVER SOLDIERS BELONGING TO THE REGIMENT.

Brown, Charles. | Holt, Harrison, 1st Lieut.

Fifty-Seventh Regiment Infantry (3 Years).
(SECOND VETERAN.)

Mustered in, April 6, 1864.   Mustered out, July 30, 1865.

ENGAGEMENTS. — Wilderness, Spottsylvania, North Anna, Cold Harbor, Petersburg, Weldon Railroad, Poplar Spring Church, and Hatcher's Run.

Killed in action,	112	Discharged: promoted,	44
Died of wounds and disease,	137	Discharged, honorably,	277
Deserted,	84	Discharged, dishonorably,	2
Missing,	34	Discharged for disability,	125
Transferred,		Discharged, expiration service,	716
Unaccounted for,	12	Total,	1543

ANDOVER SOLDIERS BELONGING TO THE REGIMENT.

Farnham, Moses L. | Vinal, George A. W.

Fifty-Ninth Regiment Infantry (3 Years).
(FOURTH VETERAN).
Mustered in, from Dec. 5, '63, to Apr. 21, '64. Mustered out, July 30, 1865.

ENGAGEMENTS. — Wilderness, Spottsylvania, North Anna, Cold Harbor, Petersburg, Weldon Railroad, Poplar Spring Church, Hatcher's Run, and Fort Stedman.

Killed in action,	48	Discharged: promoted,	55
Died of wounds and disease,	99	Discharged, honorably,	93
Deserted,	109	Discharged, dishonorably,	4
Missing,	13	Discharged for disability,	93
Transferred,	464	Discharged, expiration service,	6
Unaccounted for,	70	Total,	1054

ANDOVER SOLDIERS BELONGING TO THE REGIMENT.

Chandler, Henry F.
Farnham, Moses L.
Goldsmith, Sandford K.
Goldsmith, Benjamin F.

Patrick, Andrew K.
Ryley, Leonard W.
Vinal, George A. W.
Wardman, Thomas.

Sixtieth Regiment Infantry (100 Days).
Mustered in, — — — Mustered out, Nov. 30, 1864.

This Regiment was stationed at Indianapolis, Indiana.

Killed in action,		Discharged: promoted,	11
Died of wounds and disease,	9	Discharged, honorably,	
Deserted,	3	Discharged, dishonorably,	
Missing,		Discharged for disability,	
Transferred,		Discharged, expiration service,	928
Unaccounted for,		Total,	951

ANDOVER SOLDIER BELONGING TO THE REGIMENT.

Gifford, Robert.

DURING THE REBELLION.

Sixty-First Regiment Infantry (1 Year).

Mustered in, 1864. Mustered out, June 4, and July 16, 1865.

This Regiment took part in the engagements before Petersburg.

Killed in action,	5	Discharged : promoted,	26
Died of wounds and disease,	17	Discharged, honorably,	54
Deserted,	14	Discharged, dishonorably,	1
Missing,		Discharged for disability,	3
Transferred,	3	Discharged, expiration service,	886
Unaccounted for,	4	Total,	1013

ANDOVER SOLDIER BELONGING TO THE REGIMENT.

Black, Thomas D.

Sixty-Second Regiment Infantry (1 Year).

This Regiment was under recruitment at the time of the surrender of General Lee, and was mustered out before completion, by Order of the War Department.

Killed in action,		Discharged : promoted,	6
Died of wounds and disease,	2	Discharged, honorably,	2
Deserted,	8	Discharged, dishonorably,	
Missing,		Discharged for disability,	
Transferred,		Discharged, expiration service,	393
Unaccounted for,		Total,	411

ANDOVER SOLDIER BELONGING TO THE REGIMENT.

Winthrop, Thomas F.

First Regiment Heavy Artillery (3 Years).

Mustered in, July 5, 1861. Mustered out, Aug. 16, 1865.

For a History of this Regiment see Appendix.

ENGAGEMENTS. — Spottsylvania, North Anna, Tolopotomy, Cold Harbor, Petersburg, Strawberry Plains, Deep Bottom, Poplar Spring Church, Boydton Road, Hatcher's Run, Duncan's Run, Vaughn Road, and in all the Battles in which the Second Army Corps were engaged up to the surrender of General Lee.

Killed in action,	104	Discharged: promoted,	163
Died of wounds and disease,	360	Discharged, honorably,	898
Deserted,	121	Discharged, dishonorably,	6
Missing,	9	Discharged for disability,	418
Transferred,	1	Discharged, expiration service,	1289
Unaccounted for,	70	Total,	3439

ANDOVER SOLDIERS BELONGING TO THE REGIMENT.

Abbott, Edward P.
Abbott, Noah B.
Abbott, Lewis F. F.
Anderson, James I.
Ashworth, James,
Aiken, Samuel,
Albee, Freeland N.
Allen, Timothy F.
Burton, Joseph,
Bagley, Thomas A.
Bailey, James H.
Brown, George T.
Burris, Stephen,
Bell, Joseph,
Bell, Charles H.
Bell, Robert,
Berry, Alonzo P.
Buckley, Phineas, Jr.
Bailey, Henry H.
Bailey, Thomas R.
Barnard, Charles P.
Barnard, George N.
Beal, William,
Barker, Stephen,

Blunt, Samuel W.
Bodwell, Willard G.
Bohonnon, Albert L.
Brown, Leroy S.
Bryant, Epaphrus K.
Burnham, Henry O.
Brady, James L.
Craig, William,
Clement, Moses W.
Clark, John,
Clark, George B.
Chapin, Frank B.
Cutler, Abalino B.
Cocklin, John,
Campbell, Colin,
Cheever, Benjamin,
Cheever, Samuel,
Chandler, George W.
Clark, Aaron S.
Conley, Jeremiah,
Costello, James,
Coulie, John D.
Craig, George,
Cummings, Charles S.

Curtis, Andrew F.
Currier, Charles,
Cusick, John,
Cutler, Granville K.
Chalk, Henry T.
Colange, Etienne,
Dane, George,
Davis, Charles H.
Dearborn, John S.
Dugan, Charles,
Eastes, James H.
Edwards, Frank W.
Farnham, Orrin L.
Farmer, Edward,
Farmer, George S.
Farnham, Samuel P.
Findley, James S.
Findley, John A.
Foster, Thomas E.
Foster, Charles H.
Frye, Enoch O.
Frye, Newton G.
Gilcreast, David B.
Gillespie, William,
Goldsmith, Albert,
Goldsmith, Joseph C.
Grant, Farnham P.
Grant, George W.
Gray, Jesse E.
Greene, Charles,
Greene, William H.
Gooch, John F.
Hall, William S.
Hall, Henry H.
Hatch, George F.
Hatch, Andrew J.
Hatch, Enoch M.
Hatch, Lewis G.
Hardy, Franklin,
Hardy, John, 2d,
Hart, William,
Hastie, Thomas,
Hayward, George E.
Hayes, John, Jr.

Hervey, Samuel C.
Holt, Horace,
Holt, Newton,
Holt, Jonathan A.
Holt, Warren E.
Holt, Lewis G.
Hovey, John C.
Howarth, Oberlin B.
Hunt, Amos,
Hussey, Wyman D.
Jenkins, E. Kendall,
Jenkins, W. Harrison,
Jenkins, Omar,
Jennings, William E.
Johnson, Solon,
Joice, Redmond,
Jones, Charles E.
Kennedy, John,
Lavalette, Phillip C.
Lindsey, Robert,
Logue, James,
Lovejoy, Benjamin C.
Logue, John,
Lovejoy, Henry L.
Luscomb, Aaron E.
Mahoney, Michael,
Mason, Edward,
Mason, Walter B.
McClenna, Charles W.
McCabe, Frank,
McCusker, James,
McGurk, Bernard,
McLaughlin, John,
Melcher, Sylvester C.
Mears, Calvin,
Mears, Charles,
Mears, John,
Mears, Warren, Jr.
Mears, William,
Merrill, William F.
Morgan, David S.
Morton, Douglas,
Morse, William B.
Murray, James R.

Maynard, Charles,
Messer, Cyrus,
Nichols, William W.
Nolan, Malachi,
Noonan, Daniel,
O'Brien, John,
O'Conner, Patrick,
O'Hara, Edward,
Parker, Caleb O.
Pasho, William A.
Peterson, George,
Pike, George E.
Poor, Charles H.
Parker, John F.
Rea, Aaron G. Jr.
Rothwell, James H.
Richardson, Silas, Jr.
Ridley, Charles W.
Russell, John B. A.
Russell, Augustine K.
Russell, James,
Russell, Joseph, Jr.
Russell, William,
Russell, Winslow,
Sargent, John S.
Shannon, William,

Saunders, Ziba M.
Saunders, James, Jr.
Shattuck, Leonard G.
Shattuck, Charles W.
Sherman, Henry T.
Shields, Nicholas,
Smith, Peter D.
Smith, James,
Smith, Thomas,
Stevens, James W.
Stevens, Benjamin F.
Stowe, Frederick W.
Stephens, George W.
Smart, George M.
Townsend, Milton B.
Townsend, William W.
Trull, Charles, F.
Tuck, Moses W.
Vinal, George A. W.
Wardwell, Horace W.
Wardwell, William H.
Wardwell, Alfred,
Wardwell, George E.
Winchester, Charles H.
Wood, Elliot.

Second Regiment Heavy Artillery (3 Years).

Mustered in, 1863 and 1864. Mustered out, Sept. 3, 1865.

The principal part of this Regiment was never engaged in battle. Was stationed in North Carolina and Virginia.

Killed in action,	8	Discharged : promoted,	79
Died of wounds and disease,	340	Discharged, honorably,	141
Deserted,	157	Discharged, dishonorably,	4
Missing,	11	Discharged for disability,	157
Transferred,	432	Discharged, expiration service,	1639
Unaccounted for,	77	Total,	3045

ANDOVER SOLDIERS BELONGING TO THE REGIMENT.

Dwyer, Michael,
Dwine, Daniel,
Eldridge, Hezekiah,
Mears, John,

Melendy, George,
Parker, John F.
Roberts, George,
Springer, Eugene,

Stevens, Wendell B.

Third Regiment Heavy Artillery (3 Years).

Mustered in, — — —   Mustered out, Sept. 18, 1865.

This Regiment was composed of the 3d, 6th, 7th, 8th, 9th, 10th, 11th, 12th, 13th, 14th, 15th, and 16th unattached Companies of Heavy Artillery. The first eight Companies were raised for, and for a time were on duty in the Coast Defences of this State. They were sent forward to Washington in the fall of 1864, and, with the exception of Co. I, were in the Defences of that City until discharged.

Killed in action,	1	Discharged : promoted,	110
Died of wounds and disease,	40	Discharged, honorably,	218
Deserted,	383	Discharged, dishonorably,	8
Missing,	.	Discharged for disability,	191
Transferred,	9	Discharged, expiration service,	1353
Unaccounted for,	45	Total,	2358

ANDOVER SOLDIERS BELONGING TO THE REGIMENT.

Merrill, William F. | McKenzie, John,

Trainor, John.

Fourth Regiment Heavy Artillery (1 Year).

Mustered in Aug. 1864.   Mustered out, June 17, 1865.

This Regiment was composed of the 17th, 18th, 19th, 20th, 21st, 22d, 23d, 24th, 25th, 26th, 27th, and 28th Companies of Heavy Artillery, and was consolidated into a Regiment, Nov. 12, 1864. It was on duty in the Defences of Washington during its entire term of service.

136 THE RECORD OF ANDOVER

Killed in action,		Discharged: promoted,	14
Died of wounds and disease,	22	Discharged, honorably,	8
Deserted,	13	Discharged, dishonorably,	
Missing,		Discharged for disability,	39
Transferred,		Discharged, expiration service,	1756
Unaccounted for,		Total,	1852

ANDOVER SOLDIERS BELONGING TO THE REGIMENT.

Alderson, James,
Abbott, Charles E.
Bailey, Charles W.

Fulton, Joseph W.
Harrigan, Bartholemew,
Russell, Winslow.

First Battalion Heavy Artillery (3 Years.)

This Battalion was composed of the 1st, 2d, 4th, and 5th Unattached Companies of Heavy Artillery; but in the summer of 1864, two Companies of one year men were added. It was on duty in Boston Harbor for most of the time, but Companies were detailed for duty at Champlain, N. Y., and the Fort at New Bedford. It was mustered out by Companies from June 28th to Oct. 20th, 1865.

Killed in action,		Discharged: promoted,	22
Died of wounds and disease,	15	Discharged, honorably,	108
Deserted,	221	Discharged, dishonorably,	5
Missing,		Discharged for disability,	68
Transferred,		Discharged, expiration service,	1043
Unaccounted for	4	Total,	1486

ANDOVER SOLDIER BELONGING TO THE BATTALION.

Stanwood, Lawrence.

DURING THE REBELLION. 137

Twenty-Ninth Company Heavy Artillery (1 Year).
(UNATTACHED).
Mustered in, Aug. 1864. Mustered out, June 16, 1865.

This Company was on duty in the Defences of Washington.

Killed in action,		Discharged: promoted,	
Died of wounds and disease,	2	Discharged, honorably,	1
Deserted,	1	Discharged, dishonorably,	
Missing,		Discharged for disability,	1
Transferred,	2	Discharged, expiration service,	145
Unaccounted for,	5	Total,	157

ANDOVER SOLDIERS BELONGING TO THE COMPANY.

Collins, Richard,	Russell, John R.
Condon, Nicholas,	Tomlinson, Edwin A.
Holloran, Patrick,	Trask, Elbridge P.
Joice, Redmond,	Wescott, William,
Milkins, William,	Weston, Frederick.

Second Battery Light Artillery (3 Years).
Mustered in, July 31, 1861. Mustered out, Aug. 11, 1865.

ENGAGEMENTS. — Vicksburg, Baton Rouge, Sabine Cross Roads, Jackson, Claiborne, Ala., and Daniel's Plantation.

Killed in action,	1	Discharged: promoted,	13
Died of wounds and disease,	25	Discharged, honorably,	59
Deserted,	13	Discharged, dishonorably,	
Missing,		Discharged for disability,	39
Transferred,	29	Discharged, expiration service,	232
Unaccounted for,	4	Total,	415

ANDOVER SOLDIER BELONGING TO THE BATTERY.

Marland, William.

Fourth Battery Light Artillery (3 Years).

Mustered in, Nov. 18, 1861.   Mustered out, Nov. 10, 1865.

ENGAGEMENTS. — Pontichula, Baton Rouge, Bonfouca, Bisland, Port Hudson, Vermillion, and the several engagements of the Siege of Mobile.

Killed in action,	1	Discharged: promoted,	8
Died of wounds and disease,	46	Discharged, honorably,	126
Deserted,	22	Discharged, dishonorably,	1
Missing,		Discharged for disability,	42
Transferred,	28	Discharged, expiration service,	143
Unaccounted for,	17	Total,	434

ANDOVER SOLDIER BELONGING TO THE BATTERY.

Merrill, Edward C.

Seventh Battery Light Artillery (3 Years).

Mustered in, May 21, 1861.   Mustered out, Nov. 10, 1865.

This Battery left the State, May 22, 1861, as an Independent Company of Infantry, and was changed to a Light Artillery organization, March 17, 1862. It was in the following engagements: Deserted House, South Quay, Somerton, Providence Church Road, Holland's House, Mansura, and the several engagements of the Siege of Mobile.

Killed in action,	2	Discharged: promoted,	17
Died of wounds and disease,	34	Discharged, honorably,	63
Deserted,	9	Discharged, dishonorably,	1
Missing,		Discharged for disability,	55
Transferred,	2	Discharged, expiration service,	227
Unaccounted for,	26	Total,	436

ANDOVER SOLDIER BELONGING TO THE BATTERY.

Lovejoy, Charles W.

First Company Sharpshooters (3 Years).

Mustered in, Sept. 3, 1861.   Mustered out, June 30, 1865.

This Company left the State, Sept. 3, 1861. For several months it was not connected with any Regiment, but was attached to General Lander's command on the Upper Potomac. It was afterwards attached to the 15th Regiment, and took part in its engagements; it was subsequently attached to the 19th Regiment.

Killed in action,	17	Discharged : promoted,	8
Died of wounds and disease,	22	Discharged, honorably,	38
Deserted,	14	Discharged, dishonorably,	1
Missing,	2	Discharged for disability,	64
Transferred,	16	Discharged, expiration service,	14
Unaccounted for,	37	Total,	233

ANDOVER SOLDIERS BELONGING TO THE COMPANY.

Abbott, Wesley,
Barker, Samuel S.
Bentley, Noah,
Hanson, Charles,
Mason, Josiah.

Second Company Sharpshooters (3 Years).

Mustered in, 1862.   Mustered out, July 16, 1865.

This Company was attached to the 22d Regiment. It took part in all that Regiment's engagements in 1863. It was subsequently attached to the 15th Regiment, and after this Regiment's term of service had expired, it was transferred to the 20th Regiment.

Killed in action,	8	Discharged : promoted,	7
Died of wounds and disease,	13	Discharged, honorably,	20
Deserted,	4	Discharged, dishonorably,	
Missing,		Discharged for disability,	63
Transferred,	7	Discharged, expiration service,	33
Unaccounted for,		Total,	155

ANDOVER SOLDIER BELONGING TO THE COMPANY.

Berry, Israel A.

First Regiment Cavalry (3 Years).

Mustered in, Nov. 1, 1861.   Mustered out, June 26, 1865.

ENGAGEMENTS. — Poolsville, South Mountain, Antietam, Fredericksburg, Chancellorsville, Brandy Station, Aldie, Upperville, Gettysburg, Williamsport, Culpepper, Auburn, Todd's Tavern, Fortifications of Richmond, Vaughn Road, St. Mary's Church, Cold Harbor, and Bellefield.

Killed in action,	49	Discharged : promoted,	130
Died of wounds and disease,	167	Discharged, honorably,	409
Deserted,	161	Discharged, dishonorably,	7
Missing,	24	Discharged for disability,	314
Transferred,	297	Discharged, expiration service,	1067
Unaccounted for,	142	Total,	2767

ANDOVER SOLDIERS BELONGING TO THE REGIMENT.

Hervey, Albert G.
Holt, Harrison,
Raymond, Walter L.
Stott, Joshua H.
Searles, James H.
Withey, William H.
White, Charles W.

Second Regiment Cavalry (3 Years).

Mustered in, Jan. to April, 1863.   Mustered out, July 20, 1865.

ENGAGEMENTS. — South Anna Bridge, Ashley's Gap, Drainsville, Aldie, Fort Stevens, Fort Reno, Rockville, Poolsville, Summit Point, Halltown, Opequan, Winchester, Luray, Waynesboro', Tom's Brook, Cedar Creek, South Anna, White Oak Road, Berryville, Berryville Pike, Charlestown, Dinwiddie Court House, Five Forks, Saylor's Creek, and Appomattox Court House.

Killed in action,	62	Discharged : promoted,	160
Died of wounds and disease,	147	Discharged, honorably,	31
Deserted,	622	Discharged, dishonorably,	9
Missing,	4	Discharged for disability,	228
Transferred,	93	Discharged, expiration service,	1134
Unaccounted for,	351	Total,	2841

ANDOVER SOLDIERS BELONGING TO THE REGIMENT.

Batton, William,
Duncan, Robert,

Green, Michael,
Lawrence, John H.

Third Regiment Cabalry (3 Years).

Mustered in, Nov. 1, 1862.　　　　　Mustered out, Sept. 28, 1865.

This Regiment went into service as the 41st Regiment of Infantry on June 17, 1865. The Regiment was changed to a Cavalry organization, and the 1st, 2d, and 3d unattached Companies of Massachusetts Cavalry were consolidated with, and became a part, of the organization. It was in the following engagements: Irish Bend, Henderson Hill, Cane River, Port Hudson, Sabine Cross Roads, Muddy Bayou, Piney Woods, Red River Campaign, Opequan, Fisher's Hill, Snag Point, Winchester, Cedar Creek, and others.

Killed in action,	60	Discharged: promoted,	171
Died of wounds and disease,	203	Discharged, honorably,	249
Deserted,	372	Discharged, dishonorably,	4
Missing,	5	Discharged for disability,	447
Transferred,	18	Discharged, expiration service,	966
Unaccounted for,	158	Total,	2653

ANDOVER SOLDIERS BELONGING TO THE REGIMENT.

Abbott, Frank F.
Cass, Isaac N.
Lyman, Edward E.
Mears, John,
Morrison, Charles W.

Mason, Eri,
Phillips, Patrick,
Rowley, R. Augustus,
Sargent, Herbert N.
Wescott, Solomon.

Fourth Regiment Cabalry (3 Years.)

Mustered in, — — —　　　　　Mustered out, Nov. 14, 1865.

This Regiment was composed of the Independent Battalion, formerly 3d Battalion 1st Regiment Massachusetts Cavalry, and two new Battalions .

recruited in this State. It was in the following engagements: Gainsville, Fla.; Drury's Bluff, and the several engagements in front of Petersburg and Richmond.

Killed in action,	21	Discharged: promoted,	123
Died of wounds and disease,	123	Discharged, honorably,	180
Deserted,	262	Discharged, dishonorably,	13
Missing,	1	Discharged for disability,	79
Transferred,		Discharged, expiration service,	1169
Unaccounted for	47	Total,	2018

ANDOVER SOLDIERS BELONGING TO THE REGIMENT.

Bradley, Charles W.
Godkins, Stephen F.

Hervey, Albert G.
Jones, David L.

First Battalion Frontier Cavalry (1 Year).

Mustered in, Dec. 30, '64, and Jan. 2, '65.   Mustered out, June 30, 1865.

This Battalion was attached to the 26th Regiment of New York Volunteer Cavalry, and performed guard duty on the New York Frontier.

Killed in action,		Discharged: promoted,	13
Died of wounds and disease,	2	Discharged, honorably,	5
Deserted,	7	Discharged, dishonorably,	
Missing,		Discharged for disability,	2
Transferred,		Discharged, expiration service,	502
Unaccounted for,		Total,	531

ANDOVER SOLDIERS BELONGING TO THE BATTALION.

Clark, Jesse H.
Carter, Frederick W.
Dougherty, James,
Downes, Benjamin,
Dugan, William,
Dow, Charles E.
English, Charles G.
Fox, William,

Gibbs, Robert,
Gould, Theodore F.
Goodwin, Moses F.
Lemon, William H.
Saunders, James, Jr.
Stephenson, Alba,
Smith, Robert,
Thomas, Lewis,

Weeks, Nathaniel.

Veteran Reserve Corps.

Bell, Joseph,
Cusick, John,
Findley, James S.
Joice, Redmond,

Mason, Walter B.
Parker, Caleb O.
Ryley, Leonard W.
Stott, Joshua H.

United States Army and other State Organizations.

Name.		Rank.
Oct. 10, 1864,	Brown, George T.	Captain, 26th Regt.U. S. Col. Troops.
Oct. 11, 1864,	Boston, Peter,*	Private, 3d U. S. Colored Cavalry.
Mar. 4, 1865,	Bird, Minor,*	Private, 70th Regt. U. S. Colored Inf.
Oct. 11, 1864,	Clement, Moses W.	Captain, — Regt. U. S. Col'd Troops.
Sept. 12, 1864,	Grubbs, Cam,*	Private, 51st Regt.U. S. Col'd Troops.
July 29, 1864,	Hill, Emmett C.	Hospital Steward, U. S. Army.
Sept. 28, 1861,	Jones, Ambrose,	Private, 1st Regt. Minnesota Vols.
Sept. 12, 1864,	Jupiter, Isaac,*	Private, 51st Regt. U. S.Col'd Troops.
Dec. 27, 1864,	Jourdan, Henry,*	Private, 1st Regt. U. S. Colored Cav.
Jan. 24, 1865,	Jennings, George,*	Private, 103d Regt. U. S. Col'd T.
April, 1862,	Lovejoy, Newton,	Private, Co. F. 13th Regt. U. S. Inf.
June 2, 1864,	Owens, Redman,	Private, 19th Regt. U. S. Infantry.
Mar. 31, 1864,	Shattuck, Charles M.	Private, 3d U. S. Artillery.
June 2, 1864,	Smith, George,	Private, 19th Regt. U. S. Infantry.
Jan. 27, 1863,	Stowe, Frederick W.	Captain, and Assist. Adjt.-Gen.U.S.A.
Dec. 24, 1864,	Spradley, Randal,*	Private, 1st Regt.U. S. Col'd Cavalry.
Jan. 23, 1865,	Stephens, Andrew,*	Private, 103d Regt. U. S. Colored T.
Nov. 1863,	Taylor, George H.	1st Lieut. on General Staff.
Mar. 4, 1865,	Thomas, Nicholas,*	Private, 5th Regt. U. S. Col'd H. A.
Oct. 20, 1864,	Wardrobe, Fred.	Hospital Steward, U. S. Army.
Oct. 9, 1864,	Whideman, John,	Private, 20th Regt. N. Y. Cavalry.
Feb. 20, 1865,	Withsby, Thomas,*	Private, 70th Regt. U. S. Col'd Inf.

* Colored.

PERSONAL ARMY RECORDS.

ABBOTT, ALSON B. Son of William 2d, and Sarah J., born in Greenfield, N. H., Nov. 3, 1844. Mustered, July 23, 1864. Private, Co. C., 5th Regiment Infantry (100 days). Discharged by expiration of service, Nov. 16, 1864.

ABBOTT, CHARLES E. Son of Orlando and Lydia C., born in Andover, June 15, 1832. Mustered, Aug. 18, 1864. Corporal, Co. K., 4th Heavy Artillery. Discharged by expiration of service, June 17, 1865.

ABBOTT, EDWARD P. (Veteran). Son of Henry and Lucy T., born in Andover, Oct. 17, 1833. Mustered, July 22, 1862. Private, Co. H., 1st Heavy Artillery. Re-enlisted in the field, Feb. 29, 1864. Wounded in the hand. Discharged for disability, Oct. 25, 1864.

ABBOTT, FRANK F. Son of Enoch and Roxanna, born in Andover, Dec. 17, 1843. Mustered, Aug. 6, 1862. Private, Co. K., 3d Regiment Cavalry. Discharged by expiration of service, June 5, 1865.

ABBOTT, GEORGE B. Son of Moses. Mustered, Aug. 30, 1862. Co. G., 27th Regiment Infantry. Discharged for disability, Feb. 12, 1863.

ABBOTT, LEWIS, F. F. (Veteran). Mustered, Aug. 8, 1862. Private, Co. B., 1st Heavy Artillery, to the credit of Methuen. Re-enlisted in the field to the credit of Andover, Dec. 29, 1863. Discharged by expiration of service, Aug. 16, 1865.

ABBOTT, MOSES B. Son of William and Mary P., born in Andover, Dec. 5, 1842. Mustered, Aug. 24, 1861. Band 18th Regiment Infantry. Discharged, Aug. 11, 1862, by order of the War Department.

ABBOTT, NOAH B. (Veteran). Son of Noah B., and Augusta, born in Andover, Nov. 3, 1840. Mustered, July 22, 1862. Private, Co. H., 1st Heavy Artillery. Re-enlisted in the field, Feb. 29, 1864. Discharged, Aug. 16, 1865, by expiration of service in Co. B.

ABBOTT, WESLEY. Son of Orlando and Lydia C., born in Andover, March 9, 1834. Mustered, Sept. 2, 1861, 1st Co. Sharpshooters. Discharged for disability, caused by typhoid fever, Dec. 8, 1862.

AIKEN, SAMUEL (Veteran). Son of James and Catherine, born in Dundee, Scotland, Jan. 17, 1826. Mustered, July 22, 1862. Private, Co. H., 1st Heavy Artillery. Re-enlisted in the field, Feb. 29, 1864. Killed in battle at Spottsylvania, May 19, 1864. Buried on the battle-field.

ALBEE, FREELAND N. Mustered, Nov. 7, 1863. Private, Co. H., 1st Heavy Artillery. Deserted,* July 30, 1865, from Co. B.

ALDERSON JAMES. Mustered, Aug. 17, 1864. Private, Co. C., 4th Heavy Artillery. Discharged June 17, 1865, by expiration of service.

ALLEN, TIMOTHY FLETCHER. Son of Thaddeus P. and Timna, born in Andover, Jan. 14, 1842. Mustered, July 21, 1862. Private, Co. H., 1st Heavy Artillery. Discharged by expiration of service, July 8, 1864. Wounded June 16, 1864, at Bryant's Farm, near Petersburg, Va.

ALLEN, WALTER B. (Veteran). Son of Joseph V. and Lucy, born in Andover, Aug. 23, 1831. Mustered, Sept. 12, 1862. Private Co. G., 44th Regiment Infantry. Discharged, June 18, 1863, by expiration of service. Re-mustered Aug. 31, 1864. Private, Co. B., 11th Regiment Infantry. Discharged June 4, 1865, by expiration of service.

ANDERSON, JAMES I. (Veteran). Son of Samuel and Isabella, born Andover, May 8, 1833. Mustered, July 5, 1861. Private, Co. H., 1st Heavy Artillery. Re-enlisted in the field, Dec. 15, 1863. Promoted Corporal. Discharged, July 31, 1865, as supernumerary.

ARMSTRONG, THOMAS. Mustered, Aug. 23, 1861. Sergeant, Co. H., 20th Regiment Infantry. Discharged, Jan. 20, 1863, for disability.

ASHWORTH, JAMES. Son of John and Sarah, born in Wandsworth, England. Dec. 25, 1830. Mustered, July 5, 1861. Artificer, Co. H., 1st Heavy Artillery. Discharged, July 8, 1864, by expiration of service.

---

* See note in Appendix.

BAGLEY, THOMAS A. Son of Francis and Ann, born in Whitehaven, Cumberland, England, Oct. 6, 1841. Mustered, July 5, 1861. Private, Co. B., 1st Heavy Artillery. Captured near the Weldon Railroad, June 22, 1864. Died, a prisoner of war, at Andersonville, Ga., Aug. 28, 1864. Buried in the trenches.

BAILEY, CHARLES W. Son of Timothy and Lucy A., born in Andover, Nov. 27, 1845. Mustered, Aug. 19, 1864. Private, Co. I., 4th Heavy Artillery. Discharged, June 17, 1865, by expiration of service.

BAILEY, GEORGE A. (Veteran). Son of Joseph and Lucy, born in Andover, May 11, 1843. Mustered, Oct. 22, 1861. Private, Co. A., 26th Regiment Infantry. Re-enlisted in the field, Jan. 1, 1864. Killed, Sept. 19, 1864, at Winchester, Va. Body not recovered.

BAILEY, HENRY H. Son of Timothy 1st and Henrietta, born in Andover, Jan. 21, 1835. Mustered, July 21, 1862. Private, Co. H., 1st Heavy Artillery. Deserted, Dec. 21, 1862.

BAILEY, JAMES H. Son of Timothy and Lucy A., born in Andover. Mustered, July 5, 1861. Private, Co. B., 1st Heavy Artillery. Fell from a parapet at Fort Albany, Va., and broke his thigh. Died, Sept. 14, 1861, at Washington, D. C., and was buried there.

BAILEY, THOMAS R: (Veteran). Son of Theodore and Lernia W., born in Andover, Aug. 6, 1843. Mustered, July 5, 1861. Private, Co. H., 1st Heavy Artillery. Re-enlisted in the field, Dec. 12, 1863. Deserted,* July 30, 1865, from Co. B.

BANKER, MELVIN. Mustered, Feb. 20, 1864. Private, Co. E., 26th Regiment Infantry. Discharged, May 25, 1865, by expiration of service.

BARKER, SAMUEL S. Son of Asa A. and Mary G., born in Charlestown, 1838. Mustered, May 1, 1861. Private, Co. B., 5th Regiment Infantry (three months). Discharged, July 31, 1861, by expiration of service. Re-mustered, Sept. 2, 1861. Private, 1st Co. Sharpshooters. Deserted,† Sept. 17, 1862. Is down on State rolls as "Baker" on second enlistment.

---

* See note in Appendix.

† It is in evidence that Mr. Barker subsequently enlisted under the name of Samuel Sprague, in the 1st Maryland Cavalry, Col. Cole, where he served for about two years, and was honorably discharged, June 28, 1865.

BARKER, STEPHEN. Son of Henry and Lois S., born in Londonderry, N. H., Jan. 14, 1829. Mustered, July 16, 1861. Chaplain, 1st Heavy Artillery. Discharged, July 8, 1864, by expiration of service.

BARKER, WILLIAM. Son of Alexander and Elizabeth. Mustered, July 14, 1864. Private, Co. K., 6th Regiment Infantry (100 days). Discharged, Oct. 27, 1864, by expiration of service.

BARNARD, CHARLES P. Son of Hermon and Elizabeth, born in Andover, Oct. 25, 1844. Mustered, Aug. 7, 1862. Private, Co. H., 1st Heavy Artillery. Captured by the rebels in battle at Spottsylvania, May 19, 1864. Paroled, and died at Annapolis, Md., Dec. 2, 1864, from privation while a prisoner of war at Andersonville, Ga. Buried in West Parish Cemetery.

BARNARD, GEORGE N. Son of Isaac O. and Eliza, born in Andover, July 21, 1841. Mustered, Aug. 5, 1862. Private, Co. H., 1st Heavy Artillery. Discharged, July 8, 1864, by expiration of service.

BARNARD, HENRY F. Son of Isaac O. and Eliza A., born in Andover, July 11, 1848. Mustered, July 14, 1864. Private, Co. K., 6th Regiment Infantry (100 days). Discharged, Oct. 27, 1864, by expiration of service.

BARROWS, WILLIAM E. Son of Elijah P. and Sarah M., born in Hudson, Ohio, July 14, 1842. Mustered, Aug. 22, 1861. Hospital Steward, 19th Regiment Infantry. Promoted 2d Lieutenant, March 25, 1863; promoted 1st Lieutenant, July 11, 1863; promoted Captain, July 28, 1864. Discharged, July 22, 1865, by expiration of service.

BATTON, WILLIAM. Son of William and Elizabeth, born in New York City. Mustered, Nov. 23, 1863. Private, Co. K., 2d.Regiment Cavalry. Discharged, July 20, 1865, by expiration of service.

BEAL, WILLIAM. Born in England. Mustered, July 5, 1861. Private Co. H., 1st Heavy Artillery. Discharged, July 15, 1862, for disability.

BECKER, CHARLES. Substitute for James Shaw. Mustered, Aug. 31, 1864. Unassigned recruit, 30th Infantry.

BELANGER, WILLIAM F. Mustered, July 14, 1864. Private, Co. K., 6th Regiment Infantry (100 days). Discharged, Oct. 27, 1864, by expiration of service.

BELL, CHARLES H. Son of Peter and Mary, born in Andover, June 15, 1831. Mustered, Aug. 5, 1862. Private, Co. H., 1st Heavy Artillery. Discharged, July 8, 1864, by expiration of service. Lost right arm in battle at Spottsylvania, May 19, 1864.

BELL, JOSEPH, (Veteran). Son of Peter and Mary, born in Goffstown, N. H., in 1837. Mustered, July 5, 1861. Private, Co. H., 1st Heavy Artillery, to the credit of North Andover. Re-enlisted in the field to the credit of Andover, Dec. 7, 1863. Promoted Corporal. Wounded near Petersburg, Va., June 22, 1864. Transferred to Veteran Reserve Corps, March 19, 1865. Discharged, Aug. 20, 1865. Found dead in the woods near Lawrence, Sept. 22, 1865. Buried in Lawrence.

BELL, ROBERT. Son of William and Ann, born in Great Falls, N. H. Mustered, March 10, 1862. Private, Co. H., 1st Heavy Artillery. Discharged, Dec. 10, 1862, for disability.

BENTLEY, NOAH. Mustered, March 24, 1862. Private, 1st Company Sharpshooters. Transferred to Co. K., 19th Regiment Infantry. Discharged, March, 1865.

BERRY, ALBERT. Son of Israel and Serena, Mustered, Aug. 27, 1864. Private, Co. B., 11th Regiment Infantry. Discharged, June 4, 1865, by expiration of service.

BERRY, ALONZO P. Son of Israel and Serena, born in Middleton, July 10, 1836. Mustered, July 5, 1861. Corporal, Co. H., 1st Heavy Artillery. Discharged, Jan. 19, 1863, for disability.

BERRY, ISRAEL A. Son of Israel and Serena, born in Middleton, June 16, 1827. Mustered, Aug. 29, 1861. Private, 2d Co. Sharpshooters. Discharged, Aug. 8, 1862, for disability. Re-enlisted in 5th Regiment New Hampshire Volunteers, under the name of John Stone. Was wounded April 6, 1865, and died on the 22d, at City Point, Va.

BLACK, JAMES B. Son of Hugh and Mary F., born in Paisley, Scotland, Dec. 4, 1838. Mustered, Sept. 24, 1861. Private, Co. B., 30th Regiment Infantry. Died, Aug. 30, 1864, at Fortress Monroe, Va.

BLACK, THOMAS D. Son of James and Rebecca, born in Cincinnati, Ohio, Aug. 21, 1822. Mustered, Aug. 27, 1864. Corporal, Co. B., 61st Regiment Infantry. Discharged, June 4, 1865, by expiration of service.

BLAKE, JOHN. Mustered, Feb. 7, 1865. Private, Co. A., 26th Regiment Infantry. Discharged, Aug. 26, 1865, by expiration of service.

BIRD, MINOR (Colored). Of Franklin Co., Miss., Representative Recruit for the Town of Andover. Mustered in at Vicksburg, Miss., March 4, 1865. Private, 70th Regiment United States Colored Infantry.

BLUNT, JOSHUA MILTON. Son of Samuel and Persis. Mustered, Aug. 27, 1864. Private, Co. B., 11th Regiment Infantry. Discharged, June 4, 1865, by expiration of service.

BLUNT, SAMUEL W. Son of Samuel and Persis, born in Andover, April 5, 1822. Mustered, Aug. 26, 1862. Private, Co. H., 1st Heavy Artillery. Discharged, July 8, 1864, by expiration of service. Down on "Record of Massachusetts Volunteers" as "Blood."

BODWELL, WILLARD G. Son of Horace and Mary, born in Vermont, near Stansted, C. E., Aug. 22, 1842. Mustered, July 5, 1861. Private, Co. H., 1st Heavy Artillery. Died of disease at Fort Strong, Va., March 24, 1864. Buried near Stansted, Canada East.

BOHONNON, ALBERT L. Born in Washington, Vt. Mustered, July 5, 1861. Private, Co. H., 1st Heavy Artillery. Deserted, April 29, 1862.

BOLTON, WILLIAM A. Mustered, June 13, 1861. Private Co. H., 11th Regiment Infantry. Died, Jan. 30, 1863, at New York. A note from "Soldiers' Relief Committee, Boston, states that Mrs. Johanna Coleman, mother of F. Coleman (who enlisted under the name of William A. Bolton), has applied," etc. On the State Records is the following : "Bolton died Jan. 30, 1863, at New England Rooms, N.Y., and was buried at Cyprus Hill Cemetery, L.I., grave 2766, under the name of George A. Wardwell, this man having G. A. Wardwell's papers in his possession at his death ; was buried under that name.

BOND, JOHN. Mustered, July 14, 1864. Private, Co. K., 6th Regiment Infantry (100 days). Discharged, Oct. 27, 1864, by expiration of service.

BOSTON; PETER (Colored). Of Loundes Co., Miss. Representative Recruit for Francis Cogswell. Mustered in at Vicksburg, Miss., Oct. 11, 1864. Private, 3d United States Colored Cavalry.

BOWEN, ALBERT L. Mustered, Oct. 7, 1862. Musician, Co. K., 45th Regiment Infantry. Discharged by expiration of service, July 7, 1863. This Recruit's name appears among those rejected; but it was subsequently proved that he was put into the service by Frederick L. Church, who paid him a bounty.

BOYCE, THOMAS. Born in Dublin, Ireland, and recruited in Boston. Mustered, Dec. 10, 1862. Unassigned recruit, 22d Infantry. " Bounty Jumper"; never joined the Regiment.

BOYD, PATRICK. Born in Sligo, Ireland, and recruited in Boston. Mustered, Dec 12, 1862. Unassigned recruit, 22d Infantry. " Bounty Jumper"; never joined the Regiment.

BOYDEN, JAMES. Born in Providence, R. I., and recruited in Boston. Mustered, Dec. 11, 1862. Unassigned recruit, 22d Infantry. " Bounty Jumper"; never joined the Regiment.

BOYLE, JOHN. Born in Sligo, Ireland, and recruited in Boston. Mustered, Dec. 5, 1862. Unassigned recruit, 22d Infantry. " Bounty Jumper"; never joined the Regiment.

BRADLEY, CHARLES W. Mustered, Dec. 31, 1864. Private, Co. I., 4th Cavalry. Discharged, Nov. 14, 1865, by expiration of service.

BRADY, JAMES L. Mustered, July 5, 1861. Private, Co. I., 1st Heavy Artillery. Discharged, July 8, 1864, by expiration of service. This man is said to have been captured by the rebels on the 22d of June, 1864, since which nothing has been heard from him. A James L. Brady is reported from the Adjutant-General's Office, Jan. 17, 1862, as from Andover, on the rolls of the 17th Regiment as a recruit, mustered, Aug. 9, 1861. See, also, James Brady of Lawrence, Co. I., 17th Regiment.

BROWN, CHARLES (Colored). Son of Luther and Hannah, born in Florida, in 1814. Mustered, Aug. 24, 1864. Unassigned recruit, 54th Regiment. Transferred to Co. I., 55th Regiment Infantry. Discharged, Aug. 29, 1865, by expiration of service.

BROWN, GEORGE T. Son of John J. and Emily W., born in Andover, Aug. 5, 1840. Mustered, Aug. 5, 1861. Sergeant, Co. H., 1st Heavy Artillery. Promoted, 2d Lieutenant, Feb. 15, 1862; 1st Lieutenant, Jan. 28, 1863. Wounded and captured in front of Petersburg, Va. Discharged, Oct. 10, 1864. Captain, 36th Regiment U. S. Col'd Troops.

DURING THE REBELLION. 151

BROWN, LEROY S. Son of Jacob and Mary, born in Andover, Sept. 2, 1835. Mustered, July 5, 1861. Private, Co. H., 1st Heavy Artillery. Discharged, July 8, 1864, by expiration of service. Wounded, June 16, 1864.

BRYANT, EPAPHRUS K. Son of Thomas J. and Cordelia M., born in Lee, Maine, April 26, 1827. Mustered, July 5, 1861. Private, Co. H., 1st Heavy Artillery. Wounded in battle at Spottsylvania, May 19, 1864. Died, at Mount Pleasant Hospital, Washington, D. C., July 3, 1864. Buried, at New Market, N. H.

BUCHAN, GEORGE. Son of William and Jessie G., born in Arbroath, Scotland, Feb. 28, 1836. Mustered, July 14, 1864. Private, Co. K., 6th Regiment Infantry (100 days). Discharged, Oct. 27, 1864, by expiration of service.

BUCKLEY, PHINEAS, Jr. Son of Phineas and Hannah, born in Andover, Dec. 21, 1842. Mustered, July 5, 1861. Corporal, Co. H., 1st Heavy Artillery. Promoted Corporal, July 15, 1862. Corporal of Color Guard; acted as Sergeant of Color Guard until discharged. Discharged, July 8, 1864, by expiration of service.

BUGUAY, GEORGE A. Mustered, July 18, 1861. Sergeant Co. G., 20th Regiment Infantry. Deserted, June 15, 1862, from Co. I.

BURNHAM, HENRY O. (Veteran). Son of Oliver and Rebecca, born in South Reading, Jan. 15, 1824. Mustered, July 29, 1862. Private, Co. H., 1st Heavy Artillery. Re-enlisted in the field, Jan. 2, 1864. Discharged, June 10, 1865, by expiration of service, in Co. B.

BURRIS, STEPHEN. Son of John and Joanna, born in Prince Edward Island, Nov. 30, 1831. Mustered, July 5, 1861. Private, Co. H., 1st Heavy Artillery. Promoted Corporal, Feb. 16, 1862. Promoted Sergeant. Discharged, July 8, 1864, by expiration of service.

BURTT, JOSEPH A. Son of Jedediah. Mustered, Sept. 20, 1862, Co. H., 43d Regiment Infantry. Discharged, July 30, 1863, by expiration of service.

BURTON, JOSEPH. Son of Peter and Ann, born in England, Oct. 9, 1820. Mustered, July 22, 1862. Private, Co. H., 1st Heavy Artillery. Discharged, April 18, 1865, by Order of the War Department; says the last three or four months of his time was in the Veteran Reserve Corps, 1st Regiment, Co. D., Captain King.

BUSFIELD, JOHN, Jr. Son of John and Elizabeth, born in Leeds, England, Jan. 10, 1826. Mustered, July 14, 1864. Private, Co. K., 6th Regiment Infantry (100 days). Discharged, Oct. 27, 1864, by expiration of service.

CALLAHAN, ALBERT J. Son of James and Catherine K., born in Andover, July 28, 1846. Mustered, Aug. 26, 1864. Private, Co. B., 11th Regiment Infantry. Discharged, Aug. 14, 1865, by expiration of service.

CALLAHAN, CHARLES, H. Son of James and Catherine K., born in Andover, April 13, 1833. Mustered, Aug. 24, 1861. Private, Co. H., 20th Regiment Infantry. Discharged, April 14, 1862, for disability. Died, May 29, 1862, of disease contracted in service. Buried in South Cemetery.

CAMPBELL, COLIN. Born in Scotland. Mustered, March 8, 1862. Private, Co. H., 1st Heavy Artillery. Deserted, Jan. 29, 1863.

CARLTON, OSCAR F. Corporal, Co. B., 29th Regiment Infantry.

CARRUTH, ISAAC S. Son of Isaac and Ann D., born in Andover, March 14, 1840. Mustered Sept. 20, 1862. Private, Co. H., 43d Regiment Infantry. Discharged, July 30, 1863, by expiration of service.

CARTER, FREDERICK W. Mustered, Jan. 2, 1865. Private, Co. D., 1st Battalion Frontier Cavalry. Discharged, June 30, 1865, by expiration of service.

CARTER, WILLIAM S. Mustered, April 22, 1861. Private, Co. F., 6th Regiment Infantry (3 months). Discharged, Aug. 2, 1861, by expiration of service.

CASS, ISAAC N. Mustered, Dec. 30, 1864. Private, Co. L., 3d Cavalry. Discharged, Sept. 28, 1865, by expiration of service.

CHALK, HENRY T. (Veteran). Mustered, July 5, 1861. Private, Co. I., 1st Heavy Artillery, to the credit of Danvers. Re-enlisted in the field, Dec. 11, 1863, to the credit of Andover. Promoted Corporal Discharged, June 5, 1865, for disability.

DURING THE REBELLION. 153

CHANDLER, GEORGE W. Son of John and Phebe, born in Andover, Feb. 18, 1842. Mustered, July 5, 1861. Private, Co. H., 1st Heavy Artillery. Discharged, July 8, 1864, by expiration of service. Wounded in the leg, June 16, 1864.

CHANDLER, HENRY F. Son of Joshua and Eliza F., born in Andover, Sept. 26, 1835. Mustered, April 21, 1864. Private, Co. K., 59th Regiment Infantry. Discharged, June 8, 1865, for disability. Wounded June 17, 1864, in front of Petersburg, and at Poplar Grove Church, and was discharged by reason of latter wound.

CHANDLER, JOSEPH, Jr. Son of Joseph and Lucy R., born in Andover, April 13, 1836. Mustered, Oct. 1, 1861. Sergeant, Co. A., 26th Regiment Infantry. Died, March 10, 1863, in St. James' Hospital, New Orleans, La. Buried, in West Parish Cemetery, May 1, 1863.

CHAPIN, FRANK B. Son of Jarius and Sarah, born in Sudbury, April 30, 1834. Mustered, July 5, 1861. Sergeant, Co. H., 1st Heavy Artillery. Promoted, 2d Lieutenant, Dec. 31, 1862. Discharged for disability, Sept. 17, 1864. Wounded, lost a finger before Petersburg, June 18, 1864.

CHAPIN, JOSIAH L. Son of Jarius and Sarah. Mustered, Sept. 24, 1864, 1st Lieutenant, 11th Regiment Infantry. Promoted, Captain, Nov. 3, 1864. Discharged, July 14, 1865, by expiration of service.

CHEEVER, BENJAMIN (Veteran). Son of Samuel and Sarah, born in Andover, May 28, 1827. Mustered, July 5, 1861. Private, Co. H., 1st Heavy Artillery. Re-enlisted in the field, Dec. 29, 1863. Discharged, Aug. 26, 1865, by expiration of service, in Co. B.

CHEEVER, SAMUEL. Son of Samuel and Sarah, born in Andover, April 11, 1824. Mustered, Feb. 22, 1862. Private, Co. H., 1st Heavy Artillery. Captured, at the battle of Spottsylvania, May 19, 1864. Paroled, at Andersonville, Ga. Discharged, Feb. 23, 1865.

CHRISTIAN, WILLIAM T. Mustered, Sept. 28, 1861. Corporal, Co. B., 23d Regiment Infantry. Discharged, Jan. 3, 1863, for disability.

CLARK, AARON S. Son of Ezekiel and Abigail, born in Methuen, Sept. 22, 1823. Mustered, March 3, 1862. Private, Co. H., 1st Heavy Artillery. Discharged, Jan. 19, 1864, for disability.

CLARK, EDWIN L. Mustered, June 26, 1861. Chaplain, 12th Regiment Infantry. Resigned, June 16, 1862.

CLARK, GEORGE B. Son of Robert and Mary, born in Andover, Feb. 19, 1842. Mustered, Aug. 9, 1862. Musician, Co. H., 1st Heavy Artillery. Discharged, July 8, 1864, by expiration of service.

CLARK, JESSE H. Son of Thomas and Sarah Ann, born in Andover, Aug. 7, 1844. Mustered, Jan. 2, 1865. Private, Co. G., 1st Battalion Frontier Cavalry. Discharged, June 30, 1865, by expiration of service.

CLARK, JOHN (Veteran). Son of John and Sarah W., born in Mount Desert, Maine, April 11, 1831. Mustered, July 5, 1861. Corporal, Co. H., 1st Heavy Artillery. Promoted, Sergeant, May 11, 1863. Re-enlisted in the field Jan. 2, 1864. Promoted, 2d Lieutenant, Aug. 2, 1864; 1st Lieutenant, Aug. 12, 1864, and Captain, April 9, 1865. Discharged, Aug. 16, 1865, by expiration of service. Wounded in battle June, 16, 1864, at Bryant's Farm, near Petersburg, Va., by minnie ball entering the right side and passing out at the back-bone.

CLARK, JOHN. Born in England, and recruited in Boston. Mustered, Dec. 9, 1862. Unassigned recruit, 22d Infantry. " Bounty Jumper "; never joined the Regiment.

CLARKE, AMASA. Son of Francis and Sarah, born in Andover, Jan. 14, 1844. Mustered, Sept. 12, 1862. Private, Co. G., 44th Regiment Infantry. Discharged, June 18, 1863, by expiration of service.

CLARKSON, JOHN. Born in Philadelphia, and recruited in Boston. Mustered, Dec. 12, 1862. Unassigned recruit, 22d Infantry. " Bounty Jumper "; never joined the Regiment.

CLEMENT, CHARLES A. Son of Moses and Caroline, born in Andover, Feb. 18, 1841. Mustered, July 16, 1861. Private, Co. C., 13th Regiment Infantry. Promoted Corporal. Mortally wounded, July 2, 1863, in battle of Gettysburg. Died, Sept. 30, 1863. Buried in Old South Cemetery, Oct. 14, 1863.

CLEMENT, MOSES W. Son of Moses and Caroline, born in Andover. Mustered, July 5, 1861, 2d Lieutenant, Co. H., 1st Heavy Artillery. Promoted, 1st Lieutenant, Jan. 18, 1862. Promoted Captain, Dec. 7, 1863. Discharged, Oct. 11, 1864. Captain U. S. Colored Troops.

DURING THE REBELLION. 155

CLOUGH, WILLIAM E. Son of Josiah and Dorcas B., born in Andover, Dec. 30, 1840. Mustered, Sept. 1, 1864. Private, Co. B., 11th Regiment Infantry. Discharged, June 4, 1865, by expiration of service.

COCKLIN, JOHN (Veteran). Son of John and Catherine, born in Cork Co., Ireland, May 20, 1842. Mustered, July 5, 1861. Private, Co. H., 1st Heavy Artillery. Re-enlisted in the field, Dec. 7, 1863, to the credit of Salem. Promoted Corporal. Discharged, July 31, 1865, as supernumerary.

COGSWELL, THOMAS M. Son of Francis and Mary S. M., born in Andover, July 17, 1844. Mustered, Sept. 12, 1862. Private, Co. G., 44th Regiment Infantry. Discharged, June 18, 1863, by expiration of service.

COLANGE, ETIENNE. Mustered, Nov. 10, 1863. Private, Co. K., 1st Heavy Artillery. Deserted, Aug. 26, 1864.

COLLINS, JAMES. Born in Wicklow, Ireland, and recruited in Boston. Mustered, Dec. 12, 1862. Unassigned recruit, 22d Infantry. " Bounty Jumper"; never joined the Regiment.

COLLINS, RICHARD. Mustered, Aug. 22, 1864. Private, 29th Unattached Company Heavy Artillery. Discharged, June 16, 1865, by expiration of service.

COLLINS, THOMAS E. Mustered, Aug. 21, 1861. Private, Co. B., 1st Regiment Infantry. Discharged, Dec. 1862, for disability. Wounded at Fair Oaks, June 25, 1862.

COLLINS, TIMOTHY. Mustered, Aug. 30, 1864. Private, Co. B., 11th Regiment Infantry. Discharged, June 4, 1865, by expiration of service.

COMSTOCK, ALFRED. Mustered, June 2, 1864. Unassigned recruit, 2d Regiment Infantry. Never joined the Regiment.

CONDON, NICHOLAS. Mustered, July 22, 1861. Private, Co. G., 17th Regiment Infantry, to the credit of Danvers. Discharged, Dec. 18, 1861, for disability. Mustered, Aug. 22, 1864. Private, 29th unattached Company Heavy Artillery. Discharged, June 16, 1865, by expiration of service.

CONLEY, JEREMIAH (Veteran). Son of John and Margaret, born in Ireland, Sept. 19, 1843. Mustered, June 13, 1861. Private, Co. E., 11th Regiment Infantry. Deserted, June 25, 1861; said to have been shot in the toe, obtained a furlough, and did not return. Mustered, Feb. 14, 1862. Private, Co. H., 1st Heavy Artillery. Re-enlisted in the field, Feb. 22, 1864. Discharged, Aug. 16, 1865, by expiration of service, in Co. B.

COOMBS, JAMES. Born in Oswego, N. Y., and recruited in Boston. Mustered, Dec. 9, 1862. Unassigned recruit, 22d Infantry. " Bounty Jumper"; never joined the Regiment.

COOPER, THOMAS H. Mustered, April 22, 1861. Private, Co. F., 6th Regiment Infantry (3 months). Discharged, Aug. 2, 1861, by expiration of service.

COSTELLO, JAMES. Son of Edwin and Bridget, born in Belfast, Ireland, July 12, 1844. Mustered, July 5, 1861. Private, Co. H., 1st Heavy Artillery. Discharged, July 8, 1864, by expiration of service. Wounded in battle, May 19, 1864.

COULIE, JOHN D. (Veteran). Son of James L. and Grace, born in Montrose, Scotland, July 25, 1843. Mustered, July 5, 1861. Private, Co. H., 1st Heavy Artillery. Re-enlisted in the field, Dec. 31, 1863. Promoted Corporal. Discharged, Aug. 16, 1865, by expiration of service, in Co. B.

CRAIG, DAVID. Son of William and Sarah Ann, born in England, Aug. 22, 1845. Mustered, July 7, 1862. Musician, Co. E., 15th Regiment Infantry. Transferred, July 27, 1864, to Co. E., 20th Regiment Infantry. Discharged, July 16, 1865, by expiration of service. Promoted Drum Major, 1864.

CRAIG, GEORGE. Son of James and Margaret, born in Ireland, Jan. 8, 1832. Mustered, July 5, 1861. Private, Co. H., 1st Heavy Artillery. Discharged, Nov. 6, 1862, for disability, from Co. B.

CRAIG, WILLIAM. Son of Abraham and Margaret, born in Ireland, Aug. 17, 1822. Mustered, Nov. 18, 1863. Private, Co. B., 1st Heavy Artillery. Discharged, Aug. 16, 1865, by expiration of service.

CRITCHETT, GEORGE D. Son of Thomas and Eliza C. Mustered, July 12, 1861. Private, Co. B., 15th Regiment Infantry. Discharged, April 21, 1863, for disability.

CROSBY, ALONZO. Mustered, Feb. 7. 1865. Private, Co. A., 26th Infantry. Discharged, Aug. 26, 1865, by expiration of service.

CROWTHER, WILLIAM. Mustered, Nov. 23, 1863. Private, Co. C., 40th Regiment Infantry. Transferred to Co. G., 24th Regiment. Discharged, Jan. 20, 1866, by expiration of service.

CUMMINGS, CHARLES S. Son of Asa and Sophia, born in Shelburn, N. H., Feb. 3, 1837, Mustered, July 5, 1861. Private, Co. H., 1st Heavy Artillery. Discharged, Dec. 15, 1864, for disability.

CURRIER, CHARLES. Born in Hill, N. H. Mustered, July 5, 1861. Private, Co. H., 1st Heavy Artillery. Discharged, Dec. 20, 1864, for disability.

CURTIS, ANDREW F. Son of Andrew F. and Harriet, born in Middleton, Dec. 15, 1843. Mustered, July 5, 1861. Private, Co. H., 1st Heavy Artillery. Discharged, July 8, 1864, by expiration of service.

CUSICK, JOHN (Veteran). Son of Michael and Hannah, born in Brookline, March 27, 1838. Mustered, July 5, 1861. Private, Co. H., 1st Heavy Artillery. Re-enlisted in the field, Dec. 4, 1863, to the credit of Brookline. Transferred to Veteran Reserve Corps. Severely wounded at Spottsylvania, May 19, 1864.

CUTLER, ABALINO B. Son of William and Amelia, born in Tewksbury, Dec. 25, 1841. Mustered, July 5, 1861. Private, Co. H., 1st Heavy Artillery. Promoted Corporal, March 1, 1864. Discharged, July 8, 1864, by expiration of service.

CUTLER, GRANVILLE K. Son of William and Amelia, born in Framingham, June 14, 1839. Mustered, July 5, 1861. Private, Co. H., 1st Heavy Artillery. Killed, May 19, 1864, in battle at Spottsylvania. Buried on the field.

DANE, A. L. Mustered, April 22, 1861. Private, Co. F., 6th Regiment Infantry (3 months). Discharged, Aug. 2, 1861, by expiration of service.

DANE, ELMORE (Veteran). Son of Benjamin. Mustered, Sept. 12, 1861. Private, Co. F., 26th Regiment Infantry. Re-enlisted in the field, Jan. 5, 1864. Discharged, Aug. 26, 1865, by expiration of service.

DANE, GEORGE (Veteran). Son of Chandler and Susan, born in Andover, Jan. 17, 1840. Mustered, July 5, 1861. Private, Co. H., 1st Heavy Artillery. Re-enlisted in the field, Jan. 2, 1864. Discharged, Aug. 16, 1865, by expiration of service, in Co. B.

DANE, RICHARD G. Son of Benjamin. Mustered, April 19, 1864. Private, Co. F., 26th Regiment Infantry. Discharged, Aug. 26, 1865, by expiration of service.

DAVIS, CHARLES H. Son of Sarah A. Mustered, July 27, 1862, unassigned recruit, 1st Heavy Artillery.

DEARBORN, JOHN S. (Veteran). Son of Nathaniel and Eliza J., born in Andover, Nov. 18, 1844. Mustered, July 22, 1862. Private, Co. H., 1st Heavy Artillery. Re-enlisted in the field, Feb. 29, 1864. Discharged, June 26, 1865, for disability. Lost his right arm at Petersburg, Va., March 25, 1865.

DELANY, EDWARD. Born in New York City, N.Y., and recruited in Boston. Mustered, Dec. 9, 1862. Unassigned recruit, 22d Regiment Infantry. "Bounty Jumper"; never joined the Regiment.

DODGE, JOHN A. Mustered, Sept. 2, 1864. Unassigned recruit, 11th Regiment Infantry; subsequently assigned to Co. B. Discharged, June 4, 1865, by expiration of service.

DOWNS, BENJAMIN. Mustered, Jan. 2, 1865. Private, Co. C., 1st Battalion Frontier Cavalry. Discharged, June 30, 1865, by expiration of service.

DOW, CHARLES E. Mustered, Jan. 2, 1865. Private, Co. C., 1st Battalion Frontier Cavalry. Discharged, June 30, 1865, by expiration of service.

DOUGHERTY, JAMES. Son of James and Ann. Mustered, Dec. 30, 1864. Sergeant, Co. B., 1st Battalion Frontier Cavalry. Discharged, June 30, 1865, by expiration of service. Says he first enlisted, March 27, 1861, Co. K., 4th Division U. S. Artillery, and was discharged, March 27, 1864.

DUNCAN, JAMES. Son of James and Christina, born in Andover, Aug. 2, 1848. Mustered, Aug. 24, 1864. Private, Co. B., 11th Regiment Infantry. Discharged, June 4, 1865, by expiration of service.

DUNCAN ROBERT. Son of James and Christina. Mustered, Feb. 22, 1865. Private, Co. M., 2d Regiment Cavalry. Discharged, July 20, 1865, by expiration of service.

DUNN, ALBERT H. Mustered, July 15, 1864. Private, Co. A., 6th Regiment Infantry (100 days). Discharged, Oct. 27, 1864, by expiration of service.

DUGAN, CHARLES. Son of Bartholomew and Bridget, born in Greenock, Scotland, May 22, 1839. Mustered, July 5, 1861. Private, Co. H., 1st Heavy Artillery. Discharged, July 8, 1864, by expiration of service.

DUGAN, WILLIAM. Mustered, Jan. 2, 1865. Private, Co. C., 1st Battalion Frontier Cavalry. Discharged, June 30, 1865, by expiration of service.

DURANT, GEORGE. Born, and recruited in Boston. Mustered, Dec. 8, 1862. Unassigned recruit, 22d Regiment Infantry. "Bounty Jumper"; never joined the Regiment.

DWINE, DANIEL, Jr. Son of Daniel and Mary, born in Cork County, Ireland, April 6, 1845. Mustered, Aug. 22, 1863. Private, Co. D., 2d Heavy Artillery. Discharged, Sept. 3, 1865, by expiration of service.

DWYER, MICHAEL. Mustered, Sept. 3, 1864. Private, Co. M., 2d Heavy Artillery. Transferred, Jan. 17, 1865, to Co. E., 17th Regiment Infantry. Discharged, June 30, 1865, by Order of the War Department.

EAGLETON, CHARLES (Veteran). Mustered, Nov. 14, 1861. Private, Co. G., 24th Regiment Infantry, to the credit of Berkley. Re-enlisted in the field, Jan. 4, 1864, to the credit of Andover. Discharged, Jan. 20, 1866, by expiration of service, in Co. B.

EASTES, JAMES H. (Veteran). Son of James and Mary, born in Dover, N. H., July 26, 1839. Mustered, July 22, 1862. Private, Co. H., 1st Heavy Artillery. Re-enlisted in the field, Feb. 29, 1864. Killed in battle at Spottsylvania, May 19, 1864. Buried on the field.

EDWARDS, FRANCIS W. Son of Frank A. and Tryphenia, born in Dover, N. H., Feb. 17, 1843. Mustered, July 5, 1861. Private, Co. H., 1st Heavy Artillery. Wounded, and lost right leg in battle at Spottsylvania, May 19, 1864. Discharged July 8, 1864, by expiration of service.

EELES, FREDERICK S. Mustered, Nov. 13, 1861. Private, Co. C., 32d Regiment Infantry. Discharged, Dec. 3, 1862, for disability.

ELDRIDGE, HEZEKIAH. Mustered, Dec. 22, 1863. Private, Co. L., 2d Heavy Artillery. Discharged, Sept. 3, 1865, by expiration of service.

ENGLISH, CHARLES G. (Veteran). Son of Patrick and Jane, born in Andover. Mustered, Dec. 30, 1864. Sergeant Co. B., 1st Battalion Frontier Cavalry. Discharged, June 30, 1865, by expiration of service. Says he enlisted in 1861, Co. G., 1st U. S. Cavalry, and was discharged in 1864.

FARMER, EDWARD (Veteran). Son of Silas and Anna B., born in Andover, June 16, 1839. Mustered, July 5, 1861. Private, Co. H., 1st Heavy Artillery. Promoted Sergeant, March 11, 1863. Re-enlisted in the field, Dec. 5, 1863. Killed in battle at Spottsylvania, May 19, 1864. Buried on the field.

FARMER, GEORGE S. (Veteran). Son of Joseph and Keziah, born in Salem, May 2, 1835. Mustered, July 5, 1861. Corporal, Co. H., 1st Heavy Artillery. Promoted, Sergeant, July 5, 1862. Re-enlisted in the field, Jan. 2, 1864, to the credit of Salem. Captured in front of Petersburg, Va. June 22, 1864. Died a prisoner of war at Andersonville, Ga., Sept. 10, 1864. Buried in the trenches.

FARNHAM, DAVID T. Mustered, Oct. 31, 1862. Private, Co. K., 47th Regiment Infantry. Discharged, Sept. 1, 1863, by expiration of service.

FARNHAM, MOSES L. Son of Ezra and Hannah, born in Acton, Me., Dec. 20, 1846. Mustered, Jan. 5, 1864. Private, Co. B., 59th Regiment Infantry. Promoted Orderly Sergeant. Transferred, June 1, 1865, to Co. E., 57th Regiment. Discharged, July 30, 1865, by expiration of service. The 57th and 59th Regiments were consolidated.

FARNHAM, ORRIN L. Son of Jeremiah and Sarah, born in Andover, June 24, 1835. Mustered, July 5, 1861. Sergeant, Co. H., 1st Heavy Artillery. Promoted Regimental Quarter-Master-Sergeant, Feb. 14, 1862. Promoted 2d Lieutenant, Oct. 25, 1862. Mortally wounded, June 16, 1864, while charging on the rebel works, and died on the 17th, at Bryant's Farm, near Petersburg, Va. Buried in West Parish Cemetery.

FARNHAM, SAMUEL P. (Veteran). Son of Samuel P. and Olive T., born in Andover, March 25, 1837. Mustered, July 5, 1861. Private, Co. H., 1st Heavy Artillery. Re-enlisted in the field, Dec. 11, 1863. Promoted, Corporal. Discharged, July 31, 1865, as Supernumerary. Wounded in battle at Spottsylvania, May 19, 1864. Died at Andover, Jan. 12, 1866, of disease contracted in the service. Buried in South Cemetery.

FINDLEY, JAMES S. (Veteran). Son of John and Catherine, born in Rockport, April 27, 1844. Mustered, July 5, 1861. Private, Co. H., 1st Heavy Artillery. Re-enlisted in the field, Dec. 7, 1863. Wounded in the arm in battle at Spottsylvania, May 19, 1864. Transferred to Veteran Reserve Corps, March 19, 1865. Died, Nov. 9, 1869, and is buried in Spring Grove Cemetery.

FINDLEY, JOHN A. Son of John and Catherine, born in Andover, Dec. 6, 1842. Mustered, July 5, 1861. Private, Co. H., 1st Heavy Artillery. Discharged, July 8, 1864, by expiration of service. Died, Jan. 5, 1871, and is buried in Spring Grove Cemetery.

FITZGERALD, JAMES. Mustered, Feb. 20, 1865, by Provost-Marshal Herrick, for one year. Company and Regiment unknown.

FLEMMING, JOHN. Mustered, July 12, 1861. Private, Co. I., 16th Regiment Infantry Deserted, Aug. 1, 1861.

FLOOD, THOMAS. Born in Limerick, Ireland, and recruited in Boston. Mustered, Dec. 9, 1862. Unassigned recruit, 22d Regiment. "Bounty Jumper"; never joined the Regiment.

FOSTER, CHARLES H. Mustered, Nov. 9, 1863. Private, Co. H., 1st Heavy Artillery. Discharged, June 10, 1865, by expiration of service, in Co. B.

FOSTER, THOMAS E. (Veteran). Son of Thomas and Mary, born in Ipswich, Sep. 1, 1840. Mustered, July 5, 1861. Private, Co. H. 1st Heavy Artillery. Re-enlisted in the field, Jan. 2, 1864. Deserted,* July 30, 1865, at Fort Bunker Hill.

FOX, WILLIAM. Mustered, Dec. 31, 1864. Private, 1st Battalion Frontier Cavalry, by Provost-Marshal Herrick; never joined the Battalion. Date of muster, Dec. 31, 1864.

FRENCH, HENRY P. Mustered, June 16, 1862. Private, Co. G., 2d Regiment Infantry. Discharged, July 14, 1865, by expiration of service.

FRORZ, JAMES A. This Recruit's name appears on Selectmen's return as in the 6th Regiment Infantry (3 months), but his name does not appear on the Regimental rolls.

FRYE, ENOCH O. Son of Enoch and Lydia B., born in Andover, Nov. 7, 1837. Mustered, July 5, 1861. Private, Co. K., 1st Heavy Artillery. Accidentally killed by the falling of a tree at Fort Albany, near Arlington, Va., Oct. 29, 1861. Buried in West Parish Cemetery.

FRYE, NEWTON G. Son of Stephen and Emily G., born in Andover, June 17, 1845. Mustered, July 5, 1861. Drummer, Co. H., 1st Heavy Artillery. Discharged, Dec. 10, 1862, for disability. Died, March 28, 1863, of disease contracted in service. Buried in West Parish Cemetery.

FULMER, ROBERT. Substitute for James A. Roberts, Mustered, July 11, 1864, by Provost-Marshal H. G. Herrick for three years service. Regiment and Co. unknown.

FULTON, JOSEPH W. (Veteran). Son of James and Eunice, born in Deering, N. H., Sept. 7, 1839. Mustered, Sept. 19, 1862. Private, Co. D., 50th Regiment Infantry. Discharged, Aug. 24, 1863, by expiration of service. Re-mustered, Aug. 18, 1864. Private, Co. K., 4th Heavy Artillery. Discharged, June 17, 1865, by expiration of service.

GALLON, JAMES. Mustered, June 13, 1861. Private, Co. G., 11th Regiment Infantry. Deserted, Nov. 14, 1861.

---

* See note in Appendix.

GEORGE, WARREN. Mustered, July 14, 1864. Private, Co. K., 6th Regiment Infantry (100 days). Discharged, Oct. 27, 1864, by expiration of service.

GIBBS, ROBERT. Mustered, Dec. 30, 1864. Private, Co. B., 1st Battalion Frontier Cavalry. Discharged, June 30, 1865, by expiration of service.

GIFFORD, ROBERT. Mustered, July 21, 1864. Musician, Co. D., 60th Regt. Infantry. Discharged, Nov. 30, 1864, by expiration of service.

GILCREAST, DAVID B. (Veteran). Son of Samuel and Betsey, born in Andover, Feb. 1, 1837. Mustered, July 5, 1861. Private, Co. H., 1st Heavy Artillery. Re-enlisted in the field, Jan. 3, 1864. Promoted Corporal. Discharged, Aug. 16, 1865, by expiration of service, in Co. B. Wounded in the neck, May 19, 1864.

GILLESPIE, WILLIAM. Son of Isaac and Catherine D., born in Aberdeen, Scotland, Nov. 15, 1826. Mustered, July 5, 1861. Private, Co. H., 1st Heavy Artillery. Discharged, July 8, 1864, by expiration of service. Wounded in the hand at Bryant's Farm, June 16, 1864. Died, —— —— Buried in West Parish Cemetery.

GODKINS, STEPHEN F. Mustered, Dec. 31, 1864. Private, Co. L., 4th Cavalry. Discharged, Nov. 14, 1865, by expiration of service.

GOLDSMITH, ALBERT (Veteran). Son of Jeremiah and Elizabeth G., born in Andover, June 11, 1842. Mustered, July 5, 1861. Private, Co. H., 1st Heavy Artillery. Re-enlisted in the field, Dec. 11, 1863. Discharged, Aug. 16, 1865, by expiration of service, in Co. B.

GOLDSMITH, BENJAMIN F. Mustered, Dec. 5, 1863. Corporal, Co. A., 59th Regiment Infantry. Discharged, Jan. 8, 1865, for disability

GOLDSMITH, JEREMIAH. Son of Jeremiah and Elizabeth G., born in Andover, March 27, 1838. Mustered, Aug. 26, 1864. Private, Co. B., 11th Regiment Infantry. Discharged, June 4, 1865, by expiration of service. Died, Aug. 10, 1871, at Gainsville, Fla.

GOLDSMITH, JOSEPH C. Son of Joseph C. and Phebe, born in Andover, April 26, 1831. Mustered, Feb. 21, 1862. Private, Co. H., 1st Heavy Artillery. Discharged, Feb. 20, 1865, by expiration of service.

GOLDSMITH, SANFORD K. Son of Daniel and Rebecca K., born in Wilton, N. H., Jan. 22, 1842. Mustered, July 16, 1861. Private, Co. C., 13th Infantry, to the credit of Boston. Promoted and transferred as 2d Lieutenant to 59th Regiment, Jan. 6, 1864. Promoted 1st Lieutenant, June 23, 1864. Promoted Captain by Brevet for "gallantry at Fort Steadman, Va., March 5, 1865, U.S. Vol." Promoted Captain, March 25, 1865. Discharged, May 15, 1865, by expiration of service. Taken prisoner at 2d Bull Run and at Gettysburg. Wounded at Gettysburg and at Fort Steadman, Va.

GOOCH, JOHN F. (Veteran). Son of John and Elizabeth C., born in Cambridge, June 11, 1843. Mustered, Aug. 4, 1862. Private, Co. H., 1st Heavy Artillery. Re-enlisted in the field, Jan. 2, 1864. Discharged, Aug. 25, 1865, by expiration of service.

GOODWIN, MOSES F. Son of David and Susan, born in North Andover, April 26, 1848. Mustered, July 14, 1864. Private, Co. K., 6th Regiment (100 days). Discharged, Oct. 27, 1864, by expiration of service. Re-mustered, Jan. 2, 1865. Private, Co. C., 1st Battalion Frontier Cavalry. Discharged, June 30, 1865, by expiration of service.

GORMAN, JOSEPH E. Born in England, and recruited in Boston. Mustered, Dec. 11, 1862. Unassigned recruit, 22d Regiment Infantry. "Bounty Jumper"; never joined the Regiment.

GRANDY, HENRY E. Mustered, May 1, 1861. Private, Co. I., 5th Regt. Infantry (3 months). Discharged, July 31, 1861, by expiration of service.

GRANT, FARNHAM P. (Veteran). Son of Benjamin P. and Fannie F., born in Andover, Feb. 11, 1841. Mustered, July 5, 1861. Private, Co. H., 1st Heavy Artillery. Re-enlisted in the field, Dec. 7, 1863. Discharged, Aug. 16, 1865, by expiration of service, in Co. B.

GRANT, GEORGE W. (Veteran). Son of Benjamin P. and Fannie F., born in Andover, Jan. 27, 1846. Mustered, Aug. 2, 1862. Private, Co. H., 1st Heavy Artillery. Re-enlisted in the field, Jan. 2, 1864. Died of disease, Sept. 7, 1864, in the 2d Corps Field Hospital. Buried in West Parish Cemetery.

GRAY, JESSE E. Son of David and Maria, born in Andover, May 15, 1832. Mustered, July 5, 1861. Private, Co. H., 1st Heavy Artillery. Discharged, July 8, 1864, by expiration of service.

GRAY, NATHAN H. Mustered, Aug. 25, 1861. Private, Co. E., 20th Regiment Infantry. Discharged, Aug. 5, 1864, by expiration of service.

GREELEY, WILLIAM. Mustered, Oct. 12, 1861. Private, Co. G., 30th Regiment Infantry. Died, Aug. 22, 1862, at Carrolton, La.

GREEN, JOSEPH. Born in Dublin, Ireland, and recruited in Boston. Mustered, Dec. 9, 1862. Unassigned recruit, 22d Regiment Infantry. "Bounty Jumper"; never joined the Regiment.

GREEN, MICHAEL. Mustered, Jan. 13, 1863. Private, Co. D., 2d Cavalry. Deserted, Jan. 17, 1863.

GREENE, CHARLES. Son of Eaton and Sarah, born in Andover. Mustered, July 5, 1861. Private, Co. H., 1st Heavy Artillery. Discharged, July 8, 1864, by expiration of service.

GREENE, WILLIAM H. (Veteran). Son of Eaton and Sarah, born in Andover, Jan. 9, 1834. Mustered, July 5, 1861. Private, Co. H., 1st Heavy Artillery. Re-enlisted in the field, Jan. 2, 1864. Discharged, July 31, 1865, by expiration of service. Wounded, June 22, 1864.

GORMAN, WILLIAM B. Born in Lowell, and recruited in Boston. Mustered, Dec. 9, 1862. Unassigned recruit, 22d Regiment Infantry. "Bounty Jumper"; never joined the Regiment.

GOULD, THEODORE F. Son of Henry A. Mustered, Dec. 30, 1864. Private, Co. B., 1st Battalion Frontier Cavalry. Discharged, June 30, 1865, by expiration of service.

GRUBBS, CAM (Colored). Of Louisiana. Representative Recruit for William T. Jackson. Mustered in at Vicksburg, Miss., Sept. 12, 1864. Private, 51st Regiment U. S. Colored Troops.

HALL, HENRY H. (Veteran). Son of Samuel and Harriet, born in Unity, Me., June 30, 1841. Mustered, July 22, 1862. Private, Co. B., Heavy Artillery. Re-enlisted in the field, Feb. 29, 1864, to the credit of Charlestown. Discharged, May 23, 1865, by expiration of service.

HALL, WILLIAM S. (Veteran). Son of Samuel and Harriet, born in Unity, Me., July 19, 1844, Mustered, July 22, 1862. Private, Co. B., 1st Heavy Artillery. Re-enlisted in the field, Feb. 29, 1864, to the credit of Charlestown, Died, Sept. 30, 1864, a prisoner of war at Andersonville, Ga. Buried in the trenches.

HANSON, CHARLES. Mustered, April 22, 1861. Private, Co. B., 4th Infantry (3 months). Discharged, July 22, 1861, by expiration of service. Re-mustered, Sept. 2, 1861. Private, 1st Co. Sharpshooters. Discharged, Sept. 2, 1864, by expiration of service.

HARDY, FRANKLIN (Veteran). Son of Isaac M. and Sibyl W., born in Woburn, Feb. 20, 1830. Mustered, July 5, 1861. Private, Co. H., 1st Heavy Artillery. Re-enlisted in the field, Dec. 7, 1863. Killed at Poplar Grove Church, near Petersburg, Va., Oct. 2, 1864. Body not recovered.

HARDY, JOHN, 2d. Son of Isaac M. and Sybil W., born in Andover, May 7, 1837. Mustered, July 5, 1861. Private, Co. H., 1st Heavy Artillery. Discharged, July 8, 1864, by expiration of service. Wounded, lost a finger, May 19, 1864.

HARNDEN, GEORGE W. Son of Jesse and Dorothy, born in Andover, Aug. 12, 1843. Mustered, Sept. 19, 1862. Private, Co. D., 50th Regiment Infantry. Discharged, Aug. 24, 1863, by expiration of service.

HARRIGAN, BARTHOLOMEW (Veteran). Son of Thomas and Hannah, born in Ireland in 1829. Mustered, Dec. 13, 1861. Private, Co. C., 28th Infantry, to the credit of Danvers. Discharged, March 14, 1863, for disability. Re-mustered, Aug. 22, 1864. Private, Co. G., 4th Heavy Artillery. Discharged, June 17, 1865, by expiration of service.

HART, WILLIAM. Son of Andrew and Ellen, born in Boston, Feb. 22, 1842. Mustered, July 5, 1861. Private, Co. H., 1st Heavy Artillery. Discharged, July 8, 1864, by expiration of service, in Co. B.

HASTIE, THOMAS. Son of William and Mary, born in Scotland, May 14, 1832. Mustered, March 10, 1862. Private, Co. H., 1st Heavy Artillery. Discharged, March 10, 1865, by expiration of service. Wounded, June 16, 1864, at Bryant's Farm.

HATCH, ANDREW J. (Veteran). Son of Ezra and Tamnah, born in Burlington, Aug. 20, 1833. Mustered, July 5, 1861. Private, Co. H., 1st Heavy Artillery. Re-enlisted in the field, Dec. 11, 1863. Wounded, May 19, 1864. Deserted,* July 30, 1865, from Co. B., at Fort Bunker Hill.

---

* See note in Appendix.

HATCH, ENOCH M. Son of Jeremiah and Betsey, born in Andover, April 14, 1822. Mustered, July 5, 1861. Private, Co. H., 1st Heavy Artillery. Killed, June 16, 1864, in front of Petersburg, Va. Buried on the field.

HATCH, GEORGE F. (Veteran). Son of Jeremiah and Betsey. Mustered, July 5, 1861. Private, Co. H., 1st Heavy Artillery. Promoted Corporal. Promoted Sergeant. Re-enlisted in the field, Dec. 22, 1863. Wounded at Cold Harbor, June, 1864.*

HATCH, LEWIS G. Son of Francis W. and Rebecca, born in Chatham, N. H., Feb. 8, 1830. Mustered, July 5, 1861. Private, Co. H., 1st Heavy Artillery. Discharged, July 8, 1864, by expiration of service. Wounded at Spottsylvania, May 19, 1864. Died, Jan. 4, 1866, of disease contracted in the service. Buried in South Cemetery.

HAYES, JOHN, Jr. Son of John and Nancy, born in Roxbury, March 15, 1844. Mustered, March 17, 1862. Private, Co. H., 1st Heavy Artillery. Discharged, July 8, 1864, by expiration of service. Wounded, May 19, 1864.

HAYES, PATRICK. Son of John and Ann. Mustered, Oct. 1, 1861. Private, Co. K., 22d Regiment Infantry. Deserted, Sept. 8, 1862.

HAYES, TIMOTHY (Veteran). Son of John and Nancy. Mustered, Nov. 25, 1861. Private, Co. F., 29th Regiment Infantry. Re-enlisted in the field, Jan. 2, 1864. Promoted Sergeant. Discharged, July 29, 1865, by expiration of service.

HAYWARD, GEORGE E. Son of Henry E. and Polly S., born in Andover, Feb. 13, 1842. Mustered, July 22, 1862. Private, Co. H., 1st Heavy Artillery. Discharged, July 8, 1864, by expiration of service. Died, July 24, 1865, from the effects of a gun shot wound through the stomach, received in battle at Spottsylvania, Va., May 19, 1864. Buried in South Cemetery.

HERVEY, ALBERT G. (Veteran). Son of Albert and Ann G., born in North Andover, Sept. 23, 1839. Mustered, Sept. 25, 1861. Sergeant, Co. L., 1st Regiment Cavalry. Transferred to 4th Cavalry. Re-enlisted in the field, April 21, 1864. Promoted Commissary-Sergeant, Dec. 2, 1864. Promoted, 2d Lieutenant, May 17, 1865. Discharged, Nov. 14, 1865, by expiration of service, as Regt'l Com. Sergeant.

---

* On the Regimental Rolls he is said to have been "discharged July 31, 1865, as supernumerary," while the fact is well established that he deserted from McLellan Hospital, Philadelphia, in the fall of 1864.

HERVEY, SAMUEL C. Son of Albert and Ann G., born in North Andover, April 17, 1835. Mustered, July 5, 1861. Sergeant, Co. H., 1st Heavy Artillery. Promoted, 2d Lieutenant, Jan. 18, 1862, and assigned to Co. B. Promoted, 1st Lieutenant, Sept. 20, 1862. Discharged, Oct. 6, 1864, by expiration of service.

HIGGINS, ARCHIBALD, Jr. Mustered, Aug. 28, 1861. Private, Co. A., 19th Regiment Infantry. Discharged, Aug. 28, 1864, by expiration of service.

HIGGINS, HENRY C. Mustered, Aug. 26, 1864. Private, Co. B., 11th Regiment Infantry. Discharged, May 3, 1865, by expiration of service.

HILL, EMMETT C. Mustered, July 29, 1864. Hospital Steward, U. S. Army.

HOLLORAN, PATRICK. Mustered, Aug. 29, 1864. Private, 29th Unattached Company Heavy Artillery. Discharged, June 16, 1865, by expiration of service.

HOLT, BALLARD, 2d (Veteran). Son of Dean and Sarah, born in Chelmsford, March 20, 1837. Mustered, Sept. 12, 1862. Private, Co. G., 44th Regiment Infantry. Discharged, June 18, 1863, by expiration of service. Re-mustered, Aug. 26, 1864. Private, Co. B., 11th Regiment Infantry. Discharged, June 4, 1865, by expiration of service.

HOLT, HARRISON. Son of Stephen and Margaret S., born at Saratoga Springs, N.Y., Aug. 4, 1842. Mustered, May 16, 1863, 2d Lieutenant 55th Regiment Infantry. Promoted, 1st Lieutenant, June 7, 1863. Resigned, Oct. 14, 1863. Re-mustered, Nov. 9, 1863, 1st Lieutenant 1st Regiment Cavalry. Discharged, July 26, 1864, for disability.

HOLT, HORACE. Son of Ezra and Elizabeth G., born in Temple, N. H., Sept. 29, 1829. Mustered, July 5, 1861. Captain, Co. H., 1st Heavy Artillery. Promoted Major, Aug. 3, 1863. Promoted Lieutenant-Colonel, Jan. 27, 1865. Discharged, Aug. 16, 1865, by expiration of service, as Major.

HOLT, JONATHAN A. Son of Solomon and Phebe A., born in Andover, April 7, 1841. Mustered, July 22, 1862. Private, Co. H., 1st Heavy Artillery. Killed, in battle at Spottsylvania, May 19, 1864. Buried on the field.

DURING THE REBELLION. 169

HOLT, JOSEPH F. Son of Joseph and Elizabeth B., born in Andover, Sept. 1, 1822. Mustered, May 23, 1861. Private, Co. G., 1st Regiment Infantry. Discharged, July 5, 1861, for disability. Re-mustered, Sept. 19, 1862. Corporal, Co. G., 50th Regiment Infantry. Discharged, Aug. 24, 1863, by expiration of service. Accidentally killed at Andover, Feb. 4, 1868. Buried in South Cemetery.

HOLT, LEWIS G. Son of Jonas and Pamelia P., born in Andover, Nov. 15, 1839. Mustered, July 5, 1861. Private, Co. H., 1st Heavy Artillery. Promoted, Corporal, March 1, 1862. Wounded at Cold Harbor, June 12, 1864. Discharged, July 8, 1864, by expiration of service.

HOLT, NEWTON. Son of Joseph and Elizabeth B., born in Andover, Feb. 13, 1830. Mustered, July 5, 1861. Sergeant, Co. H., 1st Heavy Artillery. Promoted 2d Lieutenant, Dec. 3, 1862, and assigned to Co. I. Resigned, Nov. 5, 1864.

HOLT, SAMUEL M. (Veteran). Son of Amos and Eunice E., born in Andover, April 27, 1826. Mustered, Sept. 26, 1862. Private, Co. F., 45th Regiment Infantry. Discharged, July 7, 1863, by expiration of service. Re-mustered, Aug. 25, 1864. Private, Co. B., 11th Regiment Infantry. Discharged, June 4, 1865, by expiration of service.

HOLT, WARREN E. (Veteran). Son of Jonas and Pamelia P., born in Andover, April 17, 1833. Mustered, July 5, 1861. Private, Co. H., 1st Heavy Artillery. Re-enlisted in the field, March 31, 1864, to the credit of Weymouth. Discharged, Aug. 16, 1865, by expiration of service, in Co. B.

HOTCHKISS, ARTHUR E. Mustered, July 22, 1864. Private, Co. B., 42d Regiment Infantry (100 days). Discharged, Nov. 11, 1864, by expiration of service.

HOVEY, JOHN C. (Veteran). Son of James and Mary, born in Andover, Sept. 1, 1837. Mustered, Feb. 22, 1862. Private, Co. H., 1st Heavy Artillery. Re-enlisted in the field, Feb. 22, 1864. Discharged, Aug. 16, 1865, by expiration of service, in Co. B.

HOWARTH, OBERLIN B. Son of James and Sarah, born in Andover, Aug. 14, 1839. Mustered, July 5, 1861. Private, Co. H., 1st Heavy Artillery. Discharged, July 8, 1864, by expiration of service.

HUNT, AMOS. Mustered, July 5, 1861. Private, Co. H., 1st Heavy Artillery. Discharged, Nov. 24, 1861, for disability.

HUNT, WILLIAM. Mustered, Sept. 20, 1862. Private, Co. D., 47th Regiment Infantry. Discharged, Sept. 1, 1863, by expiration of service.

HUSSEY, WYMAN D. Son of Elijah and Roxanna M., born in Andover, Feb. 14, 1843. Mustered, Aug. 5, 1862. Private, Co. H., 1st Heavy Artillery. Discharged, July 8, 1864, by expiration of service.

HUNTER, WILLIAM. Son of Ferguson and Bell, born in Scotland, Feb. 26, 1813. Mustered, April 22, 1861. Private, Co. E., 6th Regiment, New Jersey Militia for three months. Discharged, Aug. 4, 1861, by expiration of service. Re-mustered, Sept. 6, 1861. Private, Co. D., 22d Regiment Infantry. Discharged, Dec. 27, 1862, for disability.

INGALLS, JOHN E. Mustered, Aug. 27, 1864. Private, Co. B., 11th Regiment Infantry. Discharged, June 4, 1865, by expiration of service.

JAMESON, JOHN. Born in Marblehead, and recruited in Boston. Mustered, Dec. 10, 1862, Unassigned recruit, 22d Regiment Infantry. "Bounty Jumper"; never joined the Regiment.

JACQUITH, JAMES. Son of James and Phebe, born in Andover, March 15, 1818. Mustered, Nov. 16, 1861. Corporal, Co. C., 30th Regiment Infantry. Died of disease, Dec. 1, 1862, at New Orleans. Buried at New Orleans.

JENKINS, E. KENDALL. Son of Benjamin and Betsey, born in Andover, Oct. 14, 1832. Mustered, July 5, 1861. Private, Co. H., 1st Heavy Artillery. Promoted Corporal, Feb. 15, 1862. Promoted Quarter-Master-Sergeant, March 1, 1862. Wounded in the shoulder, June 16, 1864. Discharged, July 8, 1864, by expiration of service.

JENKINS, JOHN B. Son of Benjamin and Betsey. Mustered, Aug. 26, 1864. Corporal, Co. B., 11th Regiment Infantry. Discharged, June 4, 1865, by expiration of service.

JENKINS, OMAR. Son of Ebenezer and Sally, born in Andover, Jan. 9, 1840. Mustered, Aug. 4, 1862. Private, Co. H., 1st Heavy Artillery. Discharged, July 8, 1864, by expiration of service. Wounded, lost a finger, June, 1864, near Petersburg, Va,

DURING THE REBELLION. 171

JENKINS, WILLIAM HARRISON (Veteran). Son of Benjamin and Abigail, born in Buckfield, Me., Sept. 7, 1840. Mustered, July 22, 1862. Private, Co. H., 1st Heavy Artillery. Re-enlisted in the field, Feb. 29, 1864, to the credit of Roxbury. Discharged, July 13, 1865, for disability.

JENNINGS, GEORGE (Colored). Of Georgia. Representative Recruit for David I. C. Hidden. Mustered in at Hilton Head, S. C., Jan. 24, 1865. Private, 103d Regiment U. S. Colored Troops.

JENNINGS, WILLIAM E. Son of Alexander and Clarissa, born in Cambridgeport, Nov. 29, 1844. Mustered, July 5, 1861. Private, Co. H., 1st Heavy Artillery. Wounded, at Spottsylvania, May 19, 1864. Discharged, July 8, 1864, for disability.

JOHNSON, JAMES. Born, and recruited in Boston. Mustered, Dec. 9, 1862. Unassigned recruit, 22d Regiment Infantry. "Bounty Jumper"; never joined the Regiment.

JOHNSON, JOHN. Mustered, Sept. 6, 1861. Private, Co. D., 22d Regiment Infantry. Deserted, Oct. 18, 1862.

JOHNSON, SOLON (Veteran). Son of Solon N. and Hannah, born in Wilmington, Oct. 8, 1839. Mustered, July 5, 1861. Private, Co. H., 1st Heavy Artillery. Re-enlisted in the field, Dec, 22, 1863. Discharged, Aug. 16, 1865, by expiration of service, in Co. B.

JOHNSTON, DAVID. Jr. Son of David and Elizabeth, born in Scotland, April 22, 1845. Mustered, July 14, 1864. Private, Co. K., 6th Regiment Infantry (100 days). Discharged, Oct. 27, 1864, by expiration of service.

JOICE, REDMOND (Veteran). Son of Catherine, born in Ireland. Mustered, July 22, 1862. Private, Co. H., 1st Heavy Artillery. Transferred, Sept. 1, 1863, to Veteran Reserve Corps. Re-mustered, Aug. 26, 1864. Private, 29th Unattached Co., Heavy Artillery. Discharged, June 16, 1865, by expiration of service.

JONES, AMBROSE. Mustered, Sept. 28, 1861. Private, Co. I., 1st Minnesota Vols.

JONES, CHARLES E. (Veteran). Son of Reuben and Rachel S., born in Andover, March 13, 1832. Mustered, Aug. 4, 1862. Private, Co. H., 1st Heavy Artillery. Re-enlisted in the field, Feb. 29, 1864. Wounded in the left arm, June 22, 1864. Discharged, April 27, 1865, for disability.

JONES, DAVID L. Mustered, Dec. 31, 1864. Private, Co. E., 4th Regiment Cavalry. Discharged, Nov. 14, 1865, by expiration of service.

JOURDAN, HENRY (Colored). Of Pitts Co., North Carolina. Representative Recruit for John L. Taylor. Mustered in at Fortress Monroe, Va., Dec. 27, 1864. Private, 1st Regiment U. S. Colored Cavalry.

JUPITER, ISAAC (Colored). Of Tensas Co., Louisiana. Representative Recruit for Frederick L. Church. Mustered in at Vicksburg, Miss., Sept. 12, 1864. Private, 51st Regiment U. S. Colored Troops.

KAVANAGH, BERNARD. Mustered, July 18, 1861. Private, Co. G., 20th Regiment Infantry. Died, Aug. 24, 1862, at Philadelphia, Pa.

KEATING, JOHN (Veteran). Son of James and Margaret, born in Dublin, Ireland, Feb. 25, 1839. Mustered, June 13, 1861. Private, Co. C., 11th Regiment Infantry. Re-enlisted in the field, Dec. 29, 1863, to the credit of Billerica. Discharged, July 14, 1865, by expiration of service. Died, March 30, 1869. Once slightly wounded.

KELLY, JOSEPH. Mustered, June 30, 1861. Private, Co. B., 29th Regiment Infantry. Transferred to Co. E., 36th Infantry. Discharged, June 30, 1864, by expiration of service.

KENNEDY, JOHN (Veteran). Son of Dennis and Mary, born in Saugus, May 14, 1840. Mustered, July 5, 1861. Private, Co. H., 1st Heavy Artillery. Promoted Corporal. Re-enlisted in the field, Dec. 7, 1863. Discharged, Aug. 16, 1865, by expiration of service, in Co. B.

KIMBALL, HENRY, G. Son of William and Elizabeth. Mustered, Sept. 12, 1862. Private, Co. G., 44th Regiment Infantry. Died, Jan. 1, 1863, of malarious fever at Newbern, N. C. Buried at Newbern, N. C.

LAVALETTE, PHILLIP C. (Veteran). Son of Nathaniel and Elizabeth C., born in Newburyport, Aug. 12, 1840. Mustered, July 5, 1861. Private, Co. H., 1st Heavy Artillery. Re-enlisted in the field, Dec. 7, 1863, to the credit of Ipswich. Mortally wounded in battle at Spottsylvania, May 19, 1864. Died at Washington, D. C., June 6, 1864.

LAWRENCE, JOHN H. Recruited in Boston. Mustered, Dec. 22, 1862. Private, Co. D., 2d Regiment Cavalry. Deserted, Jan. 17, 1863.

LEMON, WILLIAM H. Son of William and Elizabeth G., born in Andover, Nov. 10, 1845. Mustered, Jan. 2, 1865. Corporal, Co. D., 1st Battalion Frontier Cavalry. Discharged, June 30, 1865, by expiration of service.

LINDSEY, ROBERT. Son of James and Caroline, born in Scotland, May 31, 1834. Mustered, July 30, 1862. Private, Co. H., 1st Heavy Artillery. Discharged, July 8, 1864, by expiration of service.

LOGUE, CHARLES. Mustered, Nov. 25, 1861. Private, Co. F., 29th Regiment Infantry. Discharged, Jan. 9, 1864.

LOGUE, JAMES. Son of Patrick and Bridget. Mustered, July 7, 1862. Private, Co. H., 1st Heavy Artillery; was subsequently rejected on account of height, and was re-mustered, Oct. 1, 1862. Private, Co. G., 48th Regiment Infantry. Died, May 11, 1863, at Baton Rouge, La. Body not recovered.

LOGUE, JOHN (Veteran). Son of Charles and Catherine, born in Ireland, May 11, 1833. Mustered, July 5, 1861. Private, Co. H., 1st Heavy Artillery. Re-enlisted in the field, Dec. 7, 1863. Discharged, Aug. 16, 1865, by expiration of service, in Co. B.

LOVEJOY, BENJAMIN C. (Veteran). Son of William B. and Mary Ann, born in Dracut, Jan. 10, 1842. Mustered, July 5, 1861. Private, Co. H., 1st Heavy Artillery. Promoted Corporal. Re-enlisted in the field, Dec. 7, 1863. Discharged, Aug. 16, 1865, by expiration of service, in Co. B.

LOVEJOY, CHARLES W. (Veteran). Mustered, Jan. 16, 1862. Artificer, 7th Battery. Re-enlisted in the field, Jan. 17, 1864. Discharged, Nov. 10, 1865, by expiration of service.

LOVEJOY, GEORGE W. Son of Ballard and Pamelia, born in Brentwood, N. H., April 30, 1835. Mustered, Sept.1 2, 1862. Private, Co. A., 44th Regiment Infantry. Discharged, June 18, 1863, by expiration of service.

LOVEJOY, GEORGE W. Mustered, Aug. 21, 1861. Private, Co. B., 1st Regiment Infantry. Discharged, May 25, 1864, for expiration of service, as absent sick.

LOVEJOY, HENRY L. (Veteran). Son of Augustus and Mary, born in Boxford, Feb. 27, 1843. Mustered, July 5, 1861. Private, Co. H., 1st Heavy Artillery. Promoted Corporal. Re-enlisted in the field, March 21, 1864, to the credit of North Andover. Wounded severely in the face in battle of May 19, 1864. Discharged, July 31, 1865, as supernumerary. Died from the effects of a ball or shot that remained in his head.

LOVEJOY, JOSEPH T. Son of Ebenezer and Selina. Mustered, Sept. 20, 1862. Private, Co. H., 43d Regiment Infantry. Discharged, July 30, 1863, by expiration of service.

LOVEJOY, NEWTON. Son of William B. and Mary Ann, born in Dracut, April 27, 1843. Enlisted, April, 1862. Private, Co. F., 13th U. S. Infantry. Died, July 9, 1863, of disease, in the Hospital of the 15th Army Corps at Vicksburg, Miss. Body not recovered.

LOVEJOY, WILLIAM W. Son of William B. and Mary Ann, born in Andover, Oct. 1, 1837. Mustered, May 25, 1861. Private, Co. B., 2d Regiment Infantry. Discharged, May 28, 1864, by expiration of service. Wounded at Reseca, Ga.

LUKE, WILLIAM H. Mustered, May 23, 1861. Private, Co. H., 1st Regiment Infantry. Died, Sept. 13, 1862, from wounds received in 2d Battle Bull Run, Aug. 29, 1862. Buried at North Andover.

LUSCOMB, AARON E. (Veteran). Son of Aaron N. and Margaret, born in Andover, July 25, 1840. Mustered, July 22, 1862. Private, Co. H., 1st Heavy Artillery. Re-enlisted in the field, Feb. 29, 1864, to the credit of Charlestown. Discharged, Dec. 19, 1864, for disability. Lost his right arm before Petersburg, June 22, 1864.

LYMAN, EDWARD E. Mustered, Dec. 31, 1864. Private, Co. L., 3d Regiment Cavalry. Discharged, Sept. 28, 1865, by expiration of service, in Co. E.

LYON, JOHN. Recruited in Boston. Mustered, Dec. 12, 1862. Unassigned recruit, 22d Regiment Infantry. "Bounty Jumper"; never joined the Regiment.

MAHONEY, MICHAEL (Veteran). Son of Richard and Ellen W., born in Ireland, May 10, 1827. Mustered, July 5, 1861. Private, Co. H., 1st Heavy Artillery. Re-enlisted in the field, Dec. 7, 1863. Deserted,* July 30, 1865, in Co. B.

MALONE, JOHN. Born in Liverpool, England, and recruited in Boston. Mustered, Dec. 10, 1862. Unassigned recruit, 22d Regiment Infantry. "Bounty Jumper"; never joined the Regiment.

MARLAND, CHARLES H. Son of William S. and Sarah N., born in Andover, April 5, 1843. Mustered, Sept. 12, 1862. Private, Co. G., 44th Infantry. Discharged, June 18, 1863, by expiration of service.

MARLAND, WILLIAM. Son of William S. and Sarah N., born in Andover, March 11, 1839. Mustered, April 22, 1861. Sergeant, Co. F., 6th Infantry (3 months). Discharged, Aug. 2, 1861, by expiration of service. Re-mustered, Dec. 18, 1861. 2d Lieutenant, 2d Battery. Promoted 1st Lieutenant, Oct. 22, 1862. Promoted Captain, Jan. 8, 1865. Discharged, Aug. 11, 1865, by expiration of service. Brevet Major.

MASON, EDWARD. Son of Thomas C. and Phebe, born in Andover, April 19, 1831. Mustered, Nov. 7, 1863. Private, Co. H., 1st Heavy Artillery. Discharged, Oct. 27, 1864, for disability.

MASON, ERI. Mustered, Jan. 2, 1865. Unassigned recruit, 3d Regiment Cavalry.

MASON, JOSIAH. Son of Thomas C. and Phebe, born in Andover, May 30, 1822. Mustered, Sept. 2, 1861. Private, 1st Co. Sharpshooters. Discharged, April 28, 1862, for disability. Died, April 27, 1863, of disease contracted in service. Buried in South Cemetery.

MASON, WALTER B. Mustered, Nov. 7, 1863. Private, Co. H., 1st Heavy Artillery. Transferred, May 1, 1865, to Veteran Reserve Corps. Wounded in the back, June 16, 1864, at Bryant's Farm.

MASON, WARREN. Son of Thomas C. and Phebe, born in Andover, May 15, 1826. Mustered, Sept. 10, 1861. Private, Co. F., 26th Regiment Infantry. Discharged, July 1862, for disability. Accidentally injured.

---

* See note in Appendix.

MAYNARD, CHARLES (Veteran). Son of Charles and Sophia, born in Andover, July 4, 1845. Mustered, July 22, 1862. Private, Co. H., 1st Heavy Artillery. Re-enlisted in the field, Feb. 29, 1864, to the credit of Roxbury. Discharged, July 30, 1865, by expiration of service, in Co. B.

McANDREWS, JOHN. Born in Havre-de-Grace, Md., and recruited in Boston. Mustered, Dec. 12, 1862. Unassigned recruit, 22d Regiment Infantry. " Bounty Jumper"; never joined the Regiment.

McCABE, FRANK (Veteran). Son of James and Ann T., born in Ireland, July 12, 1832. Mustered, July 21, 1862. Private, Co. H., 1st Heavy Artillery. Re-enlisted in the field, Jan. 2, 1864. Discharged, Aug. 16, 1865, by expiration of service, in Co. B.

McCARTY, CHARLES. Born, and recruited in Boston. Mustered, Dec. 10, 1862. Unassigned recruit, 22d Regiment Infantry. " Bounty Jumper"; never joined the Regiment.

McCLENNA, CHARLES W. (Veteran). Son of William and Deborah, born in Westford, Jan. 24, 1835. Mustered, July 5, 1861. Private, Co. H., 1st Heavy Artillery. Promoted Corporal, March 1, 1862. Re-enlisted in the field, Jan. 2, 1864. Promoted Sergeant. Discharged, Aug. 25, 1865, by expiration of service, in Co. B.

McCULLOUGH, JOHN. Born in Ireland, June 7, 1823. Mustered, July 14, 1864. Private, Co. K., 6th Infantry (100 days). Discharged, Oct. 27, 1864, by expiration of service. Died, Dec. 24, 1864, of disease contracted in the service. Buried in the Catholic Cemetery.

McCUSKER, JAMES. Son of James and Elizabeth, born in Ireland, May 5, 1827. Mustered, July 13, 1864. Private, Co. H., 1st Heavy Artillery. Captured by the rebels, Oct. 2, 1864. Died, Dec. 2, 1864, a prisoner of war at Salisbury, N. C. Buried in the trenches.

McGURK, BERNARD (Veteran). Son of Owen and Bridget, born in Ireland, May 18, 1826. Mustered, July 5, 1861. Private, Co. H., 1st Heavy Artillery. Re-enlisted in the field, Dec. 7, 1863. Killed at Cold Harbor, Va., June 3, 1864, while on duty with his Company and Regiment supporting a line of pickets. Was buried by his Company on the field.

DURING THE REBELLION.

McKENZIE, JOHN. Mustered, Oct. 20, 1863. Private, Co. G., 3d Heavy Artillery. Discharged, Sept. 18, 1865, by expiration of service.

McLAUGHLIN, JOHN. Son of James and Bridget, born in Ireland, June 7, 1844. Mustered, March 15, 1862. Private, Co. H., 1st Heavy Artillery. Discharged, March 14, 1865, by expiration of service. Wounded in the hip at Bryant's Farm, June 16, 1864.

MEARS, CALVIN. Son of Warren. Mustered, Feb. 22, 1864. Private, Co. H., 1st Heavy Artillery. Discharged, Aug, 16, 1865, by expiration of service, in Co. B.

MEARS, CHARLES. Son of Daniel and Mary, born in Andover, July 17, 1838. Mustered, July 5, 1861. Private, Co. H., 1st Heavy Artillery. Discharged, July 8, 1864, by expiration of service. Lost right arm in battle at Spottsylvania, May 19, 1864.

MEARS, DANIEL, Jr. Mustered, July 13, 1861. Private, Co. I., 11th Regiment Infantry. Discharged, June 24, 1864, by expiration of service.

MEARS, GEORGE (Veteran). Mustered, June 13, 1861. Private, Co. I., 11th Infantry, to the credit of Charlestown. Re-enlisted in the field, March 26, 1864, to the credit of Andover. Discharged, July 14, 1865, by expiration of service.

MEARS, JOHN (Veteran). Son of Daniel. Mustered, July 7, 1862. Private, Co. H., 1st Heavy Artillery. Was rejected, July 22, 1862. Re-mustered, Aug. 4, 1863. Private, Co. C., 2d Heavy Artillery. Transferred, May 17, 1864, to Navy. Re-mustered, Dec. 30, 1864. Private, Co. L., 3d Cavalry. Discharged, Sept. 28, 1865, by expiration of service, in Co. E.

MEARS, WARREN, Jr. Son of Warren and Abigail M., born in Andover, Aug. 8, 1830. Mustered, July 5, 1861. Private, Co. H., 1st Heavy Artillery. Discharged, July 8, 1864, by expiration of service.

MEARS, WILLIAM. Son of Zebadiah and Sarah, born in Andover, Sept. 29, 1829. Mustered, Aug. 2, 1862. Private, Co. H., 1st Heavy Artillery. Discharged, April 15, 1864, for disability.

MELCHER, SYLVESTER C. (Veteran). Son of Edward and Relief, born in Manchester, N. H., Feb. 20, 1838. Mustered, July 5, 1861. Private, Co. H., 1st Heavy Artillery. Promoted Corporal, May 11, 1863. Re-enlisted in the field, Dec. 7, 1863. Promoted Sergeant. Discharged, July 31, 1865, as supernumerary.

MELENDY, GEORGE. Mustered, Aug. 30, 1864. Private, Co. D., 2d Heavy Artillery. Transferred, Feb. 9, 1865, to 17th Regiment Infantry. Discharged, June 30, 1865, by order of War Department.

MERRILL, EDWARD C. Son of Edward S. and Sarah, born in Andover, March 17, 1838. Mustered, Nov. 7, 1861. Private, 4th Battery. Died, Aug. 27, 1862, at Carrolton, La., of congestion of the brain. Body not recovered.

MERRILL, FRANK H. Mustered, April 22, 1861. Private, Co. F., 6th Regiment Infantry (3 months). Discharged, Aug. 2, 1861, by expiration of service.

MERRILL, JAMES W. Son of James and Susan B., born in Methuen, July 23, 1842. Mustered, Sept. 26, 1862. Private, Co. F., 45th Regiment Infantry. Died, Jan. 20, 1863, at Newbern, N.C. Buried in West Parish Cemetery.

MERRILL, JOHN H. Mustered, Sept. 1, 1864. Private, Co. B., 11th Regiment Infantry. Discharged, June 4, 1865, by expiration of service.

MERRILL, WILLIAM F. Son of James H. and Lucia G., born in Montague, July 14, 1842. Mustered, July 22, 1862. Private, Co. H., 1st Heavy Artillery. Promoted 2d Lieutenant, Feb. 23, 1864. Transferred to 3d Heavy Artillery, March 6, 1864. Promoted 1st Lieutenant, April 9, 1865, and assigned to 13th Unattached Co., Heavy Artillery. Resigned, June 13, 1865.

MESSER, CYRUS (Veteran). Mustered, July 5, 1861. Private, Co. B., 1st Heavy Artillery. Re-enlisted in the field, Dec. 7, 1863, to the credit of Methuen. Discharged, Aug. 16, 1865, by expiration of service.

MILKINS, WILLIAM. Mustered, Aug. 26, 1864. Private, 29th Unattached Co., Heavy Artillery. Discharged, June 16, 1865, by expiration of service.

MOAR, CHARLES G. Son of Joshua and Mary E., born in Andover, April 1, 1842. Mustered, Sept. 12, 1862. Private, Co. I., 44th Regiment Infantry. Discharged, June 18, 1863, by expiration of service.

MORGAN, DAVID S. Son of David and Roxanna, born in Johnson, Vt., Jan. 24, 1835. Mustered, Aug. 22, 1862. Private, Co. H., 1st Heavy Artillery. Wounded, May 19, 1864. Discharged, July 8, 1864, by expiration of service.

MORRISON, CHARLES W. Mustered, Dec. 31, 1864. Bugler, Co. L., 3d Regiment Cavalry. Discharged, Sept. 28, 1865, by expiration of service.

MORRISON, JOHN. Born in Albany, N. Y., and recruited in Boston. Mustered, Dec. 8, 1862. Unassigned recruit, 22d Regiment Infantry. "Bounty Jumper"; never joined the Regiment.

MORSE, WILLIAM B. Son of John C. and Catherine, born in Andover, Sept. 14, 1841. Mustered, July 5, 1861. Private, Co. H. 1st Heavy Artillery. Discharged, July 8, 1864, by expiration of service. Slightly wounded at Spottsylvania, May 19, 1864. Lost left leg at Bryant's Farm, near Petersburg, Va., June 16, 1864.

MORTON, CHARLES H. Born in Oswego, N. Y., and recruited in Boston. Mustered, Dec. 12, 1862. Unassigned recruit, 22d Regiment Infantry. "Bounty Jumper"; never joined the Regiment.

MORTON, DOUGLAS. Son of William and Jessie, born in Scotland. Mustered, July 21, 1862. Private, Co. H., 1st Heavy Artillery. Discharged, July 8, 1864, by expiration of service.

MOULTON, CHARLES L. Mustered, Aug. 31, 1864. Private, Co. B., 11th Regiment Infantry. Discharged, June 4, 1865, by expiration of service.

MURPHY, WILLIAM. Born in London, England, and recruited in Boston. Mustered, Dec. 11, 1862. Unassigned recruit, 22d Regiment Infantry. Not on "Record of Massachusetts Volunteers." "Bounty Jumper"; never joined the Regiment.

MURRAY, JAMES R. Son of Walter and Christina, born in Andover, March 17, 1841. Mustered, July 21, 1862. Private, Co. H., 1st Heavy Artillery. Discharged, July 8, 1864, by expiration of service.

NICHOLS, WILLIAM W. Mustered, July 5, 1861. Private, Co. H., 1st Heavy Artillery. Discharged, July 8, 1864, by expiration of service.

NICKERSON, EPHRAIM N. (Veteran). Son of Elisha and Lucy R., born in Belfast, Me., Feb. 23, 1833. Mustered, Sept. 12, 1861. Private, Co. F., 26th Regiment Infantry. Promoted Sergeant. Re-enlisted in the field, Jan. 5, 1864. Discharged, Aug. 26, 1865, by expiration of service.

NOLAN, MALACHI. Son of John and Bridget, born in Galway, Ireland, Aug. 21, 1833. Mustered, July 30, 1862. Private, Co. H., 1st Heavy Artillery. Wounded, May 19, 1864. Discharged, July 8, 1864, by expiration of service.

NOONAN, DANIEL. Mustered, March 24, 1862. Unassigned recruit, 1st Heavy Artillery.

NOYES, AARON. Son of Wadleigh. Mustered, Aug. 31, 1862. Private, Co. D., 6th Regiment Infantry (9 months). Discharged, June 3, 1863, by expiration of service.

O'BRIEN, JOHN. Born in Cork, Ireland. Mustered, July 22, 1862. Private, Co. H., 1st Heavy Artillery. Discharged, July 8, 1864, by expiration of service.

O'BRIEN, JOHN. Born, and recruited in Boston. Mustered, Dec. 12, 1862. Unassigned recruit, 22d Regiment Infantry. "Bounty Jumper"; never joined the Regiment.

O'CONNER, PATRICK. Mustered, July 28, 1862. Private. Unassigned recruit, 1st Heavy Artillery.

O'HARRA, EDWARD (Veteran). Son of James and Margaret, born in Ireland, Dec. 25, 1837. Mustered, July 5, 1861. Private, Co. H., 1st Heavy Artillery. Re-enlisted in the field, Dec. 7, 1863. Killed, Oct. 27, 1864, at Hatcher's Run, Va., while making reconnoisance with his Division; being obliged to abandon the position, his body was left on the field unburied.

O'MALLY, THOMAS. Mustered, Dec. 29, 1863. Private, Co. F., 19th Regiment Infantry. Discharged, June 30, 1865, by expiration of service.

OWENS, REDMAN. Enlisted, June 2, 1864. Private, 19th Regiment U. S. Infantry.

PACKARD, EDWARD W. Son of Hubbard V. and Olive P., born in Cambridge, Oct. 7, 1846. Mustered, July 14, 1864. Private, Co. K., 6th Regiment Infantry (100 days). Discharged, Oct. 27, 1864, by expiration of service.

PARKER, CALEB O. (Veteran). Mustered, July 5, 1861. Private, Co. B., 1st Heavy Artillery. Discharged, April 28, 1864, for disability. Re-mustered, Aug. 8, 1864. Private, Veteran Reserve Corps. Discharged, Oct. 1, 1864.

PARKER, GEORGE W. Mustered, Oct. 19, 1861. Private, Co. D., 24th Regiment Infantry. Discharged, April 23, 1863, for disability.

PARKER, JOHN F. Son of Caleb O. Mustered, July 7, 1862. Private. Unassigned recruit, 1st Heavy Artillery. Discharged before the recruits left Readville for the army. Re-mustered, Aug. 4, 1863. Private, Co. C., 2d Heavy Artillery. Transferred, May, 17, 1864, to the Navy.

PASHO, WILLIAM A. (Veteran). Son of Henry F. and Nancy, born in Andover, May 3, 1838. Mustered, July 5, 1861. Private, Co. H., 1st Heavy Artillery. Re-enlisted in the field, Dec. 4, 1863. Discharged, Aug. 16, 1865, by expiration of service, in Co. B.

PATRICK, ANDREW K. Son of Andrew K. and Elizabeth, born in Patterson, N. J., Nov. 27, 1847. Mustered, April 21, 1864. Private, Co. K., 59th Infantry. Wounded in the right breast, May 12, 1865, at Spottsylvania, was in Fredericksburg Hospital on 19th same month; has not been heard from since, except by report of his comrades that "he is dead." Body not recovered.

PETERSON, GEORGE (Veteran). Mustered, July 31, 1861. Private, Co. I., 1st Heavy Artillery. Re-enlisted in the field, Dec. 7, 1863, to the credit of Danvers. Transferred, Jan. 28, 1864, to the Navy.

PHILLIPS, PATRICK. Son of Michael. Mustered, Aug. 6, 1862. Private, Co. K., 3d Regiment Cavalry. Deserted, March 1, 1863.

PIKE, GEORGE E. Son of Willard and Mary, born in Lowell, Jan. 3, 1835. Mustered, July 5, 1861. Private, Co. H., 1st Heavy Artillery. Promoted Corporal, March 1, 1862. Wounded, May 19, 1864, at Spottsylvania. Discharged, July 8, 1864, by expiration of service.

POOR, CHARLES H. Son of William and Hannah G., born in Methuen, May 25, 1832. Mustered, July 6, 1861. 1st Lieutenant, Co. H., 1st Heavy Artillery. Resigned, Oct. 24, 1862.

PORTER, THOMAS F. (Veteran). Mustered, Oct. 10, 1861. Private, Co. I., 23d Regiment Infantry, to the credit of North Andover. Re-enlisted in the field, Dec. 3, 1863, to the credit of Andover. Died of wounds, April 15, 1864, at Hampton, Va.

PRAY, SEAVER. Mustered, Aug. 27, 1861. Private, Co. K., 20th Regiment Infantry. Discharged, Oct. 31, 1862, for disability.

QUALEY, PATRICK. Mustered, Sept. 3, 1864. Private, Co. B., 11th Regiment Infantry. Discharged, June 4, 1865, by expiration of service.

RAYMOND, EDWARD G. Son of Samuel and Emily F. M., born in Charlestown, May 26, 1843. Mustered, Sept. 12, 1862. Private, Co. G., 44th Regiment Infantry. Discharged, June 18, 1863, by expiration of service.

RAYMOND, JEFFERSON N. Mustered, Sept. 18, 1861. Private, Co. D., 26th Regiment Infantry. Died, Sept. 13, 1862, at New Orleans, La.

RAYMOND, WALTER L. (Veteran). Son of Samuel and Emily F. M., born in Charlestown, Aug. 23, 1846. Mustered, Sept. 12, 1862. Private Co. G., 44th Regiment Infantry. Discharged, June 18, 1863, by expiration of service. Re-mustered, Jan. 6, 1864. Private, Co. L., new Battalion, 1st Regiment Cavalry. Captured near Malvern Hill, Va., Aug, 16, 1864. Died, a prisoner of war at Salisbury, N. C., Dec. 25, 1864. Buried in the trenches.

RAY, AARON G., Jr. Son of Aaron G. and Mary, born in Andover, March 2, 1834. Mustered, July 5, 1861. Private, Co. H., 1st Heavy Artillery. Promoted Artificer, March 1, 1862. Discharged, July 8, 1864, by expiration of service.

RICHARDSON, SILAS, Jr. Son of Silas and Sally, born in Charlestown, Jan. 16, 1830. Mustered, July 5, 1861. Private, Co. H., 1st Heavy Artillery. Promoted Corporal, March 11, 1863. Discharged, July 8, 1864, by expiration of service. Died, June, 1874, at Reading, of disease contracted in the service. Buried in South Cemetery.

RIDLEY, CHARLES. W. (Veteran). Son of Amos and Tabitha R., born in Lynn, Aug. 11, 1842. Mustered, July 22, 1862. Private, Co. H., 1st Heavy Artillery. Re-enlisted in the field, Feb. 29, 1864, to the credit of Charlestown. Killed, May 19, 1864, in battle at Spottsylvania, Va. Buried on the field.

RILEY, JOHN. Born in Ireland, and recruited in Boston. Mustered, Dec. 11, 1862. Unassigned recruit, 22d Regiment Infantry. "Bounty Jumper"; never joined the Regiment.

ROBERTS, GEORGE. Mustered, Aug. 4, 1863. Private, Co. C., 2d Heavy Artillery. Discharged, Sept. 3, 1865, by expiration of service, in Co. B.

ROGERS, L. WALDO. Son of Benjamin. Mustered, Sept. 12, 1862. Corporal, Co. A., 44th Regiment Infantry. Discharged, June 18, 1863; by expiration of service.

ROLLINS, ROBERT (Colored). Son of Robert and Nancy, born in Queenstown, Md., July 22, 1828. Mustered, Nov. 28, 1863. Private, Co. A., 54th Regiment Infantry. Discharged, Aug. 20, 1865, by expiration of service.

ROTHWELL, JAMES H. Son of George and Elizabeth, born in Andover, Aug. 31, 1842. Mustered, July 22, 1862. Private, Co. H., 1st Heavy Artillery. Killed, May 19, 1864, in battle at Spottsylvania, Va. Buried on the field.

ROWLEY, R. AUGUSTUS. Son of Reuben and Mary Ann, born in Wrentham, Jan. 6, 1843. Mustered, Oct. 19, 1861. Private Magee's Independent Co. Cavalry; subsequently attached to 41st Infantry. Promoted Corporal, Sept. 1, 1862. Sergeant, Sept. 2, 1863. 1st Lieutenant 4th U. S. Colored Cavalry, April 8, 1864. Mustered out as 1st Lieutenant, March 20, 1865, at New Orleans, La.

RUSSELL, AUGUSTINE K. (Veteran). Son of John G. and Hannah, born in Bradford, June 24, 1820. Mustered, July 29, 1862. Private, Co. H., 1st Heavy Artillery. Re-enlisted in the field, Jan. 4, 1864. Discharged, June 2, 1865, for disability. Wounded, lost a foot, at Spottsylvania, May 19, 1864.

RUSSELL, JAMES. Son of Israel and Isabella, born in Biddeford, Me., Feb. 3, 1846. Mustered, Aug. 4, 1862. Private, Co. H., 1st Heavy Artillery. Died, at Fort Albany, Va., in the Regimental Hospital, Oct. 19, 1862. Buried in South Cemetery.

RUSSELL, JOHN B. A. (Veteran). Son of Edward and Caroline A., born in Andover, Aug. 11, 1840. Mustered, July 5, 1861. Private, Co. H., 1st Heavy Artillery. Promoted Corporal, March 1, 1862. Re-enlisted in the field, Dec. 7, 1863. Promoted Sergeant. Discharged, Aug. 16, 1865, by expiration of service, in Co. B.

RUSSELL, JOHN R. Mustered, Aug. 22, 1864. Private, 29th Unattached Co., Heavy Artillery. Discharged, June 16, 1865, by expiration of service.

RUSSELL, JOSEPH, Jr. Mustered, July 5, 1861. Private, Co. H., 1st Heavy Artillery. Discharged, Nov. 24, 1861, for disability.

RUSSELL, WILLIAM (Veteran). Son of Joseph and Sarah H., born in Andover, March 13, 1833. Mustered, July 5, 1861. Private, Co. H., 1st Heavy Artillery. Re-enlisted in the field, Dec. 4, 1863. Mortally wounded at Cold Harbor, Va., June 3, 1864. Died, July 11, 1864, at Washington, D.C. Buried in South Cemetery.

RUSSELL, WINSLOW (Veteran). Son of Edward and Caroline A., born in Andover, April 17, 1833. Mustered, July 5, 1861. Private, Co. H., 1st Heavy Artillery. Discharged, July 8, 1864, by expiration of service. Re-mustered, Aug. 17, 1864. Private, Co. I., 4th Heavy Artillery. Promoted Corporal. Promoted Sergeant. Discharged, June 17, 1865, by expiration of service.

RYLEY, LEONARD W. Mustered, Jan. 5, 1864. Sergeant, Co. B., 59th Regiment Infantry. Transferred to Veteran Reserve Corps, April 25, 1865. Discharged, —— ——. Died, Aug. 30, 1865, of disease contracted in the service. Buried in the Episcopal Cemetery.

SANBORN, FRANK. Mustered, April 22, 1861. Private, Co. F., 6th Regiment Infantry (3 months). Discharged, Aug. 2, 1861, by expiration of service.

SARGENT, HERBERT N. Mustered, Dec. 31, 1864. Private, Co. L., 3d Regiment Cavalry. Discharged, Sept. 28, 1865, by expiration of service, in Co. E.

SARGENT, JOHN S. (Veteran). Son of John and Margaret, born in Brooklyn, N.Y., July 21, 1841. Mustered, July 5, 1861. Private, Co. H., 1st Heavy Artillery. Promoted Corporal, Aug. 21, 1861. Promoted Sergeant, Feb. 6, 1862. Re-enlisted in the field, Dec. 7, 1863. Promoted 1st Sergeant. Wounded, May 19, 1864. Discharged, July 31, 1865, as supernumerary.

SAUNDERS, JAMES, Jr. (Veteran). Son of James and Ann W., born in Andover, May 25, 1846. Mustered, July 22, 1862. Private, Co. H., 1st Heavy Artillery. Discharged, July 8, 1864, by expiration of service. Re-mustered, Dec. 30, 1864. Private, Co. B., 1st Battalion Frontier Cavalry. Discharged, June 30, 1865, by expiration of service.

SAUNDERS, THOMAS. Mustered, Sept. 2, 1861. Private, Co. E., 24th Regiment Infantry. Discharged, June 10, 1863, for disability.

SAUNDERS, ZIBA M. Son of Ziba and Huldah, born in Tewksbury, Feb. 20, 1840. Mustered, July 5, 1861. Private, Co. H., 1st Heavy Artillery. Discharged, July 8, 1864, by expiration of service. In hospital much of the time, sick.

SEARLES, JAMES H. Mustered, Nov. 20, 1863. Private, Co. E., 1st Regiment Cavalry. Discharged, June 26, 1865, by expiration of service.

SHANNON, JOHN. Mustered, June 13, 1861. Private, Co. D., 11th Regiment Infantry. Discharged, June 24, 1864, by expiration of service.

SHANNON, WILLIAM (Veteran). Son of John and Jane, born in Boston, July 8, 1842. Mustered, July 5, 1861. Private, Co. H., 1st Heavy Artillery. Re-enlisted in the field, Dec. 11, 1863, to the credit of Boston. Promoted Corporal. Promoted Sergeant. Discharged, Aug. 16, 1865, by expiration of service, in Co. B. .

SHATTUCK, CHARLES M. Mustered, March 31, 1864. Private, 3d U. S. Artillery.

SHATTUCK, CHARLES WM. Son of Charles and Rosetta H., born in Andover, May 24, 1843. Mustered, July 5, 1861. Private, Co. H., 1st Heavy Artillery. Discharged, Nov. 24, 1861, for disability, sick. Re-mustered, Aug. 19, 1862. Private, Co. F., 35th Regiment Infantry. Promoted Corporal. Promoted Sergeant. Discharged, June 9, 1865, by expiration of service.

SHATTUCK, LEONARD G. (Veteran). Son of Simeon and Anstiss, born in Andover, June 26, 1840. Mustered, July 22, 1862. Private, Co. H., 1st Heavy Artillery. Re-enlisted in the field, Feb. 29, 1864, to the credit of Charlestown. Transferred to Veteran Reserve Corps, Oct. 15, 1864.

SHERMAN, HENRY T. (Veteran). Son of Seth and Mary, born in Andover, Nov. 25, 1834. Mustered, July 5, 1861. Private, Co. H., 1st Heavy Artillery. Re-enlisted in the field, Dec. 4, 1863. Discharged, Aug. 16, 1865, by expiration of service, in Co. B.

SHIELDS, NICHOLAS. Son of Robert and Catherine, born in Ireland, June 26, 1826. Mustered, Feb. 24, 1862. Private, Co. H., 1st Heavy Artillery. Discharged, July 8, 1864, by expiration of service.

SKERRITT, JAMES. Mustered, Nov. 21, 1863. Private, Co. F., 19th Regiment Infantry. Captured by the rebels, July 22, 1864. Paroled at Salisbury, N. C., on termination of the war. Discharged, July 24, 1865, by expiration of service.

SMART, GEORGE M. Son of Hugh and Jane M., born in Andover, Oct. 12, 1845. Mustered, July 5, 1861. Drummer, Co. H., 1st Heavy Artillery. Died, at Fort Albany, Va., July 25, 1862, of chronic disease, the effects of fever and ague. Buried in South Cemetery.

SMITH, CHARLES. Born in Philadelphia, Pa., and recruited in Boston, Mustered, Dec. 12, 1862. Unassigned recruit, 22d Regiment Infantry. " Bounty Jumper"; never joined the Regiment.

SMITH, GEORGE. Mustered, June 2, 1864. Private, 19th Regiment U. S. Infantry.

SMITH, JAMES (Veteran). Son of John and Sarah, born in Ireland, Dec. 10, 1840. Mustered, July 5, 1861. Private, Co. H., 1st Heavy Artillery. Re-enlisted in the field, Dec. 4, 1863. Discharged, Aug. 16, 1865, by expiration of service, in Co. B.

SMITH, JAMES B. Son of Peter and Rebecca B., born in Andover, Oct. 1, 1828. Mustered, Aug. 9, 1862. Private, Co. A., 33d Regiment Infantry. Discharged, Aug. 30, 1863, for disability.

SMITH, JOHN. Mustered, Feb. 20, 1865. Private, Co. H., 17th Regiment Infantry. Discharged, July 11, 1865, by expiration of service.

SMITH, JOHN. Substitute for O. S. Morse. Mustered, July 28, 1864. Private, Co. A., 28th Regiment Infantry. Deserted, Nov., 1864.

SMITH, PETER D. Son of Peter and Esther H., born in Andover, Aug. 24, 1842. Mustered, July 5, 1861. Corporal, Co. H., 1st Heavy Artillery. Promoted Sergeant, Feb. 16, 1862. Promoted 2d Lieutenant and assigned to Co. G., Aug. 3, 1863. Wounded, lost two fingers at Spottsylvania, May 19, 1864. Discharged, for disability, Aug. 1, 1864.

SMITH, ROBERT. Mustered, Jan. 2, 1865. Private, Co. C., 1st Battalion Frontier Cavalry. Discharged, June 30, 1865, by expiration of service.

SMITH, THOMAS. Son of Thomas and Betsy, born in Andover, March 21, 1820. Mustered, July 22, 1862. Private, Co. H., 1st Heavy Artillery. Discharged, July 8, 1864, by expiration of service.

SPRADLEY, RANDAL (Colored). Of Surrey Co., Va. Representative Recruit for Edward Taylor. Mustered in at Fortress Monroe, Va., Dec. 24, 1864. Private, 1st Regiment U. S. Colored Cavalry.

SPRINGER, EUGENE. Mustered, Dec. 7, 1863. Private, Co. G., 2d Heavy Artillery. Discharged, Dec. 16, 1863, rejected recruit.

STANDING, GEORGE (Veteran). Son of William and Mary, born in England, 1828. Mustered, Dec. 13, 1861. Private, Co. F., 28th Regiment Infantry, to the credit of Lawrence. Re-enlisted in the field, Jan. 2, 1864, to the credit of Andover. Discharged, May 12, 1865, for disability.

STANTON, MICHAEL. Born in Ireland, and recruited in Boston. Mustered, Dec. 10, 1862. Unassigned recruit, 22d Regiment Infantry. "Bounty Jumper"; never joined the Regiment.

STANWOOD, LAWRENCE. Mustered, Feb. 21, 1865. Private, Co. F., 1st Battalion Heavy Artillery. Discharged, June 24, 1865, by expiration of service.

STEPHENS, ANDREW (Colored). Of Georgia. Representative Recruit for the Town of Andover. Mustered in at Hilton Head, S. C., March 4, 1865. Private, 70th Regiment, U. S. Colored Infantry.

STEPHENS, GEORGE W. Son of Thomas, born in Mt. Gilead, Ohio, Jan. 22, 1843. Mustered, July 22, 1862. Private, Co. H., 1st Heavy Artillery. Discharged, July 8, 1864, by expiration of service. Lamed by accident, not in battle.

STEPHENSON, ALBA. Mustered, Dec. 30, 1864. Private, Co. B., 1st Battalion Frontier Cavalry. Discharged, June 30, 1865, by expiration of service.

STEVENS, BENJAMIN F. (Veteran). Son of Benjamin and Huldah, born in Andover, Aug. 3, 1839. Mustered, July 5, 1861. Private, Co. H., 1st Heavy Artillery. Promoted Corporal, March 11, 1863. Re-enlisted in the field, Dec. 5, 1863. Promoted Quarter-Master-Sergeant, July 1, 1865. Discharged, Aug. 16, 1865, by expiration of service.

STEVENS, B. WENDELL. Mustered, Sept. 1, 1864. Private, Co. H., 2d Heavy Artillery. Discharged, June 29, 1865, by expiration of service.

STEVENS, DANIEL. Son of Daniel C. Mustered, July 14, 1864. Private, Co. K., 6th Regiment Infantry (100 days). Discharged, Oct. 27, 1864, by expiration of service.

STEVENS, JAMES W. Mustered, July 5, 1861. Private, Co. F., 1st Heavy Artillery. Discharged, April 9, 1864, for disability.

STEWART, GEORGE. Son of George and Helen W., born in Scotland, Jan. 18, 1825. Mustered, July 14, 1864. Private, Co. K., 6th Regiment Infantry (100 days). Discharged, Oct. 27, 1864, by expiration of service.

STEWART, JOHN W. Son of George and ———. Born in ———, 18—. Mustered, July 14, 1864. Private, Co. K., 6th Regiment Infantry (100 days). Discharged, Oct. 27, 1864, by expiration of service.

STOTT, JOSHUA H. Son of James and Phebe, born in Canada, Sept. 1, 1824. Mustered, Oct. 5, 1861. Private, Co. G., 1st Regiment Cavalry. Transferred to Veteran Reserve Corps, Jan. 15, 1864. Discharged, Oct. 1, 1864. Was hurt by the falling of his horse, July 10, 1863; was sent to hospital, where he remained until transferred to V. R. C.

STOWE, FREDERICK W. Son of Calvin E. and Harriet B., born in Cincinnati, Ohio, May 5, 1840. Mustered, May 23, 1861. Private, Co. A., 1st Regiment Infantry. Promoted Sergeant. Transferred and Promoted 2d Lieutenant 1st Heavy Artillery, Jan. 18, 1862. Promoted A. A. G., rank of Captain, Jan. 27, 1863, and transferred to General Steinwehr's Brigade. Wounded at Gettysburg.

SYLVESTER, WILLIAM. Born in England, and recruited in Boston. Mustered, Dec. 11, 1862. Unassigned recruit, 22d Regiment Infantry. "Bounty Jumper"; never joined the Regiment.

TAYLOR, GEORGE H. Son of Samuel H. and Caroline P., born in Andover, June 19, 1840. Mustered, Nov. —, 1863. 2d Lieutenant, 79th U.S. Volunteers. Promoted 1st Lieutenant, March, 1864. Served on General Staff, Department of the Gulf, through the Red River Campaign.

THOMAS, LEWIS. Mustered by Provost-Marshal Herrick, Dec. 30, 1864. 1st Battalion Frontier Cavalry. Not down in "Record Mass. Vols."

THOMAS, NICHOLAS (Colored). Of Warren Co., Miss. Representative Recruit for the Town of Andover. Mustered in at Vicksburg, Miss., March 4, 1865. Private, 5th Regiment U. S. Colored Heavy Artillery.

THOMPSON, WILLIAM. Recruited in Boston. Mustered, Dec. 8, 1862. Unassigned recruit, 22d Regiment Infantry. "Bounty Jumper"; never joined the Regiment.

TOMLINSON, EDWIN A. Mustered, Aug. 22, 1864. Private, 29th Unattached Co., Heavy Artillery. Discharged, June 16, 1865, by expiration of service.

TOWNLEY, JOHN J. Mustered, June 26, 1861. Private, Co. A., 12th Regiment Infantry. Deserted, Feb. 28, 1863. Said to have been taken prisoner at Bull Run. Paroled on exchange, and not heard from since.

TOWNSEND, MILTON B. Son of Charles J. and Mary M., born in Andover, Aug. 26, 1839. Mustered, July 5, 1861. Private, Co. H., 1st Heavy Artillery. Promoted Corporal, March 1, 1862. Discharged, July 8, 1864, by expiration of service.

TOWNSEND, WARREN W. (Veteran). Son of Charles J. and Mary M., born in Andover, Sept. 28, 1836. Mustered, July 5, 1861. Private, Co. H., 1st Heavy Artillery. Re-enlisted in the field, Dec. 11, 1863. Discharged, Aug. 16, 1865, by expiration of service, in Co. B.

TRACY, WILLIAM W. Son of Stephen and Alice H., born in Hudson, Ohio, May 21, 1845. Mustered, Sept. 26, 1862. Private, Co. D., 45th Regiment Infantry. Discharged, July 7, 1863, by expiration of service.

TRAINOR, JOHN. Mustered, Oct. 20, 1863. Private, Co. G., 3d Heavy Artillery. Discharged, Sept. 18, 1865, by expiration of service.

TRASK, ELBRIDGE P. Mustered, Aug. 22, 1864. Private, 29th Unattached Co., Heavy Artillery. Discharged, June 16, 1865, by expiration of service.

TRULAN, WILLIAM. Son of Hugh and Sarah, born in Andover, July 22, 1823. Mustered, Sept. 26, 1861. Private, Co. K., 22d Regiment Infantry. Wounded, June 27, 1862; sent to the hospital, and returned to the ranks, June 1, 1863. Discharged, Oct. 17, 1864, by expiration of service.

TRULL, CHARLES F. (Veteran). Son of John and Mary, born in Andover, July 18, 1842. Mustered, July 21, 1862. Private, Co. H., 1st Heavy Artillery. Re-enlisted in the field, Feb. 29, 1864. Wounded at Spottsylvania, May 19, 1864. Discharged, Aug. 16, 1865, by expiration of service, in Co. B.

TUCK, MOSES W. Son of John and Hannah A., born in Andover, July 11, 1836. Mustered, July 22, 1862. Private, Co. H., 1st Heavy Artillery. Discharged, July 8, 1864, by expiration of service.

TUCKER, WILLIAM H. Son of Samuel and Eliza H., born in Andover, May 2, 1846. Mustered, Aug. 26, 1864. Private, Co. B., 11th Regiment Infantry. Discharged, June 4, 1865, by expiration of service.

TURKINGTON, HENRY. Mustered, April 22, 1861. Private, Co. F., 6th Regiment Infantry (3 months). Discharged, Aug. 2, 1861, by expiration of service.

TURNER, JOHN (Veteran). Son of John. Born in Germany. Mustered, Sept. 5, 1861. Private, Co. F., 26th Regiment Infantry. Re-enlisted in the field, Jan. 1, 1864. Discharged, Aug. 26, 1865, by expiration of service.

TUMEY, PETER. Born in Galway, Ireland. Mustered, Dec. 9, 1862. Unassigned recruit, 22d Regiment Infantry. Never joined the Regiment; probably deserted as soon as he received his bounty, and before he arrived at the Rendezvous at Galloup Island. Not down on " Record of Mass. Vols."

DURING THE REBELLION. 191

TYLER, HERBERT. Son of Eben. Mustered, Sept. 12, 1862. Private, Co. I., 44th Regiment Infantry. Discharged, June 18, 1863, by expiration of service.

VAUX, WALTER R. Mustered, June 13, 1861. Private, Co. G., 11th Regiment Infantry. Deserted, Sept. 24, 1861.

VINALL, GEORGE A. W. (Veteran). Son of William D. and N. K. J., born in North Reading, Oct. 17, 1833. Mustered, July 5, 1861. Corporal, Co. H., 1st Heavy Artillery. Promoted Sergeant, Feb. 1862. Discharged, July 15, 1862, for disability, fever and ague. Re-mustered, Aug. 31, 1862. Sergeant, Co. K., 6th Regiment Infantry (9 months). Discharged, June 3, 1863, by expiration of service. Re-mustered, Feb. 9, 1864. Sergeant, Co. D., 59th Regiment Infantry. Transferred, June 1, 1865, to 57th Regiment Infantry. His name does not appear on the rolls of the latter Regiment on " Mass. Vols. Records."

WALLACE, ALEXANDER. Son of William and Margaret, born in County Down, Ireland, Feb. 23, 1822. Mustered, June 13, 1861. Private, Co. B., 11th Regiment Infantry. Discharged, June 24, 1864, by expiration of service.

WALSH, WILLIAM. Born in Cork, Ireland, and recruited in Boston. Mustered, Dec. 9, 1862. Unassigned recruit, 22d Regiment Infantry. " Bounty Jumper "; never joined the Regiment.

WARD, JAMES. Mustered, July 14, 1863. Private, Co. B., 9th Regiment Infantry. Transferred to Co. B., 32d Regiment Infantry. Killed, May 5, 1864, in battle of the Wilderness. This man was drafted in July, 1863, and was the only man of the seventy-seven who entered the service from that draft. He left town to avoid reporting himself, and was subsequently arrested, and was in some way permitted to go as substitute.

WARDMAN, THOMAS. Son of Samuel and Sophia, born in Bradford, England, Aug. 6, 1846. Mustered, Jan. 5, 1864. Private, Co. B., 59th Regiment Infantry. Captured by the rebels July 30, 1864. Died, Dec. 20, 1864, a prisoner of war at Danville, Va. Buried in the trenches.

WARDROBE, FREDERICK. Mustered, Oct. 20, 1864. Hospital Steward, U. S. Army.

WARDWELL, ALFRED. Son of Simon and Margaret E. F., born in Andover, Dec. 9, 1841. Mustered, July 5, 1861. Private, Co. H., 1st Heavy Artillery. Discharged, Nov. 7, 1861, for disability.

WARDWELL, GEORGE E. Son of Charles and Mehitable K., born in Andover, April 5, 1839. Private, Co. B., 1st Heavy Artillery. The date of his muster in and discharge does not appear on the rolls of the Regiment. Re-mustered, Aug. 28, 1861. Private, Co. A., 19th Regiment Infantry. Deserted, Sept. 16, 1862.

WARDWELL, HORACE W. (Veteran). Son of Thomas G. and Mary, born in Andover, May 16, 1842. Mustered, July 5, 1861. Private, Co. H., 1st Heavy Artillery. Promoted Corporal. Promoted Sergeant, March 1, 1862. Re-enlisted in the field, Dec. 29, 1863. Transferred to the Navy, May 12, 1864.

WARDWELL, JOSEPH W. Mustered, Aug. 19, 1862. Private, Co. F., 35th Regiment Infantry. Discharged, June 9, 1865, by expiration of service.

WARDWELL, WILLIAM H. Son of Henry and Angeline G., born in Amesbury, March 25, 1839. Mustered, July 5, 1861. Private, Co. H., 1st Heavy Artillery. Killed, Aug. 1, 1863; accidentally run over by a siege gun on Maryland Heights. Buried in North Andover Cemetery.

WEEKS, NATHANIEL. Mustered, Jan. 2, 1865. Private, Co. D., 1st Battalion Frontier Cavalry. Discharged, June 30, 1865, by expiration of service.

WELCH, ROBERT. This Recruit's name appears on the Selectmen's list as in the 11th Regiment Infantry, but does not appear on the Regimental Rolls.

WESCOTT, SOLOMON. Mustered, Dec. 30, 1864. Private, Co. L., 3d Regiment Cavalry. Discharged, Sept. 28, 1865, by expiration of service, in Co. E.

WESCOTT, WILLIAM. Mustered, Aug. 23, 1864. Private, 29th Unattached Co., Heavy Artillery. Discharged, June 16, 1865, by expiration of service.

WESTON, FREDERICK. Mustered, Aug. 24, 1864. Private, 29th Unattached Co., Heavy Artillery. Discharged, June 16, 1865, by expiration of service.

WHIDEMAN, JOHN. Born in Germany. Representative Recruit for William Jenkins. Mustered in at Fortress Monroe, Va., Oct. 9, 1864. Private, 20th Regiment, New York Cavalry.

WHITE, CHARLES W. Son of William and Mary Ann, born in Hampton Falls, N. H., April 4, 1844. Mustered, Jan. 14, 1864. Farrier, Co. M., New Battalion 1st Regiment Cavalry. Discharged, June 26, 1865, by expiration of service, in Co. H.

WHITTAKER, AMOS. Mustered, Sept. 6, 1861. Private, Co. D., 22d Regiment Infantry. Killed, June 27, 1862, at Gaines' Mills, Va.

WHITTEMORE, HARRISON. Mustered, May 24, 1861. Sergeant, Co. K., 1st Regiment Infantry. Discharged, May 25, 1864, by expiration of service.

WILSON, CHARLES. Born in Salem, and recruited in Boston. Mustered, Dec. 5, 1862. Unassigned recruit, 22d Regiment Infantry. "Bounty Jumper"; never joined the Regiment.

WINCHESTER, CHARLES H. Son of Charles and Betsey, born in Tewksbury, Oct. 22, 1828. Mustered, July 31, 1862. Private, Co. H., 1st Heavy Artillery. Wounded, June 16, 1864, at Bryant's Farm, near Petersburg, Va. Discharged, July 8, 1864, by expiration of service.

WINTHROP, THOMAS F. (Veteran). Son of Thomas and Ellen M., born in Andover, May 1, 1842. Mustered, Aug. 28, 1861. Private, Co. A., 19th Regiment Infantry. Promoted Quarter-Master-Sergeant, Oct. 13, 1862. Promoted 2d Lieutenant, Dec. 21, 1862. Promoted 1st Lieutenant, April 16, 1863. Promoted Captain, June 30, 1864. Discharged, Oct. 9, 1864, by expiration of service, as 1st Lieutenant. Re-mustered, March 11, 1865. 2d Lieutenant, 62d Infantry. Promoted Captain, April 17, 1865. Discharged, May 5, 1865, by expiration of service.

WITHEY, WILLIAM H. Mustered, Nov. 23, 1863. Bugler, Co. E., 1st Regiment Cavalry. Discharged, June 26, 1865, by expiration of service.

WITHSBY, THOMAS (Colored). Of Amitie Co., Miss. Representative recruit for the Town of Andover. Mustered in at Vicksburg, Miss., Feb. 20, 1865. Private, 70th Regiment, U. S. Colored Infantry.

WOOD, ELLIOT. Son of John and Margaret, born in Ireland, Sept. 24, 1842. Mustered, July 5, 1861. Private, Co. H., 1st Heavy Artillery. Discharged, July 8, 1864, by expiration of service.

WOODS, WILLIAM. Born in Salem, and recruited in Boston. Mustered, Dec 12, 1862. Unassigned recruit, 22d Regiment Infantry. "Bounty Jumper"; never joined the Regiment.

WOODBRIDGE, FRANCIS. Son of William and Mary H., born in Andover, April 2, 1836. Mustered, Sept. 15, 1864. Musician, Co. B., 11th Regiment Infantry. Discharged, July 14, 1865, by expiration of service. Died, ——. Buried in South Cemetery.

WOODLIN, ELGIN. Son of William H. and Rebecca M., born in Andover, Nov. 17, 1842. Mustered, June 13, 1861. Private, Co. H., 11th Regiment Infantry. Was reported from the Adjutant-General's office as having deserted Oct. 16, 1863; but it was subsequently ascertained that he was captured with forty others of his Regiment by Stuart's Cavalry two days before, and taken to Libby Prison, thence to Andersonville, thence to Millen, on the advance of Sherman, thence to Savannah, where he escaped on a dead man's parole, after thirteen months imprisonment, during which time all but about half a dozen of those captured with him died. Discharged, June 24, 1864, by expiration of service. Died, at Great Falls, N. H., May 1870, from injuries received while in the employ of the Boston and Maine Railroad.

WORTHLEY, DANIEL E. (Veteran). Son of Luke and Elizabeth P., born in Hinsdale, N. H., April 1, 1836. Mustered, Oct. 5, 1861. Private, Co. I., 26th Regiment Infantry. Re-enlisted in the field, Jan. 4, 1864, to the credit of Lawrence. Discharged, Aug. 26, 1865, by expiration of service.

YOUNG, FRANCIS C. Son of Jeremiah S. and Harriet F., born in North Andover, Dec. 31, 1843. Mustered, Sept. 12, 1862. Private, Co. G., 44th Regiment Infantry. Discharged, June 18, 1863, by expiration of service.

YOUNG, GEORGE W. Son of Jeremiah S. and Harriet F., born in Dover, N. H., Nov. 9, 1841. Mustered, Sept. 12, 1862. 3d Sergeant, Co. G., 44th Regiment Infantry. Promoted 1st Sergeant. Discharged, June 18, 1863, by expiration of service.

YOUNG, SAMUEL. Born in Philadelphia, Pa., and recruited in Boston. Mustered, Dec. 11, 1862. Unassigned recruit, 22d Regiment Infantry. No evidence that this man ever joined the Regiment. "Bounty Jumper."

PERSONAL NAVY RECORDS.

ABBOTT, WILLIAM A. Son of Amos and Esther M. Entered the United States Navy, May, 1861, as Master's Mate. Served on board the South Carolina, Choctaw, Alabama, Stars and Stripes, and sloops of war, Dale and Ohio; also in the batteries at Portsmouth, N. H. Captured off Cape Hatteras, Aug. 9, 1861. Released, Dec., 1861. Promoted Acting Ensign, Oct., 1862. Wounded in the attack of the Squadron on Haines' Bluff Batteries in the rear of Vicksburg, Miss. Pensioned for disability.

ABBOTT, WILLIAM. Born in Portland, Me. Enlisted for one year, Sept. 30, 1862. Served on board the Onward.

AURICK, JOSEPH. Enlisted July 2, 1864, for three years, as a substitute for S. Charles Jackson.

BUTLER, WILLIAM. Son of Isaac and Catherine, born in Dennisville, N. J., July 5, 1827. Enlisted, April 3, 1862, on board the iron-clad Pittsburg. Discharged, May 20, 1864. Re-enlisted for two years as a substitute for Moses Foster, Aug. 30, 1864. Served on board the Grand Gulf in the Red River expedition. Wounded in the head at Fort Fisher. Discharged, Feb. 25, 1865, for disability.

DOVE, GEORGE W. W. Son of John and Helen McL., born in Andover, June 4, 1835. Lieutenant 1st Mass. Heavy Artillery. Resigned before muster and entered the U. S. Navy as 3d Assistant Engineer. Served on board the Richmond in the Gulf Squadron under Admiral Farragut. Was in the attack upon Pensacola, in the taking of Forts Jackson and St. Phillip, and in the attacks upon Port Hudson and Vicksburg. Promoted 2d Engineer. Hostilities having ceased, he resigned.

DONNELLY, THOMAS. Enlisted, Aug. 17, 1864, for three years, as a substitute for George H. Chandler.

DUDLEY, LYSANDER. Enlisted, July 18, 1864, for three years, as a substitute for E. Francis Holt.

MAKIN, JOSEPH. An assigned Seaman. Born in Watertown, Mass. Enlisted, March 2, 1862, for three years. Assigned to the South Carolina.

MAKIN, SAMUEL. An assigned Seaman. Born in Watertown, Mass. Enlisted, March 2, 1862, for three years. Assigned to the South Carolina. Died, Jan. 10, 1865.

MASON, AARON W. An assigned Seaman. Born in Boston. Enlisted, March 2, 1862, for three years. Assigned to the Wachusett.

MASON, HENRY G. An assigned Seaman. Born in Boston. Enlisted, March 2, 1862, for three years. Assigned to the Tioga.

McCANN, JEREMIAH. An assigned Seaman. Born in Boston. Enlisted June 8, 1863, for one year. Assigned to Philadelphia Navy Yard.

McCARTY, JEREMIAH. An assigned Seaman. Born in Boston. Enlisted, June 9, 1863, for one year. Assigned to the Montgomery.

McGUIRE, JOHN. An assigned Seaman. Born in Ireland. Enlisted, June 12, 1863, for one year. Assigned to the Montgomery.

McGINNISS, JOHN. An assigned Seaman. Born in Ireland. Enlisted, June 3, 1863, for one year. Assigned to Philadelphia Navy Yard.

McHUGO, WILLIAM. An assigned Seaman. Born in Boston. Enlisted, March 6, 1862, for three years. Assigned to the Penobscot.

McKENZIE, NICHOLAS. An assigned Seaman. Born in Boston. Enlisted, June 11, 1863, for one year. Assigned to the Philadelphia.

McLEAN, JAMES. An assigned Seaman. Born in Scotland. Enlisted, June 9, 1863, for one year. Assigned to the Philadelphia.

McLARTY, WILLIAM A. An assigned Seaman. Born in Boston. Enlisted, June 9, 1863, for one year. Assigned to the Montgomery.

McLAUGHLIN, MICHAEL. An assigned Seaman. Born in Ireland. Enlisted, March 8, 1862, for three years. Discharged, April 1, 1862.

McNAUGHTON, JOHN. An assigned Seaman. Born in Scotland. Enlisted, March 11, 1862, for three years. Assigned to the Penobscot.

MEARS, JOHN. Transferred to the Navy, May 17, 1864, from 2d Regiment Mass. Heavy Artillery.

MINAR, ANDREW J. An assigned Seaman. Born in Connecticut. Enlisted, June 9, 1863, for one year. Assigned to the Ethan Allen.

MILLIKEN, GEORGE E. An assigned Seaman. Born in Boston. Enlisted, March 3, 1862, for three years. Assigned to the Penobscot.

MORTON, CHARLES. An assigned Seaman. Born in Savannah, Ga. Enlisted, March 7, 1862, for three years. Assigned to the Marblehead.

MOORE, JOHN. An assigned Seaman. Born in Ireland. Enlisted, June 5, 1863, for one year. Assigned to the Ethan Allen.

MURRAY, PATRICK. An assigned Seaman. Born in Ireland. Enlisted, June 4, 1863, for one year. Assigned to Philadelphia Navy Yard.

MURRAY, MICHAEL. An assigned Seaman. Born in Ireland. Enlisted, June 11, 1863, for one year. Assigned to the Philadelphia.

MURRAY, TIMOTHY. An assigned Seaman. Born in Boston. Enlisted, Feb. 24, 1862, for two years. Assigned to the Penobscot.

MURPHY, MILES. An assigned Seaman. Born in Ireland. Enlisted, June 2, 1863, for one year.

MURPHY, ROBERT. An assigned Seaman. Born in Eastport, Maine. Enlisted, March 3, 1862, for two years. Assigned to the West Flotilla.

MURPHY, PETER. An assigned Seaman. Born in Charlestown, Mass. Enlisted, Feb. 24, 1862, for two years. Assigned to the San Jacinto.

NAUGHTY, LEWIS A. An assigned Seaman. Discharged, April 5, 1862.

NICHOLS, JOHN S. An assigned Seaman. Born in Salem, Mass. Enlisted, Feb. 15, 1862, for three years. Assigned to the Constellation.

NOBLE, WILLIAM F. An assigned Seaman. Born in Bangor, Maine. Enlisted, Feb. 12, 1862, for three years. Assigned to the Kensington.

NOLAN, JOSEPH. An assigned Seaman. Born in Halifax, N. S. Enlisted, Feb. 16, 1862, for three years. Assigned to the Constellation.

NORRIS, THOMAS R. An assigned Seaman. Born in Portland, Me. Enlisted, Feb. 16, 1862, for two years. Assigned to the San Jacinto.

NUGENT, GEORGE. An assigned Seaman. Born in Boston. Enlisted, March 12, 1862, for three years. Assigned to the Mercedita.

PARKER, JOHN F. Transferred to the Navy, May 17, 1864, from 2d Regiment, Mass. Heavy Artillery.

PAUL, DAVID E. An assigned Seaman. Born in Nova Scotia. Enlisted, April 18, 1863, for one year. Died, in Chelsea Hospital, May 9, 1863.

PETERSON, GEORGE. Transferred to the Navy, Jan. 28, 1864, from 1st Regiment, Mass. Heavy Artillery.

PERRY, JAMES E. An assigned Seaman. Born in Nova Scotia. Enlisted, April 9, 1863, for one year. Assigned to New York Navy Yard.

PHILLIPS, SETH. An assigned Seaman. Born in Portland, Maine. Enlisted, April 7, 1863, for one year. Assigned to the Mercedita.

POTTER, WILLIAM. An assigned Seaman. Born in Providence, R. I. Enlisted, May 20, 1863, for one year. Assigned to the Montgomery.

POOL, ROBERT. An assigned Seaman. Born in Salem, Mass. Enlisted, May 20, 1863, for one year. Assigned to the Montgomery.

ROGERS, GEORGE. Enlisted, July 14, 1864, for three years, as a substitute for Henry A. Bodwell.

ROUNDY, THOMAS. Enlisted, Aug. 20, 1864, for three years, as a substitute for Perry M. Jefferson.

ROBINSON, JOSEPH P. Son of Thomas and Rachel. Born in Bolton, Lancashire, England. Enlisted, May 30, 1861. Served on board the S. S. Minnesota.

SAWYER, EDWIN. Enlisted, July 18, 1864, for three years, as a substitute for James S. Dodge.

SMITH, DAVID. Son of John N. and Mary. Born in Forfarshire, Scotland, Dec. 13, 1834. Entered U.S. Navy as 3d Assistant Engineer, Aug. 26, 1859. Served on board the Pocahontus in the Gulf Squadron. Promoted, 2d Assistant Engineer, July 8, 1861, and ordered on board the Lancaster, of the Pacific Squadron. Promoted, 1st Assistant Engineer, Oct. 1, 1863. Ordered to the Tallapoosa, Oct. 3, 1864. Ordered to the Wampanoag, Sept. 8, 1867; detached, and ordered Assistant Inspector Morgan Iron Works, New York. Promoted Chief Engineer, March 5, 1871.

TAYLOR, GEORGE. Enlisted, July 19, 1864, for three years, as a substitute for Horace P. Beard.

WALSH, PETER. Enlisted, July 20, 1864, for three years, as a substitute for I. Alvin Farley.

WARDWELL, HORACE W. Transferred to the Navy, May 12, 1864, from 1st Regiment Mass. Heavy Artillery.

APPENDIX.

History of the First Regiment Massachusetts Heavy Artillery.

[COPIED FROM THE OFFICIAL REPORTS OF ITS OFFICERS].

This Regiment, organized as the 14th Infantry, commonly known as the "Essex County Regiment," from its having been mostly raised in this part of the State, was mustered into the service of the United States, July 5th, 1861, at Fort Warren. On the 7th of August it left Fort Warren, Boston Harbor, for Washington, under command of Colonel William B. Greene, and upon arriving there, was ordered to Camp Kalorama, Meridian Heights, Maryland, where it remained until the 18th of the same month, when it was ordered to cross the Potomac and garrison Fort Albany, considered at that time the key to Washington. Shortly after it was called upon to furnish a garrison for Fort Runyon, and the works at the head of the Long Bridge. On the 1st of January, 1862, by order from the War Department, the regiment was changed from an Infantry to a Heavy Artillery Regiment; consequently requiring an increase in its number, of fifty men to each company, and two additional companies of one hundred and fifty men each, to raise it to the standard, which was duly accomplished. Early in April following, the regiment was required, in addition to the forts already occupied by them, to furnish garrisons for Forts Scott, Richardson, Barnard, Craig, and Tillinghast, vacated by infantry regiments detached for other service. They remained in garrison in these Forts until August 23d, when they were ordered to Cloud's Mills, where they remained until the 26th, when orders were received to march to Manassas, to participate in the Battle of Bull Run. While on the march to this point, on the morning of the 27th, between Annandale and Fairfax Court House, they were met by squads of flying soldiers belonging to the Second New York Artillery, who had preceded them the previous day, and who had met and were repulsed by Stuart's Cavalry. The regiment kept on, passing on their route a long supply train of four or five miles in length, belonging to General Banks' army, which had been ordered back for safety. When about a mile beyond Fairfax Court House they were met by two pieces of the Twelfth New York Battery (the remainder having been captured by the enemy), rapidly retreating, followed in close pursuit by the enemy's cavalry. Colonel Wm. B. Greene of this Regiment ordered them to stop, and placed them in position, under the charge of one of his captains, at the same time deploying his regiment through the woods on both sides of the road. They remained in line all day, and lay on their arms during the following night. Early on the morning of the next day, one of their pickets was shot by the enemy and subsequently taken to a house in the rear for surgical treatment. While the surgeons were engaged in their duty, the house in which they were occupied was surrounded by the enemy's cavalry and the whole party taken prisoners, including the capture of an ambulance, a hospital wagon, and a four-horse regimental wagon with their drivers. After being taken a few miles the surgeons were unconditionally released, and the remainder of the party paroled by the enemy. Late in the day the Regiment received orders to return to Cloud's Mills where they arrived late the same evening, having marched seventeen miles in five hours and a half. The day following the regiment was ordered to garrison Forts Albany, Craig, Tillinghast, Woodbury, Whipple, De Kalb, Corcoran, Haggerty, and Bennett. After doing duty in these forts for more than a week the regiment was relieved from duty at the three last named. About the middle of September Companies H and I were ordered to Maryland Heights for garrison duty; and about a month later Co. C was ordered to join them.

The history of the regiment during the year 1863, so honorable to Massachusetts, and the officers and men comprising it, is so well told in the following letter of Colonel Tannatt, and the Reports of Major Rolfe and Major Holt, that nothing need be added.

HEAD-QUARTERS FIRST MASS. HEAVY ARTILLERY,
FORT WHIPPLE, VA., Jan. 1, 1864.

GENERAL : — Your request for data to embody in your Annual Report, has been deferred in order to obtain a correct account of the nature of service performed by the battalion then serving at Maryland Heights, but since returned to the regiment.

Notice of my transfer from the Sixteenth to this regiment reached me a few days prior to the first battle of Fredericksburg. At the request of my old and esteemed officers I remained with the Sixteenth until the return of the army to Falmouth, joining this regiment for duty, January 1st 1863. Upon assuming command, I found certain reforms necessary, but passing to the present time, I will but remark, that the regiment is to-day held in high esteem for its proficiency in drill, good discipline, and military appearance. With the exception of a transfer of three companies from lesser Forts to Fort Whipple, the largest and most complete earthwork in the defences of Washington, no change has been made in the station of the eight companies here on duty.

Companies B, C, H, and I, detached until December 1, 1863, have seen service alike creditable to the officers and men. Company I was in the battle of Winchester, gaining much praise for their good conduct, and artillery skill; being ordered by General Milroy to remain and spike the guns left by his command. Captain Martin and forty men were taken prisoners; the men are exchanged and again on duty; Captain Martin is in Libby prison.

The regiment has performed a vast amount of labor during the year, having erected fine quarters for officers and men; completed and occupied one forty-three-gun fort, besides erecting three large bomb-proof barracks, capable of quartering the men.

The system of promoting from the ranks has in no case been set aside, but preceded by a thorough examination of such sergeants as desired to compete for commissions. This system, extended to the issue of warrants, has given to the regiment a valuable class of junior officers, correct in habits, and efficient in drill and command, whilst the scale of warrant officers has reached a highly desirable degree of proficiency. During the year, twenty-one vacancies in the roster of officers have been well filled by the promotion of sergeants.

Finding the records of the regiment very defective, some time elapsed before your office could be furnished with the returns so necessary to you. During the presence of the rebel army in Pennsylvania, the troops of this command were called upon to picket in front of their line, thus doing the double duty of infantry and artillery. Several marches to the assistance of points threatened by guerillas, proved that, although garrison troops, the men were ever ready for any duty regardless of exposure. A more careful performance of picket duty I have yet to see.

Since joining this regiment I have been much of the time called upon to command the brigade, of which the regiment forms a part, and for two months the line of defences south of the Potomac, retaining command of my regiment during the time, thus being obliged to leave undone many things necessary in my immediate command.

Your attention is called to the enclosed Reports from Majors Rolfe and Holt.

In closing I desire to convey to his Excellency and yourself, my personal thanks for the uniform courtesy extended to me upon all points of interest to the men of my command.

In no case has political or social influence been allowed to govern the position, promotion, or conduct of any officer or soldier, but a clear and conscientious consideration has greatly assisted me in my feeble efforts to make my regiment capable of maintaining an honorable place among the troops sent from Massachusetts. This regiment is now filled by recruits; a large proportion of the *old* and *original* members having re-enlisted. Of the present condition of the regiment it is more proper that others should speak.

I have the honor to be, very respectfully, your obedient servant,

THOS. R. TANNATT,
Colonel First Mass. Heavy Artillery.

To General WM. SCHOULER,
Adjutant-General of Massachusetts.

HEAD-QUARTERS, 2D BATTALION, 1ST MASS. H. A.,
FORT WOODBURY, VA., Jan. 8, 1864.

SIR: — In accordance with the Colonel's orders of the 1st instant, I have the honor to make the following report of the marches, etc., made by my former command, First Battalion, First Massachusetts Heavy Artillery, while on detached service.

On the 27th of September, 1862, in accordance with orders received from Major-General McClellan, through intermediate head-quarters, I proceeded by rail with Companies H and I, to Harper's Ferry, Va., and reported to Major-General E. V. Sumner, commanding post. He directed me to march my command up on Maryland Heights, and report to Brigadier-General A. S. Williams, commanding Twelfth Corps, and get the heavy guns, which had been spiked and rolled down the heights (by order of Colonel Miles, about twelve days previous), ready for use as soon as possible. Arriving upon the heights at a position known as the Naval Battery, we found the heavy guns to be two nine-inch J. A. D. guns, and one fifty-pounder J. A. D. gun, all spiked, dismounted and rolled down the heights, fifteen or twenty feet from their platforms.

Not having suitable machines for mounting the guns, we went into the woods, cut down trees, and made blocks, and with them succeeded in getting the guns in position, and mounting them on their carriages. While Lieutenant Guilford, in command of a few men, was getting the spikes out of the guns, others were hunting in the woods and bushes for the broken implements and equipments, which we repaired sufficiently to serve the guns with. Some ammunition was found in a tent near by, which had been but partially destroyed, and was prepared for use. On the evening of the fourth day after we arrived there, I reported to General Sumner that the guns were ready for use.

Two twenty-pounder batteries from the artillery reserve of the Army of the Potomac were stationed near the Naval Battery when we arrived there, but they were ordered away a few days after we got the heavy guns ready for use. Our tents were not pitched for a week or ten days, because every man was employed in getting the guns in order, and the ground we wanted was occupied by the batteries; but the weather was exceedingly fair.

Requisitions were then made for the necessary ordnance, commissary, and quartermaster stores, which I succeeded in getting without much trouble. There being no magazines for the ammunition, we commenced on four small ones immediately after the guns were in position. Two or three days after we got the naval guns in position I received several Parrott guns from Washington Arsenal. These were placed in position at the Naval Battery.

October 27, 1862, Captain A. G. Draper reported to me with his company (C), and a few days after commenced on a new battery (now Fort Duncan), and several Parrott guns that arrived a few days after the company did, were put in temporary position near it. December 23, 1862, Captain C. S. Heath reported to me with his company (B), which was sent to the top of the heights, one thousand and sixty-five feet above the Potomac River, to build the Howitzer

Battery, with five boat howitzers I had received a few weeks previous.

January 23, 1863, Assistant-Surgeon E. B. Mason, of our regiment, reported to me; previous to which time the sick of the battalion had been attended by assistant-surgeons detailed from regiments stationed near us. From the time we arrived at Harper's Ferry, Va., until the 10th of June, 1863, the battalion was employed most of the time in building batteries, magazines, and barracks, putting guns in position, repairing roads, and hauling up supplies of all kinds.

June 10th, Company I was ordered to Winchester. For an account of the doings of the company from that time until it arrived at Harper's Ferry, Va., I refer you to Lieutenant J. B. Hanson's Report. Nearly all of Company I, except those who were taken prisoners (Captain and forty-four men), arrived at Maryland Heights on the 16th and 17th of June, in an exhausted and destitute condition. Some of the men arrived back *via* Harrisburg, Pa., near the last of the month. Lieutenants Hoppin and Holt arrived on the 16th, and as fast as the men came in, got them together and supplied their wants. A few days after, Company I started for Winchester. Captain Hawkins, of the Eighth New York Artillery, reported to me with his company (F), from Baltimore, and was sent to the battery left by Company I. It being a small company, as soon as Company I arrived from Winchester and got rested, I sent it to its old battery, to assist the New York company in case of an attack.

We were expecting an attack from the 16th of June to the 1st of July, — the day we evacuated. A great many changes were made at the batteries just previous to the evacuation, and a portion of the battalion worked day and night. The battalion, with a very little assistance, built before the evacuation, log barracks for two companies, twelve magazines, and four batteries, hauled up thirty-five pieces of artillery, and two hundred and twenty tons of ammunition of the best quality, besides a large amount of quartermaster and commissary stores.

June 29th, received orders to evacuate Maryland Heights, and destroy everything but the guns. During the night hauled the guns away from Fort Duncan and Howitzer Battery, and destroyed the ammunition.

June 30th, hauled the guns down from the Thirty-Pounder Battery, destroyed the ammunition, and loaded a part of the guns from the three batteries dismantled, aboard canal-boats. While destroying the ammunition at Fort Duncan, a shell exploded, and Sergeant E. J. Graham, privates Wm. Bachellor and J. M. Cutter, Company C, were wounded; the sergeant badly. Also, while destroying the ammunition at Thirty-Pounder Battery, an explosion occurred outside the battery, killing five or six, and wounding eight or ten. No one of this regiment was injured at the last explosion. Both explosions were the results of excitement and carelessness. The battalion was ordered to march with General Kenley's (Maryland) brigade, but subsequently was ordered to remain behind until all the guns (except a few old ones, which were to be left, to protect the retreat of General Elliott's brigade, having in charge the good guns), were loaded upon the canal-boats. Those guns for the protection of General Elliott were in charge of Captain Horace Holt.

July 1st, about 10 o'clock, all the guns having been loaded, and put in charge of General Elliott's brigade, I marched with Companies B, C, and I, of this regiment, and Company F, of the Eighth New York Artillery, about fourteen miles towards Frederick, Maryland, and bivouacked for the night. This was a hard march for the battalion, as it was a very hot day, the road very muddy, and a part of the men had been obliged to work thirty-six hours, just before starting, in mud and water; their feet became soft and tender, and the men were not used to marching. Before starting on the march, all the sick and wounded were put aboard canal-boats, and went safely to Washington, and shortly after nearly all reported to regimental head-quarters.

July 2d, marched to Frederick, and reported to Brigadier-General Kenley. At 4 o'clock, P.M., the same day, marched with Tenth Vermont Regiment and Tenth Massachusetts Battery to Frederick Junction. Just as we were starting, Captain Holt arrived with his company, and, being very tired, was allowed to remain in Frederick until next morning, when he was directed to report to me at Frederick Junction. July 4th, received orders to leave two companies of my command to guard the Junction, and march with the other three to Frederick, and guard the public property and approaches to the town. After marching about half way to Frederick the order was countermanded, and the battalion marched back to the Junction.

July 7th, sent Captain Holt and his company to Maryland Heights, by rail, by order of Major-General French. For an account of the doings of Company H, from the time it was left on Maryland Heights until it joined the battalion at Frederick Junction, and from the time it left Frederick Junction until it joined the battalion again, on the Boonsboro' and Hagerstown turnpike, I refer you to Captain Holt's Report, enclosed herewith.

July 8th, sent Company F, Eighth New York Artillery, to Maryland Heights to relieve Captain Holt's company, by order of Major-General French, and then marched through Frederick towards Middletown, until 9 o'clock in the evening, when we bivouacked for the night, and in the morning started for Middletown, which place we reached about 9 o'clock A.M. After resting a short time, marched towards South Mountain Pass, which place we reached about noon. In the evening we marched through the pass, in the rear of the Third Corps, and bivouacked for the night. July 10th, marched through Kedersville and bivouacked for the night on the road to Sharpsburg, one mile from Kedersville, and in rear of the Third Corps.

July 11th, marched through Boonsboro', to near head-quarters Third Corps, on Williamsport road, two miles from Boonsboro', and reported to Major-General French, who ordered me to report to Brigadier-General Hunt, Chief of Artillery, Army of the Potomac. The battalion was assigned by him to duty with the artillery reserve, Brigadier-General R. O. Tyler, commanding. Marched to the camp of artillery reserve on the Boonsboro' and Hagerstown Turnpike, three miles from Boonsboro', and reported to General Tyler. In the evening Captain Holt joined the battalion with his company.

July 12th, detailed one hundred and forty-eight men for the different batteries of the reserve, by order of General Tyler. Captain Fuller, Thirty-Second Massachusetts Volunteers, with his company, was temporarily attached to my command. July 13th, marched with the reserve about eight miles towards Williamsport, and then marched back to near camp left in the morning. In the evening detailed forty men to report to Captain Robinson, Fourth Maine Battery, by order of General Tyler.

July 15th, marched through Boonsboro', Middletown, and Jefferson, to within two miles of Berlin, Maryland. On the 18th, marched from Berlin across Potomac River, through Lovettsville to within a mile of Wheatland, Va. On the 19th, marched through Wheatland to Purcellville. On the 20th, marched to Union. On the 21st, all men detailed into batteries, ordered by General Meade to be sent back to their companies, and I was ordered to march with the battalion to Harper's Ferry, Va., and report to the commanding officer.

On the 22d, all men detailed in batteries, except eighteen of Company B, detailed in Company C, Fifth United States Artillery, and ordered to New York with the battery, arrived, and the battalion marched through Purcellville, Wheatland, and Lovettsville to Berlin. On the 23d, marched on the tow-path of the canal to Harper's Ferry, Va., and reported to Brigadier-General H. H. Lockwood, commanding post. The Eighth New York Artillery was occupying our old batteries, and had mounted the guns Captain Holt's company had spiked and rolled down the heights. The battalion went into camp near the Naval Battery.

On the 25th, the battalion was ordered to occupy Fort Duncan. On the 27th, the Eight New York Artillery were ordered to vacate the batteries, and the battalion to re-occupy them. I was directed to inspect the works on Maryland Heights, report upon their condition and take measures to get guns and ammunition, and put the works in the best possible condition.

On the 29th, I was sent to Washington by General Lockwood, with a letter to Generals Ripley and Barry (Chief of Ordnance, and Inspector of Artillery), requesting that the guns I might call for be sent to Maryland Heights as soon as possible. The armament I suggested was approved, and ordered to be sent immediately; and the old guns and material left on the heights at the evacuation gathered up and sent to Washington Arsenal. I immediately went back to Maryland Heights, and set the battalion to work gathering up the two hundred tons of ammunition it had destroyed a month previous, had it hauled down from the heights, and, with the old guns spiked by Captain Holt's company, loaded aboard cars, and sent to Washington Arsenal. At the same time the new guns and ammunition arrived. The guns were hauled up by the men,— from 200 to 500 being required to haul up each gun. A part of the new guns were put in the old batteries, and the rest on new and commanding positions, and batteries built around them.

Nearly the whole month of August was spent in replacing what had been destroyed in three days in June.

August 11th, an order was received discharging Assistant-Surgeon E. B. Mason, to receive an appointment in the Second Massachusetts Cavalry. From that time the sick of the battalion were attended by assistant-surgeons detailed from regiments around us, until August 24th, when Assistant-Surgeon Samuel L. Dalton of our Regiment reported to me.

October 14th, thirty-six men of Company I, captured at Winchester, reported to their company from Parole Camp, Annapolis, Md. From the time we arrived back at Harper's Ferry, until we were relieved by the Third Battalion, Fifth New York Artillery, on the 30th day of November, and ordered to report to regimental head-quarters, our duty was the same as before the evacuation, viz. building batteries, magazines, barracks, etc. In all the moving of guns which the battalion did, some of which was in the night, only one accident occurred, the circumstances of which are as follows:

On the first of August, 1863, two hundred men were hauling a thirty-pounder Parrott gun up a very steep, rough place. It was a very long, hard pull, and when the gun arrived at the top, and commenced to go easy, the men gave a cheer, and started on the run. Private William H. Wardwell, Company H, who was pulling on the rope near the gun, fell down, and the men being crowded on the rope, broke his hold, and, before the gun could be stopped, fell under the wheels of the gun-carriage, and was killed.

In order to appreciate the difficulties under which the battalion labored, it must be known that the batteries were situated from 250 to 1,065 feet above the river, and the roads leading to them very rocky, steep, and crooked, and barely wide enough for a wagon. Over these roads the guns, ammunition, and supplies of all kinds were hauled. Several times during the winter it was impossible to get down the mountain with a team for several days in succession, on account of the steep places in the road being covered with ice.

During the whole time the battalion was on detached service, officers and men obeyed all orders given them, cheerfully and promptly, and evinced a desire to practise upon the enemy with what they had studied for two years and a half, and gain a little honor for the regiment, so that in July next, when the regiment is mustered out of service, it could not be said that the largest regiment in the United States service served a three-years' enlistment without even seeing a rebel in arms, while every other regiment from the State had participated in one or more of the glorious achievements of the war, covered itself with glory, and reflected honor upon the old Bay State.

Earnestly hoping that in the spring our regiment will be ordered to active duty with our arm of the service,

I am, very respectfully, your obedient servant,

FRANK A. ROLFE,
Major, First Mass. Heavy Artillery, Commanding.

REPORT OF MAJOR HORACE HOLT.

FORT WHIPPLE, VA., Jan. 9, 1864.

I have the honor to respectfully submit the following report of the operations, marches, etc., of Company H, First Massachusetts Heavy Artillery, while detached from the first battalion of said regiment of which you were in command at Maryland Heights, Md.

When General French evacuated Maryland Heights, on the first of July, 1863, Company H, which I had the honor of commanding, was detailed to remain in charge of some heavy guns that were left upon the heights to cover the retreat, as large quantities of ordnance and quartermaster's stores were being shipped upon canal-boats to Washington for safe keeping. After you had left the heights with General French, I reported (as directed) to General Elliott, who was in charge of the shipping of the stores, and with his brigade guards the canal-boats to Washington. He gave me orders to remain at the guns till dark that night, then to "spike" my guns and destroy the ammunition, and march for Frederick City, Md. As I was about to ' spike," I received orders from General Elliott to delay a few hours, as it was reported the enemy were advancing from the direction of Sharpsburg to destroy the canal-boats and stores. I accordingly delayed until past ten o'clock; saw no enemy, and learned the boats and all the troops were out of range of my guns. I then "spiked" and otherwise destroyed, and marched for Frederick City, Md., as directed. Seven miles out from Sandy Hook we came up with Captain Pengaskill, with a company of engineers and a small train of wagons, encamped for the night. Glad was Company H to join them.

The next morning (July 2d), marched for Frederick City, where we arrived at five o'clock, P.M., all safe, but very much fatigued; but found your command in line, and about to march for Frederick Junction. As I reported to you the condition of my company from fatigue, you obtained permission for us to remain at Frederick City that night. Next morning we joined you at Frederick Junction. On the evening of the sixth of July, I received orders from you to proceed with Company H to Maryland Heights again. I obtained transportation on the Baltimore and Ohio Railroad, in open cars, attached to a train of four iron-clad cars; each car was armed with a light field-piece, without the gun-carriages; the pieces were slung with ropes from the top of the cars, and served through port-holes. The train was in charge of Lieutenant Meigs, of U. S. A., with orders to run up the railroad as far as Harper's Ferry, and learn the condition of the road and telegraph wires.

We left Frederick Junction at 8 o'clock, A.M., July 7th; arrived at Sandy Hook, Md., about 3 P.M., where we found Brigadier-General John R. Kenley, with the Maryland Brigade, just coming in from Frederick City. He immediately ordered Lieutenant Meigs and myself, with Company H, up to the Harper's Ferry bridge, to cover the advance of his brigade past the bridge and up the heights. On our arrival at the bridge we found the enemy strongly posted, on the Harper's Ferry side, behind the railroad and old brick walls. As the brigade arrived, they (the rebels) opened with musketry. I ordered Lieutenant Carter, of Company H, with twenty men, to deploy as skirmishers along the Maryland bank of the river, under cover of timbers, rocks, etc., and Lieutenant Meigs opened fire with a twelve-pounder howitzer; but as he could not bring his rear cars up to get range with the guns, he let me have two six-pounder brass pieces. I ordered Lieutenant Guilford, of Company H, to take them out of the cars, and rig them on logs in the road, for shelling the town. Lieutenant Guilford accordingly took two gun detachments of Company H, and in ten minutes the guns were both rigged, each trunnion resting upon a log, using a piece of plank for a quoin, and the rebels were soon made to quit their hiding-place and get out of range. Quite a brisk skirmish was kept up until dark that night.

There were seventeen men wounded in the Maryland Brigade; Company H came out *without a scratch*. On the 8th, Company F, of the Eighth New York Heavy Artillery, reported from Frederick Junction, with orders relieving me, and ordering me to join you at

Middletown, Md. As I was about to march with my company, I received orders from Brigadier-General Naglee (who had just arrived and assumed command of the forces at Maryland Heights), to remain at the bridge, as he had orders to hold all troops that were then in his command. The next morning (9th) I received orders from General Naglee to march my company up to the Naval Battery, and occupy my old quarters, and put the heavy guns in position that I had spiked, by order of General Elliott, at the time of the first evacuation. On the morning of the 10th, I received orders from General Naglee to march with Brigadier-General Kenley's brigade (who was then under orders to report at Boonsboro', Md.), and report to you as soon as I could *find* you. I was accordingly attached to the Eighth Maryland Regiment, under Colonel Denison. We marched that day to Boonsboro', Md. The next day (11th) we marched about seven miles beyond Boonsboro', halted, and commenced throwing up breastworks, as an attack was hourly expected. At 5 o'clock, P.M., same day, you rode into camp, and had me relieved from the Maryland Brigade. I joined your battalion, then attached to the reserve artillery of the Army of the Potomac, camped by the Boonsboro' Pike.

With regrets that the First Massachusetts Heavy Artillery cannot show upon her records an equal share of gallant deeds upon the battle-field with other Massachusetts regiments, and hoping yet that we shall have an opportunity of relieving an equal number of worn-out heroes from the front, and they have an opportunity of resting from long-continued hardships behind these breastworks on Arlington Heights, or some place equally safe.

With great respect, Major, I am yours, etc.

HORACE HOLT,
Major First Mass. Heavy Artillery.

To Major FRANK A. ROLFE, *First Mass. Heavy Artillery.*

The Regiment continued to occupy a portion of the fortifications of Washington, south of the Potomac, until the 15th of May, 1864. During the time it was engaged in performing garrison duty, it accomplished a great deal in building fortifications, mounting and dismounting heavy guns, and moving ordnance from one fortification to another. In addition it was employed in building and repairing military roads and bridges on each side of the several fortifications, etc.

May 15th, 1864. The regiment marched to Alexandria (five miles), with orders to join the Army of the Potomac. Took transports the same day for Belle Plain. Arrived at Belle Plain the 16th. Disembarked and bivouacked on the ridge near the landing. Reported to Brigadier-General R. O. Tyler, and was assigned to the Second Brigade of his (Tyler's) Division (Colonel Tannatt commanding), composed mainly of heavy artillery regiments from the fortifications of Washington and Baltimore.

May 17th, marched with the division to Head-Quarters Army of the Potomac, near Spottsylvania, Va. (twenty-three miles), passing through Fredericksburg. On arriving at army head-quarters at 2 o'clock, A.M., May 18th, bivouacked on the left of the Fredericksburg Road until 6, A.M., then moved about one mile to the right of the road and took up a position as support for a battery. It was here the command, except Company I, was first under fire of the enemy, being frequently shelled during the forenoon. At 4, P.M., marched up the road two miles, and bivouacked in the woods for the night. At 2, P.M., on the 19th, marched two miles to the Harris Farm. The brigade was massed near the house in support of a battery stationed at that point. At 4, P.M., the enemy were reported in the woods in front, when two companies (F and D) were ordered out as skirmishers, to ascertain their position and strength. The First Battalion (Major Rolfe) advanced as support to the companies of skirmishers, and became engaged. The Second Battalion (Major Shatswell) was then ordered in on the right of the First, and for a time the regiment was alone opposed to Rhodes' Division of Ewell's Corps. The men stood up to their work manfully and held the enemy in check until reinforcements arrived, when we fell back to re-form the line and advance again.

The regiment went into the fight with sixteen hundred and seventeen officers and men, and lost two commissioned officers (Major Rolfe and Lieutenant Graham) killed, and fifteen wounded, fifty-three enlisted men killed, two hundred and ninety-seven wounded and twenty-seven missing. The engagement lasted until about 10, P.M. The regiment remained on the field all night, returning to the bivouac of the previous day at 10, A.M., of the 20th. Marched at 1, A.M., May 21st, taking the road to Milford. Passed through

Bowling Green at 11, A.M. Arrived at Milford, crossed the river, and bivouacked for the night, marching twenty-eight miles. Threw up breastworks on the 22d. 23d, Marched at 6, A.M. Arrived at the North Anna River (sixteen miles) at 3, P.M. The regiment was held as reserve, the men lying on their arms all night.

May 24th, battle of North Anna River; held as reserve. Casualties, one enlisted man killed and eleven wounded. The brigade organizations of our division being broken up, each regiment was divided into three battalions, each to act as a regiment in all movements.

May 27th, marched at 3.30, A.M. Massed in a field about one mile in rear of first line. Sent out pioneers to destroy the bridge that crossed the river above the enemy's position. Had two men wounded while destroying the bridge. 12, M., marched down the north bank of the river. Bivouacked at 2, A.M., of the 28th, having marched twenty-two miles. Marched again at 9, A.M. Crossed the Pamunkey River on pontoons below Hanover Court House. Bivouacked for the night about three miles from the river on the extreme left of the line (distance marched, fifteen miles). 29th. Was ordered to report to Major-General D. B. Birney, commanding Third Division, Second Army Corps, and assigned to the Second Brigade, Colonel Tannatt taking command. Marched at 12, M. Joined the brigade and went into position near Salem Church. Threw up breastworks in the afternoon. Moved to the right, and threw up works during the night.

May 31st, battle of Tolopotomy. Regiment held as reserve in the morning at 9, A.M. Moved to the front. Threw forward a heavy skirmish line and occupied the enemy's works. Lay under a heavy fire of artillery all day. Casualties, five enlisted men wounded on the line and three missing from the picket line.

June 1st, at daylight withdrew to position occupied the previous morning. Changed position frequently during the day. At 10, P.M., marched for Cold Harbor. Arrived at Gaines' Farm at 2, P.M., of 2d.

June 2d, weather very hot and the roads dusty. Distance marched, twenty-seven miles.

June 3d, battle of Cold Harbor. Four companies, viz. B, F, H, and K, reported to Colonel Smythe, commanding Third Brigade, Second Division, Second Army Corps. Were engaged in the charge on the enemy's works in the morning and the repulse of the enemy in his night charge.

From June 4th to 12th occupied a position on the Shady Grove Road, near Barker's Mills. Under fire nearly all the time. Two enlisted men killed, thirteen wounded and sixteen missing. At 10, P.M., of the 12th withdrew from our position, and marched to the left at 7, A.M. June 13th. Crossed the York River Railroad at Despatch Station. Crossed the Chickahominy at Long Bridge at 3, P.M. Marched all day. At 10, P.M., massed near the James River for the night (distance, thirty-three miles).

June 14th, crossed the James River near Fort Powhattan in transports.

June 15th, marched for Petersburg. Arrived at the fortifications near the Dunn House shortly after the charge and capture of the same by the colored troops (distance, twenty-three miles). Threw up works during the night.

June 16th, charged the enemy's works in our front at sunset. Were repulsed with heavy loss; viz. two commissioned officers killed, six wounded, twenty-three enlisted men killed, one hundred and twenty-six wounded, and five missing. Held our position until morning, when by flank movements to the right and left, the enemy were obliged to fall back. Loss, 17th, nine enlisted men wounded.

June 18th, charged the enemy's works near the Hare House at sunrise. Carried the works, driving the enemy through the woods and across the Petersburg Pike to a rear line of works. At 12, M., another charge was ordered, which failed for want of proper support. Held our position on the pike until 5, P.M., when the brigade was relieved, and moved to the left of the Hare House, and threw up works during the night, where we remained until the night of the 20th, under fire day and night. Casualties from 17th to 20th, including the battle of the 18th, six commissioned officers wounded, four enlisted men killed and forty-five wounded. On the night of the 20th orders were received to go to the rear.

June 21st, orders were received for another of the famous left flank movements. At 9 o'clock crossed the Petersburg and Norfolk Railroad, taking our course through the woods for the Jerusalem plank road, which we struck at the Williams House, finding the enemy's cavalry in our front and covering the Weldon Railroad.

June 22d, advanced with brigade to throw up breastworks nearer the enemy's position, a general advance of the whole corps being ordered. While engaged in this work we were flanked by the enemy breaking through the lines of General Barlow's Division, who were getting into position on our left, in the woods. Casualties, one commissioned officer (Captain J. W. Kimball) killed, one wounded, and six captured, two of whom were wounded; eight enlisted men killed, forty-five wounded, and one hundred and seventy-nine captured.

July 6th, the term of service of the original members, and the recruits enlisted in July and August, 1862, having expired, the regiment was ordered to the rear, to make out the necessary papers for the muster out of the men.

July 12th, the regiment joined the brigade, and moved to the left of the Williams House, to cover the shortening of our lines, the Sixth Army Corps having been sent to Washington; remained in line of battle forty-eight hours. No enemy appearing, and the troops and trains having been withdrawn, the division withdrew through the woods, across the Norfolk Railroad to the Petersburg and Norfolk turnpike, where the brigade went into camp near the Deserted House. July 15th was the first time the regiment had formed camp since leaving the fortifications of Washington, in May.

July 21st, moved to Fort Bross, and remained until July 26th, when the regiment marched to Deep Bottom, twenty-four miles, arriving on the morning of the 27th at daylight; were immediately ordered in as support for a skirmish line of the First Brigade of our division, having to cross an open field under the enemy's fire of artillery; fortunately, only one man was wounded in this affair. 28th, marched back to the Petersburg and City Point Railroad, crossing the Appomattox at Point of Rocks (distance marched, twenty-two miles); lay in mass all day; after dark, took up a position in the front line of intrenchments. 30th, occupied a position in the front line, about half a mile to the right of the mine "exploded in the morning"; had orders to keep up a continuous fire on the enemy in our front, whose works were about two hundred yards distant. The regiment used during the day an average of one hundred and fifty rounds per man, with a loss on our part of only one man wounded. 31st, returned to our position.

August 12th, marched to City Point, eight miles. 14th, found us up the James River, where we disembarked at Deep Bottom; advanced over Strawberry Plain, and bivouacked for the day and night. 15th, the brigade reported to Major-General D. B. Birney, now commanding the Tenth Army Corps; advanced through the woods in line of battle for more than five miles, in the direction of the Charles City Road, skirmishing nearly all the way; the day was very hot. Casualties during the day, one enlisted man killed, seven enlisted men wounded. 16th, the regiment was stationed on the right flank of the brigade as skirmishers. Casualties, one enlisted man killed. 18th, returned to front of Petersburg, arriving on the morning of the 19th; distance marched twenty-five miles.

The regiment remained on picket until the 25th of August, when it was relieved, and withdrew to near the Strong House.

September 1st, ordered to the garrison of Fort Alexander Hayes. 25th, was relieved by a regiment from the Ninth Army Corps, when it joined the brigade in rear of the Jones House on the line of the Military Railroad.

October 1st, the brigade took cars for Warren's Station, marched thence to the Peeble's House, near Poplar Grove Church; bivouacked for the night. October 2d, moved out to the left of the Peeble's House, on the Squirrel-level Road; advanced and occupied the works, then steadily advanced, making connection with a division of the Ninth Corps, on the right. At 3, P.M., we developed the enemy's second line of works. At this time, orders were received for our brigade to make a demonstration on the enemy's works, to ascertain their strength, and, if possible, carry them. The command was formed in a ravine, about five hundred yards from the work, the First occupying the first line. As we advanced, the enemy opened a battery that was masked in the angle of his works — having a raking fire with canister and spherical case. Gained a position about fifty yards from the works; our support not coming up, were obliged to retire. Casualties, two commissioned officers wounded, two enlisted men killed, nine wounded, and eight wounded and captured.

October 3d, 4th, and 5th, assisted to build Forts Cummings, Emory, Seibut, and Clarke, covering the left and rear of our position at Peeble's House. On the night of the 5th, marched to the Jones House, seven miles. 6th, returned to Fort Alexander Hayes; remained at Fort Hayes until October 26th, when the regiment was relieved; joined the brigade in rear of the Jones House, marching thence to the Weldon Railroad, near General Warren's Headquarters, at the Yellow House, and bivouacked for the night. On the 27th, marched at daylight, taking the Halifax Road, then to the right on the Vaughn Road, reaching the Boydton Plank Road at noon. At 2, P.M., the brigade formed in line of battle, supporting a battery (C, First United States Artillery). At 4, P.M., the enemy appeared on our right flank. An attempt was made to change front; but the action became general, and the enemy coming in such numbers that prisoners were captured and recaptured. Finding that the enemy could not be checked, the brigade was ordered to fall back on to the road, and re-form, leaving one section of artillery in the hands of the enemy. Re-forming on the road, I took the left of the First Massachusetts, assisted by volunteers from other regiments of the brigade and division, and by a quick dash across the field secured the section of artillery, and brought it safely off. Casualties, one enlisted man killed, six wounded, and twelve captured. About thirty more of the regiment were captured, but succeeded in making their escape, and reaching our lines after dark. 28th, withdrew, and marched to the Jones House, returning to Fort Alexander Hayes on the 30th. Distance marched, forty-three miles. Regiment remained at Fort Hayes until Nov. 28th, when it was again relieved. Joined the brigade at the rear, marched thence to the extreme left of our line, at the Peebles House, going into camp outside of the works, and near the Vaughn Road, with orders to make ourselves as comfortable as possible.

Supposing that the campaign was ended, and that we were now to have winter-quarters, the men went to work with a will, and in four days had put up comfortable log-huts, all supplied with fireplaces, in hopes of remaining to enjoy them; but on the 6th of December orders were received to march at daylight of the 7th. Accordingly, the division reported to Major-General Warren, commanding Fifth Army Corps, for operation on the Weldon Railroad. Marched down the Jerusalem Plank Road, across the Nottaway River to Sussex Court House, thence to Jarrett Station, on the Weldon Railroad, then down the railroad to Bellfield, burning the ties and bending the rails, returning over the same road, arriving at the fortifications around Petersburg on the 13th of December.

The men suffered severely on this raid, as the weather was very inclement, many of the men coming back over the frozen ground without shoes. Had no engagement on the raid. Four enlisted men straggled from the command, and fell into the enemy's hands. Distance marched, ninety-six miles.

Tabular List of Casualties from May 15, 1864, *to Dec.* 16, 1864.

	Killed.	Wounded.	Missing.	Total.
Spottsylvania, May 19th,	55	312	27	394
North Anna River, May 24th,	1	11	—	12
Tolopotomy, May 31st,	—	5	3	8
Cold Harbor, June 3d to 10th,	2	13	16	31
Petersburg, June 16th,	25	132	5	162
Petersburg, June 17th,	—	9	—	9
Petersburg, June 18th,	4	42	1	47
Petersburg, June 22d,	9	46	185	240
Deep Bottom, July 27th,	—	1	—	1
Petersburg Mine, July 30th,	—	1	—	1
Deep Bottom, Aug. 15th and 16th,	2	7	—	9
On the Line, — —,	—	2	—	2
Poplar Grove Church, Oct. 7th,	2	11	8	21
Boydton Road, Oct. 27th,	1	6	12	19
Weldon Railroad, Dec. 7th,	—	—	4	4
Total,	101	598	261	960

The regiment remained in camp in front of Petersburg, near the rear line of fortifications between the Halifax and Vaughn Roads until Feb. 4th, 1865, when orders were received to be ready to march at daylight of the 5th. Marched in accordance with said order, and took part in the battle of Hatcher's Run. The command remained as support to the first line until nearly dark, when the enemy pressed that line. We were then ordered forward, and were hotly engaged for about one hour; casualties, one enlisted man wounded. The regiment bivouacked on the field for the night, and remained in bivouac the 6th, 7th, and 8th. On the 9th moved to Humphries Station, near the Vaughn Road, and went into camp; remained in camp until March 25th, when orders were received to be ready to move at a moment's notice. Marched at 12, M.; were engaged at 4, P.M., near Duncan's Run. The Fifth Michigan and First Massachusetts Heavy Artillery were first formed as a support for the First Brigade of our division (Third Division, Second Army Corps). The First Brigade fell back to the second line, when the two regiments were moved forward and held the position of the front line, for which they were highly complimented by Generals Mott and Pierce; casualties during engagement, two enlisted men killed, seven wounded. The regiment remained on picket that night (after the rest of the brigade had returned to camp), returning to camp the next night, and remaining in camp until March 29th, when we marched at 6, A.M., out on the Vaughn Road, crossing Hatcher's Run, and a smaller run about two miles from it, when the brigade was formed in line, and advanced through the woods; took the first line of the enemy's works at 6, P.M., it being held by a very few men; advanced in line until dark; lay in line all night. Advanced again at daylight next morning; found the enemy's second line of works deserted; advanced about five hundred yards, and threw up breastworks under a heavy shell fire from a battery in our front, and remained in the works all day. At 3, A.M., of the 31st, we moved to the left, and threw up works on the right of the Boydton Plank Road. At 12, M., the regiment, together with the Fifth Michigan, were ordered to charge the battery in our front, as it was believed to be held by only a few men; charged under a heavy fire of artillery and infantry, found the *abatis* and slashing in front of the enemy's works so thick that it was impossible to get through; which fact being reported to General Pierce, the two regiments were ordered back to their position in the brigade line; casualties in the charge, one enlisted man killed, and ten wounded. Remained in line until daylight, April 2d, when a combined attack of the whole line was ordered; advanced, and found the works in our front nearly deserted, the enemy having moved off most of their artillery during the night. After crossing the works, we marched down the Plank Road to the Whitworth House, near the South-side Railroad, formed in line, and threw up works under a heavy fire of artillery; casualties, one enlisted man killed, two wounded. April 3d, the enemy having evacuated their works during the night, the Second Army Corps marched in pursuit at 6, A.M., taking the road between the Appomattox River and the South-side Railroad; bivouacked for the night at $9\frac{1}{2}$, P.M.; distance marched, 18 miles. April 4th, marched at 6, A.M. At 8, A.M., the regiment was detailed to repair the road, and assist the artillery and trains to pass; worked until dark, then joined the brigade; distance marched eight miles. April 5th, marched at 4, A.M., crossed the Danville Railroad at 8 P.M.; bivouacked for the night at 9 P.M.,; distance marched, sixteen miles. April 6th, marched at 6, A.M.; at 8, A.M., formed in line of battle, the right of the Second Brigade resting on the road; advanced in line all day. At 6, P.M., the First and Third Divisions, Second Army Corps, charged and captured about three hundred wagons and three pieces of artillery. The regiment went on picket at night; distance marched, ten miles. April 7th, marched at 7, A.M., crossed the Appomattox River at High Bridge, found the enemy entrenched about two miles beyond; formed in line to charge, lay in line all night; distance marched, seven miles. April 8th, marched at 6, A.M. (the enemy evacuated their position during the night), halted at Sydney Church at 1, P.M.; struck the Lynchburg Road at 3, P.M., passed through the town of New Store at 7, P.M., and halted for the night; distance marched, eighteen miles. April 9th, marched at $3\frac{1}{2}$, A.M., halted at 12, M., near Clover Hill; distance marched, ten miles. At 5, P.M., Major-General Meade rode along the lines and said that "*Lee* had surrendered his whole army." The scene beggars *all* description. Bivouacked at Clover Hill until the morning of April 11th, then marched for Burkesville, arriving the evening of April 13th; distance marched, 48 miles. Remained in camp until May 2d, then marched with the corps for Manchester, Va., arriving at 11, A. M., May 5th; distance marched, fifty-eight miles. May 6th, crossed the James River, and marched through Richmond; bivouacked for the night three miles from the city. May 7th, the corps marched for Washington, D. C., *via* Fredericksburg. Arrived at Bailey's Cross Roads, and went into camp May 15th, just one year from the day the regiment left the fortifications of Washington to join the Army of the Potomac. Remained in camp until June 15th, when orders were received for the regiment to be reported to Major-General Hancock for duty in the fortifications of Washington; reported in accordance with said order, and were assigned to duty at Forts Ethan Allen and Macy, near Chain Bridge.

June 27th, moved to Forts C. F. Smith and Strong.

July 19th, orders were received from the War Department to consolidate the remaining veterans and recruits into four companies, and consolidate with the 3d Massachusetts Heavy Artillery; which, for said purpose, was formed into eight companies; the consolidated force still bearing the name of the 1st Massachusetts Heavy Artillery. Aug. 11th, Orders were received from the Adjutant-General's office for the command to be at once mustered out of the United States service and to report to the mustering officer of Massachusetts for final payment. The regiment left Washington on the evening of 17th of August, and arrived in Boston on Sunday the 20th. Were then ordered to Gallop's Island, where it received its final discharge on the 25th, having been in the United States' service four years one month and twenty-one days.

The following is the Roll of Andover Soldiers, belonging to the Regiment at the close of the Rebellion, April 9, 1865.

Lieut.-Col. — Horace Holt. | *Captain* — John Clark.

Quarter-Master-Sergeant — Benjamin F. Stevens.

Sergeants:

John S. Sargent,
William H. Greene,
Charles W. McClenna,
Sylvester C. Melcher,
John B. A. Russell.

Corporals:

James I. Anderson,
Samuel P. Farnham,
David B. Gilcreast,
John Kennedy,
Benjamin C. Lovejoy.

Privates:

Abbott, Lewis F. F.
Abbott, Noah B.
Albe, Freeland N.*
Bailey, Thomas R.*
Burnham, Henry O.
Burton, Joseph,
Chalk, Henry T.
Cheever, Benjamin,
Conley, Jeremiah,
Coulie, John D.
Craig, William,
Dane, George,
Dearborn, John S.
Foster, Thomas E.*
Goldsmith,* Albert,
Gooch, John F.
Grant, Farnham P.
Hatch, Andrew J.*
Hovey, John C.
Johnson, Solon,
Jones, Charles E.
Logue, John,
Mahoney, Michael,*
Mason, Walter B.
McCabe, Frank,
Mears, Calvin,
Pasho, William A.
Russell, Augustine K.
Sherman, Henry T.
Smith, James,
Townsend, Warren W.
Trull, Charles F.

---

* On the 30th of July, 1865, this Soldier with four of his comrades, without authority, left the Regiment then stationed at Fort Bunker Hill, Maryland, on its return from the front, but rejoined the Regiment when it arrived in Boston.

INDEX TO SOLDIERS' NAMES.

Abbott, Alson B., 77, 110, 144
Abbott, Charles E., 80, 103, 136, 144
Abbott, E. P., 26, 34, 66, 72, 132, 144
Abbott, Frank F., 34, 141, 144
Abbott, George B., 34, 124, 144
Abbott, Lewis F. F., 66, 132, 144, 223
Abbott, Moses B., 34, 48, 55, 116, 144
Abbott, Noah B., 26, 34, 66, 74, 132, 144, 223
Abbott, Wesley, 83, 139, 145
Aiken, Samuel, 26, 34, 66, 74, 132, 145
Albee, Freeland N., 60, 132, 145, 223
Alderson, James, 80, 136, 145
Allen, T. F., 26, 34, 74, 132, 145
Allen, Walter B., 38, 80, 103, 105, 113, 126, 145
Anderson, James I., 20, 34, 67, 104, 132, 145, 223
Armstrong, Thomas, 34, 117, 145
Ashworth, James, 20, 34, 132, 145

Bagley, Thomas A., 34, 132, 146
Bailey, Charles W., 80, 104, 136, 146
Bailey, George A., 34, 67, 120, 146
Bailey, Henry H., 26, 34, 132, 146
Bailey, James H., 83, 132, 146
Bailey, T. R., 20, 34, 67, 132, 146, 223
Banker, Melvin, 60, 120, 146
Barker, S. S., 34, 38, 83, 109, 139, 146
Barker, Stephen, 83, 132, 147
Barker, William, 77, 111, 147
Barnard, C. P., 26, 34, 75, 132, 147
Barnard, Geo. N., 26, 34, 132, 147
Barnard, Henry F., 77, 111, 147
Barrows, William E., 34, 116, 147

Batton, William, 60, 141, 147
Beal, William, 20, 83, 132, 147
Becker, Charles, 80, 121, 147
Belanger, William F., 77, 111, 147
Bell, C. H., 26, 34, 73, 84, 101, 132, 148
Bell, Joseph, 20, 67, 74, 132, 143, 148
Bell, Robert, 34, 132, 148
Bentley, Noah, 83, 116, 139, 148
Berry, Albert, 80, 104, 113, 148
Berry, Alonzo P., 20, 34, 55, 132, 148
Berry, Israel A., 34, 139, 148
Bird, Minor, 78, 143, 149
Black, James B., 83, 121, 148
Black, Thomas D., 80, 104, 131, 148
Blake, John, 81, 107, 120, 149
Blunt, Joshua M., 80, 104, 113, 149
Blunt, Samuel W., 26, 34, 132, 149
Bodwell, Willard G., 20, 34, 132, 149
Bohonnon, Albert L., 20, 34, 132, 149
Bolton, William A., 34, 113, 149
Bond, John, 77, 111, 149
Boston, Peter, 78, 143, 149
Bowen, Albert L., 38, 99, 126, 150
Boyce, Thomas, 50, 118, 150
Boyd, Patrick, 50, 118, 150
Boyden, James, 50, 118, 150
Boyle, John, 50, 118, 150
Bradley, C. W., 81, 107, 142, 150
Brady, James L., 34, 132, 150
Brown, Charles, 80, 104, 128, 129, 150
Brown, Geo. T., 20, 34, 132, 143, 150
Brown, Leroy S., 20, 34, 74, 132, 151
Bryant, E. K., 20, 34, 74, 101, 132, 151
Buchan, Geo., 77, 105, 107, 111, 151
Buckley, Phineas, Jr., 20, 34, 132, 151

INDEX TO SOLDIERS' NAMES.

Buguay, George A., 34, 117, 151
Burnham, Henry O., 26, 34, 67, 132, 151, 223
Burris, Stephen, 20, 34, 132, 151
Burtt, Joseph A., 38, 125, 151
Burton, Joseph, 26, 34, 132, 151, 223
Busfield, John, Jr., 77, 105, 111, 152

Callahan, Albert J., 80, 104, 113, 152
Callahan, Charles, H., 34, 117, 152
Campbell, Colin, 34, 132, 152
Carlton, Oscar F., 34, 121, 152
Carruth, Isaac S., 38, 104, 125, 152
Carter, Fred. W., 82, 107, 142, 152
Carter, William S., 34, 110, 152
Cass, Isaac N., 81, 107, 141, 152
Chalk, Henry T., 67, 133, 152, 223
Chandler, G. W., 20, 34, 74, 132, 153
Chandler, Henry F., 60, 107, 130, 153
Chandler, Joseph, Jr., 34, 120, 153
Chapin, Frank B., 20, 34, 132, 153
Chapin, Josiah L., 69, 71, 80, 104, 105, 113, 153
Cheever, B., 20, 34, 67, 132, 153, 223
Cheever, Samuel, 34, 75, 132, 153
Christian, William T., 34, 119, 153
Clark, Aaron S., 34, 132, 153
Clark, Edwin L., 16, 83, 113, 154
Clark, George B.. 34, 78 132, 154
Clark, Jesse H., 82, 107, 142, 154
Clark, John (1st H. A.), 20, 34, 67, 74, 132, 154, 223
Clark, John (22d Inf.), 50, 118, 154
Clarke, Amasa, 38, 104, 126, 154
Clarkson, John, 50, 118, 154
Clement, Charles A., 34, 114, 154
Clement, Moses W., 8, 9, 20, 34, 132, 143, 154
Clough, William E., 81, 104, 113, 155
Cocklin, John, 20, 35, 132, 155
Cogswell, Thos. M., 39, 107, 126 155
Colange, Etienne, 60, 133, 155
Collins, James, 50, 118, 155
Collins, Richard, 80, 104, 137, 155

Collins, Thomas E., 83, 108, 155
Collins, Timothy, 80, 104, 113, 155
.Comstock, Alfred, 79, 108, 155
Condon, Nich., 80, 104, 115, 137, 155
Conley, Jeremiah, 35, 67, 74, 83, 113, 132, 156, 223
Coombs, James, 50, 118, 156
Cooper, Thomas H., 35, 110, 156
Costello, Jas., 20, 35, 38, 72, 132, 156
Coulie, John D., 20, 35, 67, 132, 156, 223
Craig, David, 83, 114, 117, 156
Craig, George, 20, 35, 132, 156
Craig, William, 60, 73, 132, 156, 223
Critchett, George D., 35, 114, 156
Crosby, Alonzo, 82, 107, 120, 157
Crowther, William, 60, 119, 124, 157
Cummings, C. S., 20, 35, 72, 132, 157
Currier, Charles, 20, 35, 133, 157
Curtis, Andrew F., 20, 35, 133, 157
Cusick, J., 20, 35, 73, 133, 143, 157
Cutler, Abalino B., 20, 35, 132, 157
Cutler, G. K., 20, 35, 74, 133, 157

Dane, A. L., 35, 110, 157
Dane, Elmore, 35, 67, 120, 157
Dane, Geo., 20, 35, 67, 133, 158, 223
Dane, Richard G., 79, 120, 158
Davis, Charles H., 26, 35, 133, 158
Dearborn, John S., 26, 35, 67, 101, 133, 158, 223
Delany, Edward, 50, 118, 158
Dodge, John A., 81, 104, 113, 158
Dow, Charles E., 82, 107, 142, 158
Downes, Benj., 82, 107, 142, 158
Dougherty, James, 82, 107, 142, 158
Duncan, James, 81, 104, 113, 158
Duncan, Robert, 82, 107, 141, 159
Dunn, Albert H., 77, 111, 159
Dugan, Charles, 20, 35, 133, 159
Dugan, William, 82, 107, 142, 159
Durant, George, 50, 118, 159
Dwine, Daniel, Jr., 60, 135, 159
Dwyer, M., 81, 104, 115, 135, 159

INDEX TO SOLDIERS' NAMES. 227

Eagleton, Charles, 67, 119, 159
Eastes, J. H., 26, 35, 67, 74, 133, 159
Edwards, F. W., 20, 35, 72, 133, 160
Eeles, Frederick S., 83, 122, 160
Eldridge, Hezekiah, 60, 135, 160
English, Charles G., 82, 107, 142, 160

Farmer, E., 20, 35, 67, 74, 133, 160
Farmer, G. S., 20, 35, 75, 133, 160
Farnham, David T., 51, 127, 160
Farnham, Moses L., 60, 129, 130, 160
Farnham, O. L., 8, 20, 35, 74, 133, 161
Farnham, Samuel P., 20, 35, 67, 75, 133, 161, 223
Findley, James S., 20, 35, 67, 72, 133, 143, 161
Findley, John A., 20, 35, 133, 161
Fitzgerald, James, 79, 107, 161
Flemming, John, 83, 115, 161
Flood, Thomas, 50, 118, 161
Foster, Charles H., 60, 133, 161
Foster, T. E., 20, 35, 67, 133, 162, 223
Fox, William, 82, 107, 142, 162
French, Henry P., 35, 108, 162
Frorz, James A., 35, 38, 162
Frye, Enoch O., 35, 133, 162
Frye, Newton G., 20, 35, 133, 162
Fulmer, Robert, 80, 162
Fulton, J. W., 39, 81, 104, 128, 136, 162

Gallon, James, 35, 113, 162
George, Warren, 77, 111, 163
Gibbs, Robert, 82, 107, 142, 163
Gifford, Robert, 77, 130, 163
Gilcreast, David B., 20, 35, 67, 72, 133, 163, 223
Gillespie, W., 20, 35, 75, 133, 163
Godkins, S. F., 82, 107, 142, 163
Goldsmith, Albert, 20, 35, 67, 75, 133, 163, 223
Goldsmith, Benjamin F., 60, 130, 163
Goldsmith, Jer., 81, 104, 105, 113, 163
Goldsmith, Joseph C., 35, 133, 163
Goldsmith, Sanford K., 60, 130, 164

Gooch, J. F., 26, 35, 67, 74, 133, 164, 223
Goodwin, Moses F., 77, 82, 107, 111, 142, 164
Gorman, Joseph E., 50, 118, 164
Gorman, William B., 50, 118, 165
Gould, Theodore F., 82, 107, 142, 165
Grandy, Henry E., 35, 109, 164
Grant, F. P., 20, 35, 67, 133, 164, 223
Grant, G. W., 26, 35, 67, 133, 164
Gray, Jesse E., 20, 35, 133, 164
Gray, Nathan H., 35, 117, 165
Greeley, William, 83, 121, 165
Green, Joseph, 50, 118, 165
Green, Michael, 51, 141, 165
Greene, Charles, 20, 83, 133, 165
Greene, William H., 20, 35, 67, 74, 133, 165, 223
Grubbs, Cam, 78, 143, 165

Hall, Henry H., 26, 35, 133, 165
Hall, William S., 26, 35, 133, 165
Hanson, C., 25, 38, 83, 109, 139, 166
Hardy, Franklin, 20, 35, 67, 133, 166
Hardy, John 2d., 20, 35, 74, 133, 166
Harnden, George W., 39, 128, 166
Harrigan, Barth., 81, 104, 136, 166
Hart, William, 20, 35, 133, 166
Hastie, Thomas, 35, 75, 133, 166
Hatch, Andrew J., 20, 35, 67, 72, 107, 133, 166, 223
Hatch, Enoch M., 20, 35, 74, 133, 167
Hatch, G. F., 20, 35, 67, 74, 133, 167
Hatch, L. G., 20, 35, 73, 133, 167
Hayes, John H., 35, 72, 133, 167
Hayes, Patrick, 35, 118, 167
Hayes, Timothy, 67, 83, 121, 167
Hayward, G., E., 26, 35, 72, 133, 167
Hervey, A. G., 35, 67, 140, 142, 167
Hervey, Samuel C., 20, 35, 133, 168
Higgins, Archibald, Jr., 35, 116, 168
Higgins, Henry C., 81, 104, 113, 168
Hill, Emmett C., 79, 99, 104, 106, 107, 143, 168
Holloran, Patrick, 81, 104, 137, 168

INDEX TO SOLDIERS' NAMES.

Holt, B., 2d., 39, 81, 104, 113, 126, 168
Holt, Harrison, 60, 129, 140, 168
Holt, Horace, 8, 9, 16, 17, 18, 20, 35, 133, 168, 202, 204, 207, 208, 209, 211, 213, 223
Holt, Jonathan A., 26, 35, 74, 133, 168
Holt, Joseph F., 51, 83, 108, 128, 169
Holt, Lewis G., 20, 35, 74, 133, 169
Holt, Newton, 20, 35, 133, 169, 206
Holt, S. M., 39, 81, 104, 113, 126, 169
Holt, Warren E., 20, 35, 133, 169
Hotchkiss, Arthur E., 77, 125, 169
Hovey, John C., 35, 67, 133, 169, 223
Howarth, O. B., 21, 35, 133, 169
Hunt, Amos, 21, 83, 133, 170
Hunt, William, 51, 127, 170
Hunter, William, 35, 118, 170
Hussey, Wyman D., 26, 35, 133, 170

Ingalls, J. E., 81, 104, 105, 113, 170

Jameson, John, 50, 118, 170
Jaquith, James, 83, 121, 170
Jenkins, E. K., 21, 35, 74, 133, 170
Jenkins, John B., 12, 13, 14, 81, 104, 113, 170
Jenkins, Omar, 26, 35, 133, 170
Jenkins, W. H., 26, 35, 71, 133, 171
Jennings, George, 78, 143, 171
Jennings, W. E., 21, 35, 75, 133, 171
Johnson, James, 50, 118, 171
Johnson, John, 35, 38, 118, 171
Johnson, S., 38, 67, 83, 133, 171, 223
Johnston, David, Jr., 77, 111, 171
Joice, Redmond, 26, 35, 81, 104, 133, 137, 143, 171
Jones, Ambrose, 83, 143, 171
Jones, Charles E., 26, 35, 67, 75, 133, 172, 223
Jones, David L., 82, 107, 142, 172
Jourdan, Henry, 78, 143, 172
Jupiter, Isaac, 78, 143, 172

Kavanagh, Bernard, 83, 117, 172

Keating, John, 35, 113, 172
Kelly, Joseph, 83, 121, 123, 172
Kennedy, J., 21, 35, 67, 133, 172, 223
Kimball, Henry G., 39, 102, 126, 172

Lavalette, P. C., 21, 35, 71, 133, 173
Lawrence, John H., 51, 141, 173
Lemon, W. H., 82, 107, 142, 173
Lindsey, Robert, 26, 35, 133, 173
Logue, C., 83, 106, 107, 121, 173
Logue, J., 27, 36, 51, 127, 133, 173
Logue, John, 21, 35, 67, 133, 173, 223
Lovejoy, B. C., 21, 35, 67, 133, 173, 223
Lovejoy, Chas. W., 67, 83, 138, 173
Lovejoy, George W. (1st Reg.), 35, 108, 174
Lovejoy, George W. (44th Reg.), 39, 126, 174
Lovejoy, H. L., 17, 21, 75, 83, 133, 174
Lovejoy, J. T., 39, 105, 125, 174
Lovejoy, Newton, 35, 143, 174
Lovejoy, William W., 35, 108, 174
Luke, William H., 83, 108, 174
Luscomb, A. E., 27, 36, 75, 133, 174
Lyman, Edw. E., 82, 107, 141, 174
Lyon, John, 51, 118, 175

Mahoney, Michael, 21, 36, 67, 73, 133, 175, 223
Malone, John, 51, 118, 175
Marland, Chas. H., 39, 105, 126, 175
Marland, W., 36, 38, 83, 110, 137, 175
Mason, Edward, 60, 133, 175
Mason, Eri, 82, 107, 141, 175
Mason, Josiah, 36, 139, 175
Mason, W. B., 60, 75, 133, 143, 175, 223
Mason, Warren, 36, 120, 175
Maynard, Charles, 27, 36, 134, 176
McAndrews, John, 51, 118, 176
McCabe, F., 27, 36, 67, 133, 176, 223
McCarty, Charles, 51, 118, 176
McClenna, Charles W., 21, 36, 67, 133, 176, 223
McCullough, John, 77, 105, 111, 176

INDEX TO SOLDIERS' NAMES. 229

McCusker, J., 56, 79, 104, 133, 176
McGurk, B., 21, 36, 67, 74, 133, 176
McKenzie, John, 60, 135, 177
McLaughlin, John, 36, 75, 133, 177
Mears, Calvin, 60, 133, 177, 223
Mears, Chas., 21, 36, 73, 101, 133, 177
Mears, Daniel, Jr., 36, 113, 177
Mears, George, 36, 67, 113, 177
Mears, John, 27, 36, 60, 82, 107, 133, 135, 141, 177
Mears, Warren, Jr., 21, 36, 133, 177
Mears, William, 27, 36, 133, 177
Melcher, S. C., 21, 36, 67, 133, 178, 223
Melendy, G., 81, 104, 115, 135, 178
Merrill, Edward C., 83, 138, 178
Merrill, Frank H., 36, 110, 178
Merrill, James W., 39, 126, 178
Merrill, John H., 81, 104, 113, 178
Merrill, W. F., 27, 36, 133, 135, 178
Messer, Cyrus, 83, 134, 178
Milkins, William, 81, 104, 137, 178
Moar, Charles J., 51, 126, 179
Morgan, D. S., 27, 36, 72, 133, 179
Morrison, C. W., 82, 107, 141, 179
Morrison, John, 51, 118, 179
Morse, W. B., 21, 36, 74, 101, 133, 179
Morton, Charles H., 51, 118, 179
Morton, Douglas, 27, 36, 133, 179
Moulton, Chas. L., 81, 104, 113, 179
Murphy, William, 51, 118, 179
Murray, James R., 27, 36, 133, 179

Nichols, Wm. W., 21, 36, 134, 180
Nickerson, Eph. N., 36, 68, 120, 180
Nolan, Malachi, 27, 36, 74, 134, 180
Noonan, Daniel, 83, 134, 180
Noyes, Aaron, 51, 111, 180

O'Brien, J. (1st H.A.), 27, 36, 134, 180
O'Brien, J. (22d Reg.), 51, 118, 180
O'Connor, Patrick, 27, 36, 134, 180
O'Hara, E., 21, 36, 68, 72, 134, 180
O'Malley, Thomas, 60, 116, 180
Owens, Redman, 79, 143, 181

Packard, Edward W., 77, 111, 181
Parker, C.O., 81, 83, 104, 134, 143, 181
Parker, George W., 36, 119, 181
Parker, J. F., 27, 36, 60, 134, 135, 181
Pasho, William A., 21, 36, 68, 134, 181, 223
Patrick, Andrew K., 60, 130, 181
Peterson, George, 36, 134, 181
Phillips, Patrick, 83, 141, 181
Pike, George E., 21, 36, 72, 134, 181
Poor, Charles H., 8, 20, 36, 134, 182
Porter, Thomas F., 68, 119, 182
Pray, Seaver, 83, 117, 182

Qualey, Patrick, 81, 104, 113, 182

Raymond, Edward G., 39, 126, 182
Raymond, Jefferson N., 36, 120, 182
Raymond, W. L., 39, 60, 126, 140, 182
Rea, Aaron G., Jr., 21, 36, 134, 182
Richardson, Silas, Jr., 21, 36, 134, 182
Ridley, C. W., 27, 36, 74, 134, 183
Riley, John, 51, 118, 183
Roberts, George, 60, 135, 183
Rogers, L. Waldo, 39, 126, 183
Rollins, Robert, 60, 128, 183
Rothwell, J. H., 27, 74, 83, 134, 183
Rowley, R. Augustus, 36, 141, 183
Russell, Augustine K., 27, 36, 68, 73, 134, 183, 223
Russell, James, 27, 36, 134, 183
Russell, John B. A., 21, 36, 68, 134, 184, 223
Russell, John R., 81, 104, 137, 184
Russell, J., Jr., 21, 56, 83, 134, 184
Russell, Wm., 21, 36, 68, 74, 134, 184
Russell, Winslow, 21, 36, 81, 104, 134, 136, 184
Ryley, Leonard W., 60, 130, 143, 184

Sanborn, Frank, 36, 110, 184
Sargent, H. N., 82, 107, 141, 184 •
Sargent, John S., 21, 36, 68, 75, 134, 184, 223

INDEX TO SOLDIERS' NAMES.

Saunders, James, Jr., 27, 36, 82, 107, 134, 142, 185
Saunders, Thomas, 36, 119, 185
Saunders, Z. M., 21, 36, 71, 73, 134, 185
Searles, James H., 60, 140, 185
Shannon, John, 36, 113, 185
Shannon, William, 21, 36, 134, 185
Shattuck, Charles M., 60, 143, 185
Shattuck, Charles Wm., 21, 27, 36, 83, 123, 134, 185
Shattuck, L. G., 27, 36, 134, 185
Sherman, Henry T., 21, 36, 68, 134, 186, 223
Shields, Nicholas, 36, 134, 186
Skerritt, James, 60, 116, 186
Smart, George M., 20, 84, 134, 186
Smith, Charles, 51, 118, 186
Smith, George, 79, 143, 186
Smith, Jas., 21, 36, 68, 134, 186, 223
Smith, James B., 36, 122, 186
Smith, John (28th Reg.), 80, 120, 186
Smith, John (17th Reg.), 82, 107, 115, 186
Smith, Peter D., 20, 36, 134, 187
Smith, Robert, 82, 107, 142, 187
Smith, Thomas, 27, 36, 87, 134, 187
Spradley, Randal, 78, 143, 187
Springer, Eugene, 60, 135, 187
Standing, George, 68, 120, 187
Stanton, Michael, 51, 118, 187
Stanwood, L., 82, 107, 136, 187
Stephens, Andrew, 78, 143, 187
Stephens, G. W., 23, 27, 36, 73, 134, 187
Stephenson, Alba, 82, 142, 188
Stevens, Benjamin F., 21, 36, 68, 134, 188, 223
Stevens, B. W., 81, 104, 135, 188
Stevens, Daniel, 77, 111, 188
Stevens, James W., 84, 134, 188
Stewart, G., 77, 102, 105, 111, 188
Stewart, John W., 77, 111, 188
• Stott, Joshua H., 36, 140, 143, 188
Stowe, F. W., 36, 108, 134, 143, 188
Sylvester, William, 51, 118, 189

Taylor, George H., 60, 143, 189
Thomas, Lewis, 82, 107, 142, 189
Thomas, Nicholas, 78, 143, 189
Thompson, William, 51, 118, 189
Tomlinson, E. A., 81, 104, 137, 189
Townley, John J., 36, 113, 189
Townsend, M. B., 21, 36, 134, 189
Townsend, Warren W., 21, 36, 68, 134, 189, 223
Tracy, William W., 39, 126, 189
Trainor, John, 60, 135, 190
Trask, Elbridge P., 81, 104, 137, 190
Trulan, William, 36, 118, 190
Trull, Charles F., 27, 36, 68, 75, 134, 190, 223
Tuck, Moses W., 27, 36, 134, 190
Tucker, William H., 81, 104, 113, 190
Tumey, Peter, 51, 118, 190
Turkington, Henry, 36, 110, 190
Turner, John, 36, 68, 120, 190
Tyler, Herbert, 39, 126, 191

Vaux, Walter R., 36, 113, 191
Vinal, George A. W., 20, 39, 60, 84, 111, 129, 130, 134, 191

Wallace, Alexander, 36, 113, 191
Walsh, William, 51, 118, 191
Ward, James, 57, 60, 112, 122, 191
Wardman, Thomas, 60, 130, 191
Wardrobe, Frederick, 81, 143, 191
Wardwell, Alfred, 21, 84, 134, 192
Wardwell, G. E., 84, 116, 134, 192
Wardwell, H. W., 20, 36, 68, 134, 192
Wardwell, Joseph W., 36, 123, 192
Wardwell, W. H., 21, 36, 134, 192, 210
Weeks, Nathaniel, 82, 107, 142, 192
Welch, Robert, 36, 38, 192
Wescott, Solomon, 82, 107, 141, 192
Wescott, William, 81, 104, 137, 192
Weston, Frederick, 81, 104, 137, 193
Whideman, John, 78, 143, 193
White, Charles W., 60, 140, 193
Whittaker, Amos, 84, 118, 193

INDEX TO SOLDIERS' NAMES.

Whittemore, Harrison, 84, 108, 193	Woods, William, 51, 118, 194
Wilson, Charles, 51, 118, 193	Woodbridge, F., 57, 81, 106, 113, 194
Winchester, C. H., 27, 36, 74, 134, 193	Woodlin, Elgin, 36, 113, 194
Winthrop, Thomas F., 36, 82, 116, 131, 193	Worthley, Daniel E., 36, 120, 194
Withey, William H., 60, 140, 193	Young, Francis C., 39, 126, 194
Withsby, Thomas, 78, 143, 194	Young, George W., 39, 126, 195
Woods, Elliot, 21, 36, 134, 194	Young, Samuel, 51, 118, 195

INDEX TO SEAMEN'S NAMES.

Abbott, William,	65, 196	Murphy, Peter,	65, 198
Abbott, William A.,	62, 65, 82, 196	Murphy, Robert,	65, 198
Aurick, Joseph,	66, 196	Murray, Michael,	65, 198
		Murray, Patrick,	65, 198
Butler, William,	62, 65, 66, 196	Murray, Timothy,	65, 198
Donnelly, Thomas,	66, 196	Naughty, Lewis A.,	65, 199
Dove, G. W. W.,	8, 13, 17, 82, 196	Nichols, John S.,	65, 199
Dudley, Lysander,	66, 197	Noble, William F.,	65, 199
		Nolan, Joseph,	65, 199
Henriques, Joseph.	*See* Aurick.	Norris, Thomas R.,	65, 199
		Nugent, George,	65, 199
Makin, Joseph,	65, 197		
Makin, Samuel,	65, 197	Parker, John F.,	181, 199
Mason, Aaron W.,	65, 197	Paul, David E.,	65, 199
Mason, Henry G.,	65, 197	Peterson, George,	181, 199
McCann, Jeremiah,	65, 197	Perry, James E.,	65, 199
McCarty, Jeremiah,	65, 197	Phillips, Seth,	65, 199
McGinness, John,	65, 197	Pool, Robert,	65, 199
McGuire, John,	65, 197	Potter, William,	65, 199
McHugo, William,	65, 197		
McKenzie, Nicholas,	65, 197	Robinson, Joseph P.,	62, 65, 200
McLean, James,	65, 197	Rogers, George,	66, 200
McLarty, William A.,	65, 197	Roundy, Thomas,	66, 200
McLaughlin, Michael,	65, 198		
McNaughton, John,	65, 198	Sawyer, Edwin,	66, 200
Mears, John,	177, 198	Smith, David,	62, 65, 82, 200
Milliken, George E.,	65, 198		
Minar, Andrew G.,	65, 198	Taylor, George,	66, 200
Moore, John,	65; 198		
Morton, Charles,	65, 198	Walsh, Peter,	66, 200
Murphy, Miles,	65, 198	Wardwell, Horace W.,	192, 200

Printed in Dunstable, United Kingdom